'This is one of the most attractiv
read in recent years. Through critical reflection on the
foundation stones of our political thought—conservatism,
liberalism and socialism—and through an easy mastery of the
most important contemporary political debates, David
McKnight has managed to write something that is at once
original, courageous, realistic and fresh. For those who are
uneasy with the stale dogmas of Left and Right and whose
hopes for the creation of a more humane society remain
alive, McKnight's book will act both as an inspiration and as
a stimulus to further thought. At a peculiar historical moment,
where material prosperity and spiritual anxiety rub shoulders,
McKnight suggests the need for a new national conversation
about what we should value and how we should live. It is an
invitation we should accept.'

Robert Manne, Professor in the School of Politics
at La Trobe University

Beyond Right and Left

New politics and the culture wars

David McKnight

ALLEN&UNWIN

First published in 2005

Allen & Unwin
83 Alexander Street
Crows Nest NSW 2065
Australia
Phone: (61 2) 8425 0100
Fax: (61 2) 9906 2218
Email: info@allenandunwin.com
Web: www.allenandunwin.com

National Library of Australia
Cataloguing-in-Publication entry:

McKnight, David.
    Beyond right and left : new politics and the culture wars.

    Bibliography.
    Includes index.
    ISBN 1 74114 570 8.

    1. Conservatism - Australia. 2. Right and left (Political
    science). 3. Socialism - Australia. 4. Australia -
    Politics and government. I. Title.

320.994

Set in 12/14 pt Centaur MT by Bookhouse, Sydney
Printed by Griffin Press, Adelaide

10 9 8 7 6 5 4 3 2 1

Contents

In memory of a dear friend, Denis Freney (1936–1995)

Beyond Right and Left

*The ideas of economists and political philosophers both when they are right
and when they are wrong, are more powerful than is commonly understood.
Indeed the world is ruled by little else. Practical men, who believe themselves
quite exempt from any intellectual influence, are usually the slaves of some
defunct economist. Madmen in authority who hear voices in the air, are distilling
their frenzy from some academic scribbler of a few years back.*

John Maynard Keynes, 1936

Do the terms Right and Left still mean anything in politics?
Political pundits use these terms but, as with any words
repeated too often, the meaning starts to disappear. So many people
have become sceptical. We routinely describe John Howard's
Liberal–National Coalition government as Right. Logically, then,
Labor is Left. But is this polarisation accurate, or even helpful? The
meaning of these terms, like the ideas of those parties, has been
transformed in recent times. When Kim Beazley was elected leader
of the Labor Party for the second time in 2005, former Liberal
prime minister Malcolm Fraser commented that there was not a
single issue on which Kim Beazley was 'on the Left of me'. Then
there is Iraq. George W. Bush (on the Right) made war and was
joined by Britain's Labour government (on the Left). Meanwhile,
the French government (Right) and the German government (Left)
opposed the British–United States war. What's going on?

The Right is defined as conservative and the Left as radical in
their attitudes to social change. But the radical economic changes

in Australia over the last two decades have been driven by *both* major parties. When John Howard and Peter Costello came to government in 1996, they modified, but did not esentially change, the direction of economic policy from that advocated by Bob Hawke and Paul Keating. Yet voices on both the Right and the Left have protested this overall direction on which the mainstream parties agree.

The Right–Left model assumes that all the big questions of the day can be fitted somewhere on this spectrum. But is this true? Where do concerns about the environment fit? Is alarm about climate change and loss of biodiversity a 'left-wing' response? Is it 'right wing' to be worried about the family? Moreover, there is a widespread expectation that people must choose either Right or Left, as if all the wisdom lies on one side or the other. We often feel frustrated that policies and ideas are put into one box or the other, rather than being judged in their own terms. In fact, today, there are many 'Lefts' and many 'Rights', which is a sign that the Right–Left spectrum is breaking up.

In this book I argue that the Right–Left confusion is a symptom of a broader historic shift in cultural, social and economic ideas. This shift offers new opportunities for escaping the Right–Left bind and creating new ways of seeing the world. Quite unprecedented problems—above all in the global environment, but also in the family—require this. Untangling the Right–Left knot is the key to understanding the direction of new ideas, which take elements from both Right and Left.

In this book, I attempt to challenge a number of complacent beliefs of both the Right and Left. This is vital because these beliefs are the hidden underpinnings of decisions that affect our daily lives, and which will affect the lives of our children and their descendants. These ideas define the meaning of key terms such as 'the common good', 'individualism', 'care for others' and 'freedom'. The names of these sets of philosophical ideas are liberalism, socialism and conservatism. These ideas are little discussed today, although they motivate the policies and stances of governments and parties. Yet they have a new relevance in an era which has seen an increase in debates around 'values' in politics. These older philosophies have also been joined by historically very new ideas, such as environment-alism, feminism and multiculturalism, the meaning and application of which are the subject of intense conflict.

The new ideas and old ideas are still trapped within a linear political spectrum of Right and Left. I believe that we must recognise that the Right–Left spectrum of ideas has collapsed and that many old ways of thinking are finished. This is the first and most important step to advancing new ideas on the environment, the family, economic inequality, cultural diversity, and even deeper issues concerning purpose and meaning in our lives. All the 'isms' are now 'wasms'. Many people instinctively feel—as I do—that the established spectrum of Right and Left is inadequate; this book will explore where such feelings might take us. In the next chapter I begin this journey by examining the most powerful—yet often misunderstood—set of ideas of recent times, which are those of the Right.

Looking at Right and Left today

Originally, the idea of Right and Left stemmed from the seating arrangement of the National Assembly after the French Revolution of 1789. The deputies on the left of the chamber wanted to carry the goals of the revolution—liberty, equality and fraternity— through to their logical and radical conclusion. The right of the chamber was opposed to this. It was wary of radical experiments that implemented abstract ideas such as equality, and it tended to value traditions. In nineteenth-century Europe, the Left became more clearly defined as a socialist force, wanting to redistribute the wealth of the newly industrialising nations to the working class, while the Right became the description for those who thought the existing order worked well and was divinely ordained (and who benefited from it). This period established the tradition of defining the Right as conservative and the Left as radical.

In the twentieth century, the Left and Right came to be defined more by those supporting a greater role for government—in either its social democratic or its Marxist form—and those who opposed such a role. During the Cold War, the Right and Left were defined by their attitudes to communism and anti-communism.

The Right–Left model originated in Europe and, although it did not translate in a simple and direct way to Australian politics, enough of these ideas and traditions permeated Australia to make the Right–Left way of thinking part of a generally accepted discourse. For many reasons—among them the globalising economy and the collapse of the Cold War—this basic way of thinking about politics is now being transformed, however. Today, the Right–Left spectrum is becoming increasingly useless as a way of talking about many issues. And, while the Right–Left binary remains in popular use, what is actually meant by Right and Left has altered dramatically, since the content of the ideas of Right and Left has shifted greatly in recent decades.

At the level of major political parties in Australia, the Right–Left distinction was once very pronounced in the area of economic policy. This distinction has since narrowed dramatically, and there is now wide acceptance of what can loosely be called free-market economic theories. Since economic theories also express an attitude towards wider social and philosophical ideas, including the role of government, there is consequently a significant degree of convergence between the major parties. Debates on economic policy today are about identifying the best managers, not about the most convincing planners for change or the social goals of economic policy. This convergence has been accompanied by a certain reversal of roles: where Labor was once seen as the party of ideology, vision and conviction, today the policies of the Liberals, and even the Nationals, often have a more distinct ideological tinge. Where Labor was once influenced by the various theories of socialist ideology, today the most significant ideological input in Australian politics comes from the intellectual circles of the Right, especially from its policy 'think-tanks', and Labor prides itself on its pragmatism. Pollsters have detected a public desire for what they call 'conviction politics', but this now tends to translate into support for the Right rather than for the former partisans of principle on the Left.

The social classes that once underpinned the Right–Left spectrum have also changed. The industrial working class, once Labor's heartland, has shrunk and Labor can no longer take its allegiance for granted. Today, industrial workers are notable for their social conservatism, not their radicalism. The middle class, once the conservative Liberal Party heartland, has grown in size and diversified; part of it now consistently supports Labor and a small proportion of its members are drawn to the Greens.

In the wider political debate outside the major parties, the meaning of Right and Left is becoming harder to define simply. The rise of Pauline Hanson's One Nation Party, for example, bluntly expressed cultural fears about immigration and Indigenous Australians. It was therefore on the Right. Yet its economic policies, driven by rural bank closures and the human casualties of economic rationalisation, shared concerns with those of the socialist component of the Left.

On cultural issues, the division between Right and Left is no longer a useful descriptive tool. Is it 'left wing' to support a woman's right to abortion? Apparently not, since many members of the Liberal Party also support women's right to control their fertility. The Right once opposed policies favouring multiculturalism and cultural diversity, but today these policies continue under a conservative government. Moreover, during the Hanson outbreak, prominent members of the Liberal Party, such as Malcolm Fraser, John Hewson and Jeff Kennett, took a genuine stance against racism.

The meaning of Right and Left has been destabilised over the last two decades by a growing number of issues which cannot be understood or analysed in traditional Right–Left terms. To put this another way: political ideas and philosophies are meant to help us understand and solve problems yet, increasingly, the ideas of Right and Left offer us no ready answers. The new emerging faultlines are about issues such as:

- Problems of the *environment*, especially those with a global dimension, are historically unprecedented issues for humanity. The political ideas of Right and Left emerged to deal with the conflict between powerful social groups and conflict over moral issues. But environmental challenges represent a conflict or tension between the natural world and the whole of humanity, and this is a conflict no political theory can explain. Is it 'left wing' to be concerned about global warming? Why, then, are an increasing number of businesses and conservative governments beginning to imagine how a sustainable economy might work?
- Unending *material progress* is seen by Left and Right as one of the main ways to ensure a good life. The struggle for better living standards underpins the labour movement, and economic growth is the rationale for free-market economics. But, as many now reach a materially comfortable lifestyle, this is increasingly being questioned—not only on the grounds of its ecological sustainability, but also on whether it truly satisfies human needs. For a growing number of people the problem is not a lack of money, but a lack of meaning.
- *Poverty* was once seen as the result of low wages and unemployment, which were the result of the cyclical nature of capitalism. Today, the causes of poverty seem far more complex, and include family breakdown and drug abuse. Financial support for the poor is necessary, but it is not enough. Welfare dependency is now a recognised problem. Such issues cannot simply be understood in Right–Left terms.
- With both parents frequently in paid work, a crisis has emerged about *balancing work and family life*. Jobs require longer hours of work than before, yet still make no allowances for the needs of

children. Over 40 per cent of marriages break down. While the Right has much to say about family values, and while feminists on the Left defend the gains of women, no coherent program to deal with this crisis has emerged.

- A new collection of *ethical issues about health and the body*, focused around euthanasia, genetic engineering and human biotechnology, have emerged which do not 'fit' established paradigms. Is it left wing to support euthanasia and right wing to oppose it? Yet supporters of Left and Right can be found on both sides. Conservatives like Francis Fukuyama warn of the dangers of human biotechnology, and so do many Greens.
- *Globalisation* and *economic liberalisation* have made our lives less secure and communities less cohesive, yet we revel in the individual choice and diversity that have accompanied these. Traditions no longer limit our choices yet, increasingly, some people yearn for the security of tradition. The Right supports economic globalisation and is wary of cultural globalisation. The Left stands for the reverse. Yet there is also a great deal of crossover between individuals on the Right and Left on these issues.
- Increasingly, politics is discussed in terms of *values*. But Right and Left are both inconsistent about their stance on key values. The Right is economically liberal and the Left is socially liberal. The Right wants moral regulation, the Left wants economic regulation. Yet opposites also attract. The liberal Right and liberal Left sometimes agree (for example, on opposing censorship) and the old Right and the old Left sometimes agree (on issues such as opposing deregulation).

The trouble with the self-contained boxes of Right and Left is that we often want a bit of both. We need a society in which members support and care for each other, and we need an economy that is competitive and productive. Governments are seen as the guarantors of the former and markets as the guarantors of the latter. Getting the balance right is hard. Market forces can undermine the institutions of civil society, such as the family and community. Governments can also undermine civil society by providing services and income with little or no obligation. Also out of balance is our relationship to the natural world. We live in a high-energy society that is living off the earth's capital and not just its interest. The lifestyle of advanced industrial countries like Australia cannot be generalised to the rest of the planet's inhabitants, and will not be enjoyed in the future by our own descendants and coming generations of Australians. We need a new balance, a new sustainability. This requires that our current philosophies go beyond Right and Left.

The Right rethinks

The problems in the Right–Left dichotomy in politics are not new. But something else needs to be said. In the 1980s and 1990s, the terrain over which Right and Left were in conflict changed. In the 1980s, a new intellectual leadership emerged on the Right. Armed with new ideas generated by think-tanks which were often inspired by the Thatcher and Reagan governments, the Right took bold steps. It developed a new aggressive confidence. This was surprising—members of the Right are usually depicted as hidebound conservatives, fearful of change. This rethinking on the Right introduced an era of profound internal debate for conservatives, which is still barely understood by its opponents on the Left.

This ideological revolution of the Right had a remarkable result. The Right gained the ascendancy in the battle of ideas and values in Australia and elsewhere. Even where it did not directly succeed in taking government, the Right succeeded in dominating the political agenda and promoting its values and world view. The price of this renewal was the destruction of the older kind of Right and the creation of a new and more radical Right. The old Right had always been an alliance of at least three political ideals: social conservatism, based on family and nation; a progressive kind of social liberalism (the 'wets'); and a minority strand of economic liberalism. This revolution on the Right saw the triumph of economic liberalism, the defeat of the social liberals and the reformulation of social conservatism. The point is—and this has been hard for many commentators to grasp—that the conservatives are no longer afraid of radical change. In fact, they embrace it.

In Australia, this occurred in the 1980s with the rise of the think-tanks and the displacement within the Liberal Party of 'wet' MPs. Today, more people are referring to the contemporary Right as 'neo-liberal' or as 'radical conservatives'. The other factor which disentangled the old Right was the dissolution of the glue of anti-communism that occurred when the Soviet Union and Eastern Europe collapsed. This, too, accelerated a rethinking of the Right's purposes and goals. These changes occurred worldwide and their most successful local beneficiary was the Liberal–National Party Coalition under John Howard. I explore these crucial (and often misunderstood) changes in the ideas of the Right in chapters 3 and 4.

Any process of ideological rethinking requires vision and daring, risk-taking and radicalism. The last element, radicalism, proved to be the unexpected element of the revolution on the Right. The Right ceased to be a conservative force in any straightforward sense when it adopted the free-market economics and philosophy of thinkers like Friedrich Hayek (see Chapter 3). Setting in place market mechanisms, both in the economy and well beyond it, leads to a society being constantly transformed. In Australia, this transformation has meant the rise of commercial values in place of older social and moral values. The slow permeation of commercial values into areas far removed from the economy may turn out to be the most insidious and radical consequence of all, as I discuss in Chapter 2.

Today, the radicals are those who want to drive economic liberalism even further, while conservatives want to slow it down. The radicals want the full privatisation of Telstra along with the deregulation of the labour market. The Left, once a radical force for social change, opposes this. It has scaled down its goals to more modest and conservative tasks such as defending social welfare and trade union rights against an aggressive Right. In this sense, the market radicals of the Right have reversed the previous meaning of Right and Left as conservative and radical.

It would be tempting to claim that the ideological rethinking on the Right has been paralleled by a similar rethinking on the Left side of Australian politics, but this has not occurred. Within the Labor Party, a fitful and unproductive debate about Labor's beliefs and purpose has gone on for many years. The most public (and damaging) expression of this is the conflict between the 'traditional heartland' and the 'middle-class progressives'. This conflict about long-term beliefs and purposes underlies clashes such as those between Tasmanian forestry workers and those opposed to logging. It also exists on other social and economic issues in less dramatic form. This lack of a clear and agreed vision within Labor and the Left is one of the reasons for the hegemony of the Right.

The new, reformed political Right, while economically liberal and radical, also draws a great deal of its strength from the kind of conservatism associated with the promotion of 'conservative values'. The short-lived leader of the Labor Party, Mark Latham, put this succinctly: 'For a century or more, Labor parties won the votes of working people on the basis of economic issues. Now we are losing them in the values debate.'[1] The values debate is not some artefact of conservatism, but arises from real economic and cultural changes in Australia over the last 25 years. Social researcher Michael Pusey, for example, studied 'middle Australia' from 1996 to 2000, and described in great detail our 'moral anxiety' about damage to the 'values ecology' of communities, families and work.[2]

This cultural instability and moral anxiety is what lay behind the rise of One Nation; the name itself expressing a desire for common unifying values and a strong national identity. The Hanson upsurge began a political sea change for Australia—one we are still experiencing. Since its high tide, John Howard and the Right have continued to address the moral anxiety and cultural losses felt by many Australians. They have largely recaptured the One Nation vote for the mainstream Right, and they have done this through a 'culture war' over values. Phrases like 'family values' and 'moral values', along with 'border protection' and 'national security', capture the spirit of popular anxiety and the desire for something stable and secure. Too often, the Left has dismissed these slogans without addressing the genuine fears behind them. It can sympathise with economic insecurity, but finds it harder to do the same with cultural insecurities.

The culture war over values

One effective weapon in the culture war which has been widely used by the ideologues of the Right in parliament and the press is the characterisation of opponents as an 'elite'. Left-wing elites are said to be deaf to the needs of ordinary people while they lecture them on political values and cultural etiquette. These are the elites who sip lattés in inner-city cafes and drink chardonnay while they busily undermine the values of ordinary Australians, the 'battlers'. Just before the 2001 election, John Howard commented proudly that he was 'scorned by the elites and held in such disdain'. Playing on suspicion of elites is an enormously powerful device in a country like Australia, with a long-standing and popular streak of egalitarianism and anti-intellectualism. It is used to great effect by populist journalists such as Piers Akerman and Andrew Bolt, as well as by Liberal ministers such as Tony Abbott. This is the political rhetoric that commentator Robert Manne describes as 'conservative populism'.

The Right's dismissal of critics as 'elites' who are out of touch with 'the battlers' is, as journalist Geoffrey Barker says, 'an extraordinary charge coming from neo-liberal fundamentalists whose privileged lives rarely bring them close to anyone who has had to "battle" for anything'.[3] But, while it is true that the Right's charges of elitism are grossly hypocritical, such rebuttals cut little ice. The discourse damning cultural elites is powerful because it connects with a real weakness of the Left. The Left's world view was based on class, which had a strong populist element. Until relatively recently, it was the Left that spoke the language of 'elites' in the name of the people. This class ideology, originating in socialism, identified elites on the basis of their wealth and political power. Today, class has much less resonance and the Right has constructed an ideology around the perceived power of an elite with cultural influence.

One of the reasons for this decline is that class ideology was based on what economist Clive Hamilton calls the 'paradigm of material deprivation'.[4] This paradigm means that the main political task is the fight against material inequalities and for redistribution of wealth. In its most common form, it supported government regulation and intervention, and in its most extreme form, it involved the abolition of capitalism. This ideology had a powerful resonance for a long time because of widespread problems of deprivation. While Labor was never socialist, its ideas were grounded in this paradigm of material deprivation. It captured an essential part of the reality of much of twentieth-century Australia, and inspired a great deal of Labor's idealism. But this world view has been under siege for a long time. For many decades, capitalism has proved to be more dynamic and innovative than most imagined. One result has been the achievement of higher living standards and a degree of everyday affluence unimaginable even by trade unionists and Leftists in the 1950s.

Other related changes have long been recognised. The world view of class and deprivation grew out of a largely male working class, which performed physically hard jobs and had a more or less unified collectivist 'battlers' outlook. Each of these assumptions was slowly eroded as more women joined the workforce, white-collar work grew and workers developed a more individualist identity based on consumer choices offered by affluence. Their sense of collectivism—the ethos of battlers—is now more likely to be expressed as a cultural phenomenon defending, for example, a traditional notion of Australian cultural identity rather than an economic class identity. While modern industrial societies still have gross material inequalities and an underclass of poor people, the paradigm of deprivation is no longer adequate as the sole foundation stone for a world view. (These and other issues are explored in the second half of this book.)

The Right's charge of Left elitism also relates to issues around gender and ethnicity. These were part of a slow cultural revolution which made Australia a better place. But this cultural revolution brought losses as well as gains. Family life changed and marriage became less secure. Stable identities and expectations of mother, father, wife, husband and child changed. What it meant to be 'Australian' became less clear; assumptions based on an Anglo-Celtic population with shared values could no longer be made. Combined with the waning of the old class-based Labor paradigm, the vision of Labor and the Left became even more complicated. Above all, among the old and new supporters of Labor, there is a lack of a common unifying vision. (These ideas are further developed in chapters 6, 7 and 8.)

One consequence of this lack of an agreed common vision is a vulnerability to 'wedge politics' in which the Right has successfully identified issues on which differences exist within the Left and exploited this division. The most obvious has been 'border security', on which middle-class Labor supporters tend to differ from Labor's blue-collar constituency. Other issues have been gay marriage and the teaching of values and literacy in public schools. Culture war and wedge politics have become permanent features of modern politics, because the Left side of the spectrum is now a coalition of social forces. It lacks the unifying set of ideas once provided by class-based ideology. This is most apparent in the Labor Party, but it reflects the situation in broader progressive thought. While the Right has reconfigured its ideas, the fact that this has not yet occurred on the Left is a vital part of contemporary politics.

There are at least two Lefts in Australian politics in terms of ideas. One is an older socialist Left and the other is a newer cultural Left. Simply put, the socialist Left tends to be based in the trade unions and Labor Party and the cultural Left tends to be based in the social movements and the universities. The socialist Left tends to be influenced by variants of socialism, including Marxism, and the cultural Left by liberalism and postmodernism. In practice, the two Lefts cross-fertilise and blend into each other, and neither exists in a 'pure' form. The cultural Left usually supports economic redistribution and trade unionism, and the socialist Left usually supports cultural diversity and feminist positions.

Both Lefts share something else, however. This is their incomprehension at the triumph of their opponents—the John Howards and George Bushes of this world. Their ideas—the modern formula of a radical conservatism—involve an economic outlook based on free markets and a social outlook based on conservative moral values. This modern formula is a blend of two contradictory tendencies: libertarianism in economic theory and conservatism in terms of the family and national identity. It is an extraordinarily powerful and appealing combination. In 2004, it led to the political devestation of the US Democrats and the Australian Labor Party.

To many progressives, this winning formula of radical conservatism is a trick, a fraud, a reliance on fear. But this begs the question: if it is some sort of trick, why haven't the progressives been able to expose the trick and project a more appealing vision? Why has progressive politics failed to mobilise popular support?

Rethinking Left values

Although this book involved a great deal of traditional research and is written by someone in a university, it is not intended as an academic study of some interesting political processes. Its intended audience is those members of the public who are interested in ideas and in politics, and the connection between them. It is an extended argument with two premises. First, it argues that the problems of the Left reside at the level of ideas and philosophy. Tinkering with policies, presentation and leadership is not enough. Second, it argues that it is only by confronting certain flaws in cherished ideas that the Left can rebuild its intellectual and values framework in the wider Australian society. I use the term 'Left' in its broadest sense of the members and supporters of the Labor, Democrat and Green parties, the unions and community groups, and unaffiliated progressive opinion, which includes current and erstwhile supporters of the Liberal and National parties.

Such a rethinking in progressive politics in Australia is long overdue and will take time. Yet it is urgently necessary. The ascendancy of the Right has meant that the Left now finds itself in a defensive position, holding grimly to familiar ideas, worried that a shift will open up new vulnerabilities and new defeats. Perhaps a more appropriate metaphor for the Left is that it is standing on a sandbank which is slowly eroding from under its feet. Buffeted by the surf, it manages to hold its position. However, survival lies not in immobility but in striking out in new and scary directions. These new directions mean rethinking the Left's intellectual framework and methods, while retaining its basic values.

One positive response to the inadequacy of past Left ideas has been the emergence of the Australian Greens. The Greens not only exist in local, state and national governments, but also in the community movements so vital for progressive change. Significantly, the Greens see themselves as 'neither Right nor Left, but in front'. By basing themselves around the idea of a sustainable society and economy, they have grasped a vital truth—something no other party has done. The presence and success of the Greens is a welcome sign of the ability of progressive politics to renew itself and to grasp new ideas. Another sign of hope comes from the Right. A number of people on the Right have taken a public stance against the aggressive reborn Right of John Howard. People such as Robert

Manne, former prime minister Malcolm Fraser and Liberal MP Petro Georgiou have taken principled stances opposed to Howard's agenda. They represent a strand of 'social liberalism' that was once on the Right, but is now hard to classify.

Another sign of hope comes from within the embattled Labor Party. Often, the first step toward wisdom is recognising the problem and asking the right questions. One of Labor's more thoughtful spokespeople, Julia Gillard, argues that Labor needs a new vision—a 'new animating force'. In the face of the conservative onslaught, she argues that 'Labor and the Australian Left have not been able to articulate an answering guiding philosophy'.[5] Progressives need to define a new 'transformative ideal' and vision. The issues which appeal to Labor's tertiary educated supporters 'need to be sited within a broader vision of Australia, which is inclusive of those who rightly worry about jobs, health, education, roads, border security and the like'. Similar views have come from fellow MP Lindsay Tanner.

Developing a new vision will not be easy. It is not a simple arithmetical 'adding up' of a list of progressive causes and demands. Rather, it requires far more complex syntheses of ideas and policies. For example, it involves a synthesis of the world of paid work, class and material equality with the world of family, home and gender. Paid work and family life are intimately connected in modern societies in ways they were not before. Economic policy deeply affects family life—something I explore in chapters 2 and 7. In similar fashion, a synthesis is needed based on both the ideals of cultural diversity, and the virtues of social cohesion and common values (see Chapter 8). Another issue concerns the widely held support for ever-increasing progress in living standards. The welfare of humans has to be reconciled with the need for a sustainable economy, and this may be the challenge of the coming century.

At a less abstract level, all these syntheses which form part of a common vision must be translated into policies and practical stances. These must respond to issues as they arise and strike a resonance with ordinary Australians. This book is not the last word on all of this. In many ways, it is 'first words'. But it will, I hope, provoke and stimulate the kind of debate needed to develop this common vision.

2

A world made by markets

When we possess something of real value—doors unlocked at night, laughter in the playground—we are asked to name its price, otherwise it can't be audited. The immeasurable world is slipping away . . . Today we inhabit a perpetual 'state of emergency': politicians have short attention spans; capitalists dance to the fluctuations of the finance markets. In my youth, speed was a drug, now it's a lifestyle.

Richard Neville[1]

Market populism decries elitism while transforming CEOs as a class into one of the wealthiest elites of all time. It deplores hierarchy while making the corporation the most powerful institution on earth. It hails the empowerment of the individual and yet regards those who use that power to challenge markets as robotic stooges. It salutes choice and yet tells us the triumph of markets is inevitable.

Thomas Frank, *One Market Under God*[2]

The point is greed is good . . . greed is right . . . greed works. Greed clarifies, cuts through and captures the essence of the evolutionary spirit.

Gordon Gekko, *Wall Street*

We live in a world made by markets. The last twenty years have seen the triumph of a broad doctrine which goes by many names—economic rationalism, neo-liberalism, neo-classical economics, supply-side economics—and which argues that all kinds of economic and social issues can be successfully dealt with by a combination of individualism, competition and free markets. At the same time, older styles of conservatism and social liberalism have waned, along with socialism—in both its radical and reformist modes.

These changes and the end of the Cold War in 1989–91 have ushered in the era of the New Capitalism: more global, more efficient and more dynamic. The old capitalism of the postwar industrial world operated in a regulated economy, relying for its profitability on such industries as food processing, white goods, cars and steel-making. The New Capitalism is a deregulated economy, increasingly relying on services and knowledge. It commercialises all aspects of culture and leisure—sport, movies and music—and on the backs of them it builds industries of merchandised clothing, footwear, toys and sporting goods. Its appetite for commodities leads it to dig more mines, log more timber and pump more oil. The New Capitalism deepens the commodification of things once done within the family economy: preparing meals, caring for children and looking after the elderly. Activities once performed by government have been commercialised or privatised in recent years: education, electricity-generation, telecommunications, water and health. All of this economic activity is backed by sophisticated industries of marketing and advertising. Everything is a product and everyone is a customer.

New Capitalism is a libertarian capitalism, and libertarianism has attractive elements. It is more open and flexible. Workers are more mobile and skilled, and those whose skills are in demand have more autonomy in their working lives and good material rewards. For most people, daily life is less constrained by social conformism. Enjoyment is not constantly shadowed by moralistic guilt. Sexuality and sexual preference are not hidden in the shadows and the expectations of women (and men) are less rigid.

Indeed, the libertarian New Capitalism has embraced the libertarian cultural revolution of the 1970s. Diverse lifestyles have been converted into market niches for an endless array of new consumer products. Above all, for many, material living standards are higher than at any time in history.

Under this dispensation, a curious paradox has emerged, however. The threat of communism has collapsed and Western economies pour out a cornucopia of material goods, yet there is an uneasiness about all of this. There has been a popular revival of critiques of hyper-consumption and hyper-individualism. There is a yearning for 'moral values'. A move back to religious belief—often funda-mentalist—has been observed, both in the wealthy West and in the less developed world.

The gap between the super rich and the poorest is growing, as is a larger middle class. In a previous era, the struggle over this unequal distribution of wealth was the underlying dynamic of politics in countries like Australia. Today, resentment over the unequal distri-bution of wealth has lost its bite. But unease and resentment about something else is growing. It's hard to put your finger on, but it is about the way we live—the quality of our lives. It has something to do with that overused and slippery term, 'stress'. It is about being unable to spend as much time with your children as you'd like; it's insecurity about your job; it's about the growth of social problems like gambling, drug abuse and mental illness; it's a loss of trust in common institutions (and not just parliament). For 'old Australians', it is an unease over multiculturalism and an uncertainty over national identity. It's also about the penetration of commercial values into all parts of our lives. As we enter the twenty-first century, our world is not only faster, busier and more stressful; it is also suffused with the language and values of business.

We can now shop at the mall at midnight. Previously, we did not need to shop at midnight, but now we have choice. And, given the torrent of changes to the intensity of our lives, we now *need* to shop at midnight.

It once seemed commonsense that public goods such as water, telephone services, electricity, road-building and so on would be organised with the public good uppermost in mind. But now privatisation, marketisation, competition and deregulation have become the new commonsense—and bring with them a new set of values. Universities were once institutions whose rationale was in the knowledge they produced and passed on. Today, universities jealously guard their 'brand' in the competitive market for fee-paying overseas and local students.

An amateur pastime—sport—is today a global industry, with players bought and sold for millions of dollars. Meanwhile, obesity grows and physical exercise diminishes in the wider society.

The working lives of many people have been transformed. For many, careers and jobs have given way to contracts or casualisation.

The activities of business suffuse public space. Every hour, on the hour, we can find out the price of a barrel of West Texas Crude, or the gyrations of the FT100 Index of share prices. In the world of New Capitalism, money is slowly becoming the measure of all value. Non-commercial activities and motives exist, but they are under siege.

The market revolution

Humanity did not always live in such excessively market-driven economies. In pre-market agrarian societies, life was regulated by custom and not markets, every action performed by an individual was moralised, invested with a sense of right and wrong which was determined by whatever religious or spiritual beliefs prevailed. Money was not the sole measure of value. Every action was measured against the weight of tradition, and every action occurred within a web of obligation towards family and tribe. Such societies were stable and slow paced. Lest we over-romanticise them, they were (and are) societies of material scarcity, and sometimes people starved to death. Obligation was enforced by ostracism or violence. They were deeply conservative—marriages were arranged and women obeyed men, sometimes on pain of death.

The point of the comparison, as I said, is not to romanticise these societies, but to say this: our modern-day instincts and minds were shaped by a million years of hunter-gather society, then by agriculture-based societies for the last 10 000 years. Our human nature evolved in conditions which were utterly different from those of modern society. We always had the capacity for individual aspiration and self-interest, but this was held in check by low material levels which forced communal lifestyles for most of human history. Today, as the material wealth of society soars to new heights, these capacities are less restrained. As well, a growing gap is emerging between self-interest and the more communal human instincts.

The Great Transformation, a book by the historian of the market and the changes it wreaked on feudal society Karl Polyani, is undergoing a revival as a book for our time.[3] It documents the epochal change the market represented in the sweep of human history. In Polyani's analysis, *society* is counterposed to the *market*. The significance of the market is not that it initially generated massive inequalities of rich and poor, urban slums and exhausting factory work, but that it destroyed the protection offered by social bonds and social obligations: 'Instead of economy being embedded in social relations, social relations are embedded in the economic system.'[4] The economy in its various forms was 'submerged in [man's] social relationships'. Self-interest, in its modern form of widespread profit-seeking, barely existed. Social standing, social ties, obligations, reciprocity and redistribution were fundamental to feudal and earlier societies. Such societies were strongly cohesive: 'Custom and law, magic and religion co-operated in inducing the individual to comply with rules of behaviour which, eventually, ensured the functioning of the economic system.'[5]

Central to the coming of the market was the process of *commodification*—the turning of the necessities of life into objects for buying and selling. The most radical form of commodification involved human labour and land.

To allow the market mechanism to be the sole director of the fate of human beings and their natural environment, indeed, even of the amount and use of purchasing power, would result in the demolition of society. For the alleged commodity 'labor power' cannot be shoved about, used indiscriminately, or even left unused, without affecting the human individual who happens to be the bearer of this peculiar commodity. In disposing of a man's labor power the system would incidentally, dispose of the physical, psychological and moral entity 'man' attached to that tag. Robbed of the protective covering of cultural institutions, human beings would perish from the effects of social exposure; they would die as the victims of acute social dislocation through vice, perversion, crime and starvation. Nature would be reduced to its elements, neighborhoods and landscapes defiled, rivers polluted, military safety jeopardized, the power to produce food and raw materials destroyed.[6]

The process of the commodification of labour and nature is still with us, and opposition to it led to the rise of the trade union movement and, more recently, to the environmental movement. The significance of Polyani's approach is that it is a *conservative* critique, not a radical one. It stands in contrast to that of Marx, who built an elaborate theoretical system involving a trajectory of history which would see socialism arise as the radical negation of capitalism. Polyani has a much more modest critique, which focuses instead on the fact that human communities depend on the human values and needs that can be eroded or not fulfilled by the market. He constantly contrasts what he calls *organic societies*—where the relations between humans are direct, interpersonal ones—with the atomistic individualism encouraged by the market.

The market grew out of occasional exchanges on the periphery of human communities. In earliest times, salt was traded over long distances; in later periods, fruit, vegetables and animals were bought and sold on a cycle of 'market days'. Today, the market is the central totem of our society, active around the clock, exchanging commodities, demanding our time and defining our lives. In this kind of society, social relations are under the constant pressure of being reduced to their commercial and instrumental purpose.

Once a robust sphere of non-commercial life existed alongside the world of the market. Today, this non-commercial sphere—from the level of public institutions down to family life—is shrinking and is itself being commodified, its elements being produced or packaged and sold on commercial terms. Old-fashioned notions like the public good blur and the quality of life changes in so many ways. We live rushed lives, jamming work, fast food and leisure into the constricted space of our lives. One response is the popular radical movement in Italy today called the 'slow food movement'—which stands for a different way of living, not just of eating.

This is the era of the New Capitalism, whose outlines first emerged during the long boom which ended in the mid-1970s. It really flourished fully only after the impact of the Thatcher and Reagan eras made itself clear. It is a turbo-capitalism, a lean and mean capitalism, a capitalism with no competitors.

The junking of the old-fashioned firm

The transformation of the old capitalism has had major consequences for the wider society, but let us start—perhaps paradoxically—with the changes wrought within business itself. Historically, major companies used also to be social institutions with a degree of authority—old money, often family based, saw its role partly as a 'pillar of society'. Such companies were ruthless, but not without a sense of their own rectitude and public responsibility. That is, they felt they owed something to an idea of the public interest which was beyond the immediate interests of their shareholders—hence the philanthropy of the great families of old money. In the United States, it was the Carnegie, Rockefeller and

Mellon families. In Australia, it was the Fairfax, Myer and Baillieu families. Today we face a new kind of stripped-down, deregulated capitalism. It is a capitalism that is more open and libertarian, but one where corporate leaders have, in consequence, little sense of public duty, morality or public interest—other than what is required by law. The widespread use of the term 'the bottom line' as the final measure of all things sums this up. Rather than a modest and disinterested philanthropy, we have corporate sponsorship, developed as part of a keenly targeted marketing strategy aimed at getting concrete results for the company.

Once, a sense of public duty went along with a paternal interest in employees—especially in white-collar and old-money firms. Dedication and loyalty from employees were repaid with loyalty from the corporate board when times were tough. Today, in spite of the flowering of 'human resources' departments, the old career structures and security have been replaced by a short-termist view of employees as mere commodities to be bought and sold, or dumped. Meanwhile, CEOs flit from company to company, sacking a few hundred here, collecting obscene payouts there.

The political philosopher John Gray calls this 'the corrosion of bourgeois life' due to 'the hollowing out of the business corporation as a social institution' by outsourcing.[7] Others reflect on the unprecedented wealth that has accrued to the top 5 per cent of managers and owners, and worry. Lester Thurow, an American economist and management expert, argues that:

> . . . in the short run, capitalism can politically afford to be much tougher economically on its workforce than it used to be when socialism or communism threatened it with an internal revolution and an external threat. But at some point, something will arise to challenge capitalism and capitalism will need the political support of more than those small numbers of individuals who are actually owners of substantial amounts of capital. Where is this support to come from?[8]

Such qualms, based on a sense of history, are rare among the advocates of the New Capitalism.

Instead of the solidity of the company-as-social-pillar, we now have the weightless corporation. It has as few real employees as possible, along with lots of casual and contract workers, and numerous outsourced services. Such companies do not make *things*—that is done offshore—they make *brands*, as Naomi Klein's powerful *No Logo* maintains. Branded music, clothing, sports shoes, alcohol, takeaway food, soft drink—the big name brands like Sony, Hilfiger, Nike, McDonald's and Coke—are woven into the texture of ordinary life: 'The old paradigm had it that all marketing was selling product. In the new model, however, the product always takes back seat to the real product, the brand, and the selling of the brand acquired an extra component that can only be described as spiritual.'[9]

But perhaps even more important than brands, customer service or whether or not old money is better than new money is the fact that the economic system provides most of us with that most basic necessity for living: a job. In the New Capitalism, work has been transformed. There is no longer a standard pattern of work with fixed hours, with the consequent ability to balance work and life.[10] Australia once led the world in reducing working hours, but now we are part of a process of polarisation of overwork and underemployment. At one end of the scale, work has become a matter of spending long hours away from home. About one-third of workers now work long or very long (50+) hours per week. More than half work overtime, and much of this is unpaid. Work has intensified, with fewer rest breaks and more understaffing. Many complain of work affecting family life and causing stress. A senior nurse administrator noted: 'The wards were staffed way back for about 85 per cent occupancy of patients and now they run at over 100 per cent occupancy. The patients who used to come in for ten-day stints now come in for two. The throughput and the movement and what the nurses have to do now in the ward area is just incredible.'[11]

At the other end of the scale, unemployment remains high even during boom times. In some regional areas, it persists at above 10 per cent, while long-term unemployment is concentrated among school leavers, mature workers and the non-English-speaking. Despite apparent drops in official unemployment figures, about one in eight workers is under-employed. Casual jobs accounted for three-quarters of new jobs in the 1990s. In the 1960s, about 90 per cent of workers were in permanent full-time jobs; by 1988 this had dropped to 74 per cent and by 2002 it was 61 per cent.[12] Longer hours, casualisation and under-employment have all contributed to a growing crisis in the family, which we explore further in Chapter 7.

The culture of neo-liberalism

The New Capitalism has spawned massive and growing industries based on advertising and marketing. Their activities are by no means limited to the mass media, but affect the texture and quality of our daily lives—in our workplaces, homes, schools, sports, universities, museums and galleries.

Advertising in the mass media has traditionally been confined to certain limits: the number of minutes per hour, restrictions on content in children's viewing hours, and the strict and clear distinction between advertising and non-advertising content. Elsewhere, other restrictions applied—often responding to custom and taste rather than the law. Today, all bets are off. The aggressive instinct of the advertising and marketing industries is to break down such barriers to promotion. The process is never ending. Consumers, said one ad executive, 'are like roaches—you spray them and spray them and they get immune after a while'.[13]

Once there seemed no need for advertising on buses, taxis and other public spaces. And when it slowly began to occur, it hardly seemed worth dying on the barricades to oppose:

But somewhere along the line, the order flipped. Now buses, streetcars and taxis, with the help of digital imaging and large pieces of adhesive vinyl, have become ads on wheel, shepherding passengers around in giant chocolate bars and gum wrappers, just as Hilfiger and Polo turned clothing into wearable brand billboards.[14]

Children were once largely ignored or treated as off limits by advertisers. Today there is pressure to deregulate barriers on TV advertising to children, and even to penetrate such non-commercial havens as schools. Advertisers have discovered a new demographic, 'tweenagers'. But already the 23 000 ads watched by children annually—largely for confectionery, soft drinks, sugared cereals and fast food—are being blamed for a rise in levels of childhood obesity.[15] Some of the most probing and detailed research into the private world of children is carried out by advertisers, rather than educational psychologists. According to Stephen Kline, the marketers of children's goods have always paid more attention than educationists to children's active imaginations and fantasy life:

> The marketers didn't have to assume that children's daydreams, hero worship, absurdist humour and keen sense of group identity were meaningless distractions . . . [rather] they recognized that these attributes were the deep roots of children's culture and could be employed as effective tools for communicating with them.[16]

The toys and games advertised to children displace older patterns of family relations and lack the depth, authenticity and social richness of older non-commercialised forms. 'Something is missing from childhood, the critics argue, when we give a child a musical tape of children's songs because we don't have time to sing to or with them; when we give them a My Little Pony colouring book as a substitute for drawing; when we let them watch fantasies on TV, without reading to them or exposing them to the intimacy of personal story telling.'[17] And many parents will testify to the intensity of children's obsession with getting toys or games associated with the latest merchandised craze, or of refusing to use or wear things which are not 'branded' by that craze.

Schools were once havens from commercial pressure, and education was seen as an intellectual and moral process far removed from the marketplace. Now worried academics, child psychologists and teachers hold conferences debating the trend towards corporate sponsorship in schools.[18] In exchange for donations, companies—large and small—demand their logo on sports uniforms and equipment. Junk food manufacturers offer refrigerators to school canteens in exchange for promotional rights; supermarket chains offer computers to schools and so turn schoolchildren into a promotional army hassling their parents and neighbours to shop at their stores. All promotions support noble causes. A pizza-maker offers its products as prizes for the best readers and spellers. 'Once again we are bribing our children to read, to learn, to spell not for their own sakes but for some outside reason', said school community leader Judith Tarrant. 'Are we giving a subliminal message to children that these things are not worth doing for their own sakes?'[19]

The allied industry of marketing conquers new fields beyond advertising. The Big Brother of George Orwell's novel *1984* was everywhere, watching citizens through telescreens and controlling their behaviour. His influence also aimed to penetrate the most private places of the mind. When the hero of the novel rebels and is caught, he is tortured until the moment when he finally breaks: he realises that he loves Big Brother. Thoughtcrime and further rebellion are therefore impossible. Today, advertising and commercial values aim to penetrate our most private places and consciousness. In 1999, a TV network in Holland developed a new kind of docu-soap, called *Big Brother*—an idea later sold around the world. Like its namesake, *Big Brother* is all-seeing and it also aims to control behaviour—through advertising and product placement. According to one executive from the Ten Network: 'As we go through the planning for a series like *Big Brother*, we look at the show and see where opportunities lie for sponsors . . . it's about understanding the sponsor's brand and product and what ways we can leverage them throughout the format of the show.'[20]

In motion pictures, commercial promotion—dubbed 'product placement'—has been an established fact since 1950, when the Marx brothers staged a rooftop chase past the neon signs of companies in *Love Happy*.[21] But the movies have long gone far beyond product placement. Popular movies for kids have become vehicles for vast merchandising and marketing exercises in food, clothing, footwear, toys and electronic games. Product placement has spread to the purely literary arts. In 2001 the British author Fay Weldon published a novel, *The Bulgari Connection*, for the Italian jewellers Bulgari. Weldon said that initially she was appalled by the idea, but later reconciled herself to it. Her contract stipulated that Weldon was required to mention the name Bulgari at least twelve times, but she went much further. The London *Daily Telegraph* said one passage in the book read 'rather like a catalogue showcasing the jeweller's products'.[22]

The commercialisation of sport

In October 1999, over 30 000 fans rallied to support the South Sydney Rugby League football team. They were angry because their football code had finally capitulated to Rupert Murdoch's News Ltd plan to turn the game into 'product' for his pay television operation. As a result of this deal, their team had been dropped from the rationalised competition. The 'Super League war' and its aftermath illustrated what happens in commercialised sport. Teams with a genuine grassroots following were excluded, while artificial teams were created in order to give the new game a 'national appeal'. Players were bought and sold and politicians were warned to lay off supporting the rebels; media coverage was distorted (News Ltd owns 70 per cent of newspaper circulation). It was about 'what happens when a global juggernaut rolls through a local community'.[23]

At the rally, a lay chaplain for the team argued that the struggle between South Sydney and the National Rugby League was a microcosm of bigger events: 'What was held dear and what bonded people in terms of family and loyalty seems to have gone from their workplace and many institutions. Sport was one of the last vestiges that people held on to . . . and if you strip away 100 years of meaning and identity played out through sport, it can really cripple a community.'[24]

The values of sport were once expressed in the phrase 'physical culture', which saw values of physical achievement and of health as underpinnings of the intellectual and moral health of individuals and the nation: *sano mens in corpore sano* ('a healthy mind in a healthy body'). These now old-fashioned ideals arose at a time when sport was more local and participatory. The 'love of the game' motivated the unpaid players and volunteer administrators.

Larry Writer gives us a picture of a football match at this time, so near and yet so far from today:

> The vast spectator areas were seething with people, 69,860 of them, an Australian club record to that time. Rain had started to fall heavily and many in the throng had unfurled umbrellas and donned slick black raincoats and sou-westers. There was just one sign on the perimeter fence: 'Up Wests' it said . . . There were no monstrous club symbols burnished into the grass, no smoke-flare skydivers, crash-landing on the roofs of the stands, no Tina Turner or soap opera stars lip synching their latest hit. No media battalion, no advertising logos . . . a brass band played 'Garry Owen' and 'The Road to Gundagai'.[25]

This world of sport had almost passed by the 1970s, when the owners of television networks began to realise that coverage of sport was one of the cheapest ways to provide popular content around which advertising could be sold. Initially this was embraced by many sports administrators because it provided a massive boost of money and publicity. But the embrace is slowly crushing many of the original values of sport, replacing them with the logic of profit maximisation.

Once funding for major sports depended heavily on gate receipts, the expression of a close relationship between fans, players and the administrators. Television changed that, along with the internal structure of many sporting contests. Rules, scoring, conditions of play, timing, place and duration of events were all manipulated to accommodate TV.[26] Graham Samuel, a commissioner of the Australian Football League, recently argued that sporting competitions 'are essentially franchise operations, broadly akin to a KFC or McDonald's chain of restaurants. The franchisor, the sporting code's administrators, issue licences to teams to participate in the competition—to create and sell the company's product to their supporters, their demographic market'.[27]

The role of the players also changed. Many elite athletes systematically use performance-enhancing drugs, driven by a desire to win at any cost—including to their own health. Meanwhile, in schools, physical education is 'in a crisis state' and the 'era of commodified global sport and TV entertainment encourages watching ads, discourages the dabbler, giving preference (and rewards) to the elite performer'.[28]

An older kind of sport—played for its own sake and responsive to local community support—still exists, of course, but it is overshadowed by high-stakes sport. The intrinsic *values* which motivated the old idea of sport are fading as the extrinsic, commercially motivated values of the new sport soar to commanding heights.

The corporatisation of culture

A different set of values is under attack in the case of universities, libraries, museums and art galleries. Historically, they expressed the aesthetic and intellectual values of the world of art and science. Such institutions are central to the identity of a society like ours because they both preserve and give meaning to the wider society by embodying cultural, intellectual and spiritual values.

One of the lesser known consequences of the neo-liberal revolution is the boom in corporate sponsorship of art galleries, museums and individual artists. As government support was withdrawn, they sought private largesse. Patronage of art by the rich is nothing new. But two things have changed since the days of the Medicis: its scale and consequences. Patronage, once small time and relatively disinterested, is today a sophisticated marketing tool. The corporate art guru of Chase Manhattan bank, Manuel Gonzalez, puts it thus:

> A corporation's obligation is to its community. Art is the cheapest—by that I mean most reasonably priced—decorative element available, with a larger margin of profitability than any other commodity in history. It gives you a great cachet among the sophisticated individuals with a high net worth who are usually targeted by most businesses.[29]

This rings alarm bells with people like art critic Robert Hughes, who warns about the development of a public culture 'wholly dependent on corporate promotion budgets of white CEOs, reflecting the concerted interests of one class, one race, one mentality'.[30] The author of a study of corporate sponsorship of art, *Privatising Culture*, Chin-Tao Wu, concludes:

> By institutionalizing itself, corporate art assumes moral authority, appropriates legitimizing symbols to itself and is able to set artistic trends. In this sense one social group acquires power over one of the few sectors of society supposedly above the profit and loss principle and art becomes the unwitting accomplice of a new cultural hegemony.[31]

Another network of cultural and intellectual institutions undergoing a radical transformation is the universities. For a number of years, leading academics—from both Left and Right—have warned about the narrowing of universities' functions. Government funding of Australia's universities has dropped from about 90 per cent in 1981 to just over 50 per cent in 2000, with much of the difference being made up from student fees and from courses set up to attract full fee-paying students. Universities now compete fiercely for fee-paying students—their solvency depends on it. Academics report that increasing attention is paid to courses that attract fee-paying students and that their research priorities are affected.[32] One result is the phenomenon of 'soft marking' of the work of fee-paying students.

Increasingly, the topics for research conducted by academics are channelled towards assisting industry or existing institutions. Research that might be critical (or simply independent) of industry or existing institutions is not favoured. It is true that universities have always had strong vocational and professional content, and some fee-paying courses existed in previous years. But, prior to the current commercialisation, universities also developed a set of intellectual and cultural values which prized autonomy from the short-term demands of society. These values are since being eroded by managers who insist on narrowing and flattening the purpose of universities to short-term utilitarian ends.

For example, a great deal of academic life depends on voluntary participation in informal processes, such as refereeing articles for publication, marking theses, serving on professional academic bodies, editing journals and organising conferences. These cooperative activities are centred around particular disciplines in science, the humanities, and so on. Often reciprocal, they depend on a shared love of the knowledge and challenge of the discipline. Historian Judith Brett from La Trobe University argues that this collective ethos is being undermined as universities compete for prestige, research funding and students.[33]

Another set of cultural institutions, often overlooked but increasingly subject to commercial pressure, is the news media. In the 1990s, banks, phone companies and airlines began paying secret fees to Sydney radio talkback hosts such as Alan Jones and John Laws to promote and protect their products within their normal radio patter. More than this, when a misguided listener called in to complain about a bank or business, the disc jockey was expected to defend the company or steer the complaint on to neutral ground. The resulting scandal was dubbed 'cash for comment'. But the scandal is not confined to talkback radio. It touches on a profound problem for democracies: the growing intrusion of commercial values into journalism and into the conduct of public debate.

Since their inception, lifestyle magazines, as well as rural and suburban newspapers, have offered advertisers sympathetic coverage in news pages on payment of a premium fee. Thus the billion-dollar cosmetics industry has been protected from critical coverage in the pages most often read by its consumers. Within the industry, the deception of 'advertorials' is thought to be harmless, quarantined to mere lifestyle publications. But advertorials are now creeping into the news and current affairs coverage of major newspapers and television programs. The commercial mentality was expressed by the CEO of Fairfax newspapers, Fred Hilmer, who referred to journalists as 'content providers' and newspapers as 'advertising platforms'. Another newspaper executive recently argued that 'a newspaper was basically a media for distributing advertising and the news was wrapped around it to make it attractive'.[34] This marks a significant break with ideas of journalism as a vital force in a democracy, informing citizens and acting as a watchdog for the public interest.

News values are skewed because of the newspaper, magazine or broadcaster's hunt for desirable demographics. A former editor of the *Sydney Morning Herald* once told me there was 'too much news about losers' in the paper, which might upset its desired wealthy readership in the 'AB' demographic segment. The motivations and ideals of journalism, like those of many other professions, are cast in terms of providing a public service and a public good, which are not reducible to commercial calculation. Yet the forces ranged against such journalism, both within and outside the industry, are growing, driven by the commercial imperative.

Neo-liberalism versus family values

The effect of the new commercial values is most keenly felt when they affect our most intimate places: our immediate circle, our family and close friends.

Families, friendships and other non-market bonds are a problem for economic liberalism and the commercial culture which it promotes. Relations between families, friends and similar communities tend not to be motivated by self-interest, but by care for others and altruism. Parents raise their children because they love them, not for reward. They may receive a reward, such as the reciprocal love of their child, but it is not *because* of this calculation that they spend time and money and less tangible things in caring. Nor is this solely because children are uniquely vulnerable. Among adults, friends help each other without a thought of monetary reward.

And this happens in communities as well. While writing this book, I happened to visit the war memorial in the town of Goulburn in southern New South Wales. I was struck by an inscription honouring the dead soldiers. It read: 'Service Before Self'. The society that chose these noble but quaint words might as well have been from antiquity rather than one within living memory. An ethic of service still exists in communities, but now more than ever it works against the grain.

Care for others, altruism, non-market relations—such feelings, such motives and the actions which flow from them do not make sense for most economic theorists. They do not easily fit the model of rational, self-interested behaviour. The place where they flourish most of all is in families. One person who has done much to pinpoint the contradiction between market values and family values is the feminist economist Nancy Folbre in her book *The Invisible Heart*.[35] This American academic chose the title of her book as a play on words of the best remembered phrase in Adam Smith's 1776 book, *The Wealth of Nations*. Smith saw the 'invisible hand' of the market— composed of a multitude of self-interested actions—resulting in a common good. Smith, often credited as the intellectual founder of neo-liberalism (it is actually more complicated than that) pointed to the beneficial role of self-interest in the economy. In another memorable phrase, he argues that 'it is not from the benevolence of the butcher, the brewer or the baker that we expect our dinner, but from their regard to their own self interest'.

But Folbre points out that, even though Smith was speaking figuratively, his example is very misleading. The sale of meat by the butcher does not actually provide us with dinner at all. He provides the meat for dinner, but the preparation of dinner (like many similar acts) is usually done by a wife or mother who does not act out of self-interest. In fact, a vast, parallel political economy based on the 'invisible heart' continually lubricates and reproduces society.

> The invisible hand represents the forces of supply and demand in competitive markets. The invisible heart represents family values of love, obligation and reciprocity. The invisible hand is about achievement. The invisible heart is about care for others. The hand and heart are interdependent, but they are also in conflict. The only way to balance them successfully is to find fair ways of rewarding those who care for other people. This is not a problem that economists—or business people—have taken seriously. They have generally assumed that God, nature, the family and 'Super Mom'—or some combination thereof— would automatically provide whatever care was needed.[36]

Nancy Folbre points out that the book which launched Adam Smith's career was not *The Wealth of Nations* but *The Theory of Moral*

Sentiments. In it, Smith showed he was perfectly aware of the existence of the kind of labour about which Folbre writes. He assumed that some kind of strong moral and altruistic underpinning of society would continue indefinitely and not be fundamentally damaged by the operation of competition and markets. But the spreading and entrenchment of markets, and especially of the values they promote, is doing just that.

Since the days of Adam Smith, the functions of the family have progressively been whittled away by the rise of industrial capitalism. From the introduction of widespread wage labour and the manufacture of food and clothing to the provision of education and health, the family has been reducing continually. This has not necessarily been a uniformly bad thing. The traditional family depended almost totally on the unstinting and unpaid work of wives and mothers whose choices about their own desires and needs depended on the goodwill of their husbands. The market and the process of commodification, as we shall see later, are by no means entirely bad. Folbre argues that capitalism weakened the family in some ways that were good and in other ways that were bad. Wage employment was important for women, giving them some alternatives to immediate marriage and motherhood. Some degree of financial independence became possible. 'Most of us agree that the growth of individualism expanded personal freedom in some very healthy ways', she says.

In the era of neo-liberalism, these tendencies have rapidly intensified and are now having an opposite effect from expanding freedom. Today, the final remaining functions of the family are being squeezed as the care of young children and the provision of food are increasingly provided by the market and the pressures of work constrict the time of parents. But the question is not just how much further we can go in this commodification. The question is whether we are already experiencing the costs of the crushing of our most intimate groupings and the devaluing of care.

Outsourcing and downsizing the efficient family

It is one of the paradoxes of modern industrial society that the revolution which saw women move towards equality occurred as the neo-liberal economic revolution gathered steam. The latter transformed the workforce and the nature of work into which women were flooding from the 1970s and 1980s onwards.

The conditions of paid work, which had slowly improved for many decades, began to change. Efficiency and competitiveness became the watchwords of the economy. Australians started to work longer and longer hours, often as unpaid overtime, and, significantly, women's share of these longer hours grew and is still growing.[37] The proportion of workers spending more than 45 hours a week at work increased from 18 per cent in 1985 to 26 per cent in 2001, according to one study. And in many workplaces, work has also intensified and working hours more frequently cover weekends and unsociable times of the day. Australians now have a 'long-hours culture', which is having disastrous effects on family life (see Chapter 7).[38]

An eye-opening study of the combination of these changes is *The Time Bind: When Work Becomes Home and Home Becomes Work*, by Arlie Russell Hochschild. This study explores what happens in a large American corporation when lengthening working hours are combined with two-job marriages in which women continue to do the lion's share of raising children and housework.

The study gives no easy answers to the 'time bind'. 'Amerco', the anonymous Fortune 500 company which Hochschild studied for several years, was one of the top 'family-friendly' companies, yet its employees took little advantage of these policies. Few women or men chose to work part time—and the obvious explanations for this, such as financial need or resistance from middle management, did not explain their choice. What Hochschild found was that, for many women, work was a relief from home. 'Work' was much more homely than 'home', which had become too much like work. Home was not a place to relax; it was another workplace—and in some cases one more onerous than 'real' work.

As well, family time is succumbing to a cult of efficiency, with the rush to the child-care centre, the skipping of family meals together and the loss of other unconstrained time. That is, the cult of 'scientific management' of work time associated with F.W. Taylor has been impinging on the industrial family. Parents are subjecting their family time to imagined time-and-motion studies in order to get maximum efficiency.

To achieve maximum efficiency in the family, Hochschild found parents responded in different ways. Some developed an 'emotional asceticism'—in effect minimising how much care their child or partner really needed. 'They made do with less time, less attention, less fun, less relaxation, less understanding and less support at home than they imagined possible. They emotionally downsized life.'[39] (Ever ready to make a commercial opportunity of any of life's problems, one company has produced self-help books like *Teaching Your Child to be Home Alone*, while Hallmark manufactures greeting cards which say 'Sorry I can't be there to tuck you in' and 'Sorry I can't say good morning to you'.)

Other parents acknowledged the needs of family and paid others to meet these needs: 'They outsourced ever larger parts of the family production process.' This has been going on for many years, as industrial urban society has replaced a smaller scale agricultural society and many family functions have been commodified.

Families, once a haven from the world of work (for most husbands and some wives), are being inexorably oriented to the industrial strategies of downsizing, outsourcing, industrialising and utility maximisation. One of the results is that parents—especially mothers—spend less time with their children. Hochschild is alarmed (rather than dismissive) about studies which show that this can lead to problems in later life development.

In truth, scholars don't know yet what, if any, the exact links
are between these ominous trends and the lessening amounts
of time parents spend with children . . . It's enough to observe
that children say they want more time with their parents and
parents say they regret not spending more time with their
children.[40]

In Australia, like the United States, the commodification of
family life deepens. In 2001, a new company, ABC Learning
Centres, listed on the Australian Stock Exchange. ABC runs over
200 child-care centres, caring for more than 20 000 children. ABC
is profitable: within three years, its share value increased tenfold
and in 2001–02 it made a $12 million profit. Those supporting
community and non-profit child care, such as Alma Fleet of
Macquarie University, argue that any spare money should not be
for the shareholders, but should be ploughed back into the welfare
of children. While ABC fulfils its minimum obligations, it battles
over care standards.[41]

The benefits of commodification are immense—prepared food,
ready-made clothing, professional child care and aged care; the trouble
is that the downside and the costs of commodification are at
present seamlessly wrapped in the same package. The main cost is
the adulteration of the quality of human and family relationships.
The products of commodification make for a convenient world,
one that many of us have taken advantage of. And because
commodification has benefits as well as costs, the struggle for a
society which meets human needs is not a simple one of returning
to a world of mothers welcoming working fathers back into the
haven of the home. Rather, the problem is how we can consciously
shape or roll back the processes of commodification so that we
can make them serve the human ends we value.

Commodification smuggles certain values into our daily lives
and into our relationships. The changes brought on by each step
in the process of commodification are welcome—they meet a real

problem, whether it is takeaway food, child care or formula milk (instead of breast milk). None of these are wholly wrong or destructive in themselves; cumulatively, however, they reduce and supplant other values—family values, if you like—with those of the instrumental, the technically efficient and the self-interested.

What is happening to the family under the pressure of neo-liberalism is happening to other relationships in the wider society. Not only are families moving into crisis, but wider social cohesion is fraying.

Some neo-liberal commentators try to minimise the conflict between the ruthless desire for efficiency of liberal economics and the cohesion provided by civil society which classical conservatism always valued. The Liberal Party ideologue Andrew Norton, for example, argues accurately that his party has long been interested in civil society, which he defines as 'non-state institutions such as the family, Churches, neighborhood associations, political groups, charities and sporting clubs'.[42] But Norton's argument that modern neo-liberals value both civil society, including the family, *and* economic efficiency, is flawed. First, it is perfectly possible to hold two quite contradictory beliefs if the tension is not starkly obvious. Second, this argument, which is widely accepted, relies on artificially separating the economy from the family and civil society—that is, talking about them as quite distinct and largely unrelated concepts. In the real world, the demands of maximum economic efficiency are in constant tension with the demands of family and the network of voluntary bodies that make up civil society. Such conflict cannot be overcome by neo-liberal theorists assuring us that they value both the traditional family and maximum economic efficiency. The values promoted by a hyper-commercialised culture are slowly crushing the values of an earlier, less commercialised culture.

Moreover, the assumptions of neo-liberal economics are also biased to a masculine point of view. They assume that the individual is autonomous, taking on associations as a choice and normally competing with others. But, as Marian Sawer points out, this model ignores 'the centrality of connection in women's lives, the web of relationships that are not in any meaningful sense "chosen" and the naturalness of interdependence'.[43]

Markets and the environment

One of the best-known areas in which market values clash with other values is the environment. This is obvious in basic ways, such as the desires of property developers and construction companies to tear down heritage buildings, or for logging or mining companies to despoil the natural environment. But this is only a microcosm of what is happening globally.

Markets can harness self-interest to produce massive economic growth. In the past century, world economic output has increased twentyfold. This has brought enormous benefits in terms of living standards, but such improvements have been purchased at enormous cost to the environment and to our future.[44] Between one-third and a half of the world's forests are gone, together with about half the mangroves and other wetlands. About three-quarters of marine fisheries are over-fished. There is a crisis in the loss of biodiversity, with large numbers of species of birds, mammals, reptiles and fish facing extinction or already extinct. The use of oil and coal together with deforestation has increased the amount of carbon dioxide in the atmosphere. The result is human-made climate change, with the melting of icecaps, erratic storms and desertification. The scale of it all, and its implications, are far too difficult to contemplate for most people.

In her 1998 speech to the American Association for the Advancement of Science, the AAAS president, ecologist Jane Lubchenco, said:

> The conclusions . . . are inescapable: during the last few decades, humans have emerged as a new force of nature. We are modifying

physical, chemical, and biological systems in new ways, at faster rates and over larger spatial scales than ever recorded on Earth. Humans have unwittingly embarked on a grand experiment with our planet. The outcome of this experiment is unknown, but has profound implications for all life on Earth.

Another analysis of the global ecological crisis is aimed at the increasingly obvious glaring holes in neo-liberal theory. Economist and environmentalist David Korten argues that one of the key weaknesses of free-market economics is that corporations can 'externalise' their costs. That is, they mostly don't have to pay for, or face the consequences of, the true cost of their operations. It is basic to market theory that the producer must bear all the costs of production, and that these be included in the selling price of a commodity. In fact, corporations constantly try to externalise their costs. They try to 'free ride':

> Externalized costs don't go away—they are simply ignored by those who benefit from making the decisions that result in others incurring the costs. For example when a forest products corporation obtains rights to clear-cut Forest Service land at giveaway prices and leaves behind a devastated habitat, the company reaps the immediate profit and the society bears the long term costs. When logging companies are contracted by the Mitsubishi Corporation to cut the forests of the Penan tribespeople of Sarawak, the corporation bears no cost for devastating native culture and ways of life.[45]

Many similar situations exist when corporations thrive on pollution. But this goes way beyond, say, the illegal midnight dumping of toxic wastes in sewers and such like. We are talking, rather, of one of the systematic causes of global warming. The normal and legal expulsion of waste into the atmosphere that arises from petrol- and diesel-powered trucks and cars is an example of externalising costs. In this case, the price will be paid by some of us in old age and by our children and our grandchildren. Major coal, oil and automobile companies continually lobby against limits on carbon dioxide emissions and back this with donations to political parties.

Market theory argues that, when the seller receives a benefit from an unearned profit, it represents an important source of market inefficiency because it rewards externalising behaviour. But more than this, any chance of curbing this behaviour relies on the law and governments—yet these bodies are precisely the ones being tightly restrained by free-market theory. Korten adds: 'Market forces create substantial pressure on business to decrease costs and increase profits by increasing efficiency. The corporate rationalists fail to mention that one way firms increase their "efficiency" is to externalize more of their costs.'

Globalisation and human values

The area of commercialisation and marketisation that has caused some of the greatest political controversies is not on the home turf of advanced industrial countries, but concerns the less developed world. The social and moral crisis that is *implicit* in advanced countries is *explicit* in the under-developed world. In the latter, the crises exacerbated by the global neo-liberal economy can be a matter of life and death. For example, it can mean the denial of life-saving drugs to the dying due to intellectual property rules tightened at the insistence of pharmaceutical companies; it can mean the stripping of jungle mountains and plains of their natural cover by logging companies; it can mean the dumping of toxic waste from mining into rivers which are the lifeblood of local communities. Or it can mean something less dramatic, such as the refusal by wealthy 'free trade' nations to open their borders to the agricultural products of poorer nations. As a result, they pay $300 billion annually in farm subsidies, which distorts trade and lowers world prices to the detriment of poor countries.[46] About 25 000 American cotton farmers, for example, are paid US$1.5 billion annually in subsidies while they control 40 per cent of global cotton exports.

The main moral defence of neo-liberal globalisation is that it is necessary to assist people in less developed countries to gain some of the benefits of higher living standards—clean water, affordable food, shelter, health and education systems. It is telling, then, that one of the most powerful rebuttals comes not from a radical in the anti-globalisation movement, but from Nobel prize winner for economics Joseph Stiglitz. Apart from winning that most prestigious prize, Stiglitz was chief economist of the World Bank in 1997–2000 and from 1993–97 was on the US president's Council of Economic Advisers.

Explaining why he wrote his book *Globalization and its Discontents*, Stiglitz says his views on globalisation were changed by serving in the World Bank, where: 'I saw first hand the devastating effect that globalization can have on developing countries and especially the poor within those countries.'[47] Stiglitz argues that globalisation has the *potential* to enrich the poor, but must be 'radically rethought'. What made Stiglitz critical of his own generation of neo-liberal economists was that he had a broader notion of human values which made him sceptical of ideologically driven policy.

Thus Stiglitz's support for competition policies, for freer trade and privatisation, all have their *moral* justification in his belief that such measures, if applied sensibly and carefully, will lead to genuine economic development—above all, jobs and higher living standards. Ironically, one of his exemplars is China, which is still ruled by the Communist Party which has gradually introduced privatisation (starting with land) and gradually freed internal markets. For the same moral purpose, he also supports Western investment—for instance, in sports shoe factories. 'People in the West may regard low-paying jobs at Nike as exploitation, but for many people in the developing world, working in a factory is a far better option than staying down in the farm and growing rice.'[48] But, while criticising mindless opponents of globalisation (he doesn't specify anyone in particular), he reserves the bulk of his argument for those he regards as 'market fundamentalists', epitomised by the actions of the International Monetary Fund (IMF).

Like all fundamentalists, both political and religious, market fundamentalists apply a uniform solution to every situation, unimpeded by empirical messiness or human consequences. So wedded to a single prescription is the IMF that, at times, whole paragraphs from its draft report for one country are lifted and transferred to a different country.[49]

Stiglitz is sceptical, for example, of privatisation as a cure-all.[50] In the Third World, government action is needed to stimulate or support aspects of the economy where private business will not or cannot do so. In addition, privatisation often turns enterprises from losses to profits by sacking workers. The newly privatised company does not directly share the social costs of unemployment, which may manifest themselves in urban violence, crime and political unrest. Privatisation, which is often demanded by the IMF, is supposed to curb government corruption based on manipulation of state-owned enterprises. Yet the forced privatisations are carried out by the same corrupt governments which sell state assets cheaply to cronies (with Russia being the prime example).

On trade liberalisation, liberal economic theory argues that when protection barriers are abolished and an economy is subjected to international competition, new and more productive industries arise in place of the older, less productive and less efficient industries. Stiglitz argues that this simple and neat equation is another ideological construct which often bears little relation to reality. Many workers and their families pay a terrible price for this. But the essential difference between the market fundamentalists and an economist like Stiglitz is not that they have diametrically opposed views on privatisation, trade and investment—they don't. Rather, the difference is the yardstick against which such policies are measured. For Stiglitz, this involves caring for the vulnerable:

the lack of concern about the poor was not just a matter of
views of markets and government, views that said that markets
would take care of everything and government would only make
matters worse; it was also a matter of values—how concerned
we should be about the poor and who should bear what risks.[51]

Again, while discussing the IMF's demands, which worsened the
East Asian economic crisis of 1997–98, he compares the values
inherent in the IMF's priorities: 'there are billions available to bail
out banks, but not the paltry sums to provide food subsidies for
those thrown out of work as a result of IMF programs'.

The point of this chapter is not that markets are inherently evil.
In later chapters I will argue that non-market societies are inevitably
tyrannical and repressive. Rather, my point is that when a society
relies excessively on market mechanisms this has consequences for
the values and culture of that society. Markets encourage the values
of self-interest at the expense of common interests; they promote
commercial and utilitarian values in place of human and traditional
values.

Market mechanisms can be useful in the economic sphere but
are destructive when routinely applied to the wider society.
Individuals, families and communities depend on human values in
order to flourish. The relentless march of markets is slowly but
inexorably corroding these human values in ways that even their
enthusiasts fail to comprehend. In order to understand this process,
it is necessary to investigate the intellectual framework of neo-
liberalism and how this set of ideas transformed many advanced
industrial countries, including Australia.

3

The triumph of an idea

A system that takes the pursuit of self-interest and profit as its guiding light does not necessarily satisfy the yearnings in the human soul for belief and some higher meaning beyond materialism. In the Spanish Civil War in the late 1930s, Republican soldiers are said to have died with the word Stalin *on their lips. Their idealised vision of Soviet communism, however misguided, provided justification for their ultimate sacrifice. Few people would die with the words* free markets *on their lips.*[1]

Daniel Yergin and Joseph Stanislaw

We must make the building of a free society once more an intellectual adventure, a deed of courage. If we can regain that belief in the power of ideas which was the mark of liberalism at its best, the battle is not lost.

Friedrich Hayek

The power of ideas to shape societies is profound, although we remain largely unaware of their effect in our day-to-day lives. Underneath the commonsense of an epoch and the slogans of its political parties are buried sets of philosophical ideas and values. These new ideas often begin as the property of a small group, then filter out into the surrounding society. If they find fertile ground, they can spread and transform societies in a relatively rapid space of time. This has occurred with many religious ideas, such as Christianity, and it also occurred with the ideas of the socialists in the nineteenth century. The ideas of democracy, equality and reason fermented in French society before they burst out in 1789 in a revolution which transformed not only France, but Europe and beyond.

Australians have lived through a more modest revolution over the last twenty years. Like similar changes, it was preceded by a ferment of ideas which were originally the property of a small group, but then struck a chord and changed society.

Today, our world is not just made by markets, but by 'free markets'—a phrase which operates as a code word for the triumph of a politico-philosophical trend known by various names, but increasingly by the phrase *neo-liberalism*. In popular Australian parlance, it is known as 'economic rationalism'. Other critics, like George Soros, use the term 'market fundamentalism'. I prefer the term 'neo-liberalism' because it conveys the profoundly important philosophical ideas which underlie what are often seen as merely economic policies. Conversely, to oppose the logic of neo-liberalism requires a different set of philosophical ideas and values, not just different policies or a set of slogans.

Neo-liberalism stands for a range of ideas, but the most popular expressions of its best-known stances are:

- Individual choice expressed in markets is better in principle and gives better outcomes than any other economic arrangement.
- Government regulation of private business should be abolished in favour of self-regulation and greater competition.
- The public sector should be commercialised and state-owned enterprises sold to shareholders.
- Tax should be as low as possible, with a user-pays principle for many government services.
- Barriers to trade between nations should be eliminated.
- The market principle should be applied far beyond the economy to all public goods—education, health, the environment, and so on.

There is more to this than meets the eye, including certain deeper assumptions about human nature. But 25 years ago, the small group of economists and philosophers who held these views were regarded as rather eccentric—even by the mainstream Right. They met in small discussion groups and debated each other in obscure magazines and economic journals. They dreamt of a world reshaped by these ideas. We now live in this world.

Looked at coolly, this transformation is an inspiring testament to the power of ideas to shape society. It can give us hope that other ideas might also reshape the world and fashion it to more human ends. But first the ideas of neo-liberalism need to be understood. In fact, the success of neo-liberalism contains many lessons for those who oppose its relentless commercial logic. The fact that its critics have understood neither its ideas (including their strengths) nor why they have taken root means that the emergence of new political philosophies beyond Right and Left continues to be delayed.

Neo-liberal ideas trace their origins to the Scottish economist Adam Smith. Smith's weighty book *The Wealth of Nations* is still a reference point, and in Britain his name is commemorated by the Adam Smith Institute, a think-tank founded in 1977. The glory days of economic liberalism occured in mid-nineteenth century Britain, still an idealised reference point for modern neo-liberals. But perhaps the key date for us is 1947, when the Austrian economist Friedrich Hayek founded the Mont Pelerin Society. The Society was no secret cabal of conspirators, but a regular forum for discussion by the tiny minority of postwar economic liberals who swam against the tide of opinion which favoured the welfare state and government intervention.

But the tide changed, as it always does. By the late 1960s, the ideas of Hayek, and of other economic liberals such as US economist Milton Friedman, had won important ground among academic and professional economists in universities, governments and corporations. Global institutions such as the International Monetary Fund (IMF) and the World Bank had increasingly been staffed by people who described themselves as 'neo-classical economists'. The tide of opinion was slowly but inexorably turning among elite economists, but this was not enough. Their target—the welfare state and government regulation of the economy—was the product of both conservative and social-democratic governments. Both had been pragmatic in their economic theory, adjusting their policy sails to the winds of key constituencies such as farmers, manufacturers, trade unions and exporters. When it finally succeeded, the neo-liberal revolution trampled as much on an older conservatism as it did on the beliefs of socialism (see Chapter 4).

Two processes opened the door to the storm that was to come in the 1980s and 1990s. The first was a series of events in 1971–74 which crystallised problems in managed capitalism. In 1971, after a series of trade deficits that could be attributed to the costly war in Vietnam, US President Nixon removed the US dollar from a system of fixed exchange rates—in other words, the dollar was floated. In 1973, the largely Arab organisation of oil exporters (OPEC) dramatically raised the price of oil to industrialised countries. As well, for some time the unusual combination of both inflation and lack of growth ('stagflation') had become apparent in industrialised economies. This meant that the Keynesian approaches to managing the economy, supported by both conservatives and non-conservatives, simply did not work. The Keynesian approach to inflation recommended higher interest rates and tightening government spending, but these measures would further deepen stagnation and worsen unemployment.

The second process was a quite different phenomenon. It was not an economic crisis, but a slow-building, deeper social and cultural change. The long boom of the 1950s and 1960s in advanced industrial countries had increased material wealth for nearly all their citizens. The expansion and cheapening of the number of consumer goods led to a growing expectation of greater individual choice in satisfying material wants and, more importantly, desires elsewhere. For example, owning a motor car came within the reach of far more people, resulting in a decline in state-supported public transport. Personal choice for women was widened by the widespread availability of the contraceptive pill. All of this generated a climate in which individuals chafed at the restraints of a narrow-minded moral uniformity favoured by church and state. The result was the cultural and political revolt of the 1960s, which saw a blossoming of libertarianism.

Credit for this revolt has been largely claimed by the Left, but its effects were far deeper and more complex. While the conservative moral order enforced by government and churches was flouted, it was only a matter of time before all sorts of other restrictive regulatory policies, including those on businesses (small and large), came under fire. When the twenty-year-olds who asked why government should censor films turned 30, they were open to neo-liberalism's questions: 'Why should a government run a national bank, an airline or a phone company?' As one commentator on Thatcherism notes, on moral issues the British New Right worked against the grain of the 1960s, but it worked with the grain on economy–state issues: 'Many of the Thatcherites viewed their politics as a crusade against the pettiness, restrictiveness, traditionalism and inertia that characterised the post-war settlement,' argues Richard Cockett.[2] Such were also the terms of Left libertarianism of the 1960s.

The Thatcher revolution

This deeper sea change first came to public view in Britain in the late 1970s. The emergence of 'Thatcherism' deeply influenced conservative ideas globally, including in Australia. In 1975, the British Conservative Party elected a new leader, Margaret Thatcher, who became prime minister when her party won the 1979 election. Margaret Thatcher drew many of her ideas about economic policy from the new ideas of Hayek and Friedman. In her first term, Thatcher began deregulating the finance industry, contributing her step to globalisation, and cut government spending savagely, influenced by what were then called the 'monetarist' economic theories of Friedman. In 1981, Margaret Thatcher revealed to the House of Commons the source of her unorthodox conservative views: 'I am a great admirer of Professor Hayek. Some of his books are absolutely supreme—*The Constitution of Liberty* and the three volumes of *Law, Legislation and Liberty*—and would well be read by almost every honourable member.'[3]

In her second term, an even more unexpected policy was added to the mix; it went by the ugly neologism of 'privatisation'. In 1984, British Telecom was sold to investors, followed by British Gas, British Petroleum, British Airways and British Steel. All of this was done rapidly and was radically new—not just to the British public, but also to the Conservative Party. As well, the language of politics began to change. Where conservatism once appealed to authority, social cohesion and tradition, Thatcher's political discourse was that of freedom, individualism and choice.

Although endorsed by Conservative governments, the ideas of Hayek and Friedman could not be described as conservative at all, but sprang from a quite different philosophy—one with its roots in liberalism. These ideas had been nurtured through the 1960s and 1970s by what we now call 'think-tanks' such as the Institute of Economic Affairs and the Centre for Policy Studies, the latter having been sponsored from 1974 by Thatcher herself and her colleague Keith Joseph. For many years, this subsidiary tradition of liberalism had been glued to a dominant conservative tradition. When Keynesianism floundered in the 1970s, this glue came unstuck.

Dealing with these political philosophies is not made any easier by the popular tags used in politics. The long-term commitment of Conservative governments to the welfare state and social justice was made possible by a fusion of traditional conservative instincts for stability, cohesion and a strong state, with a version of liberalism called 'social liberalism', which emerged in the late nineteenth century.[4] Social liberalism, originally known as 'New Liberalism', favoured government intervention to achieve social cohesion, and to that extent was in accord with the Conservative outlook. One of the goals of the revived neo-liberalism of Hayek was to reclaim pure liberalism and destroy social liberalism.

The tide of ideas changed in the United States as well. There, the basic ideas of free-market economics and neo-liberalism had different and more populist roots than they did in Britain. The US Right had a stronger tradition of anti-government individualism than British conservatism did, and this was mobilised to cut government programs and deregulate economic conditions. To make all this more confusing, in the US political lexicon, the term 'liberal' tends to denote someone on the Left of the spectrum who supports the welfare state (rather like the 'social liberal' tradition in Britain and Australia). In the United States, 'conservative' is a catch-all term to embrace neo-liberals as well as moral conservatives. Thus the 'neo-conservatives' who in 2003 led the Bush administration into war in Iraq, such as Dick Cheney, Paul Wolfowitz, Condoleeza Rice and Donald Rumsfeld, are economic *neo-liberals*. They are increasingly criticised by US conservatives, who point out that they are far removed from the conservative tradition which is cautious about experimental leaps into the unknown.

Neo-liberalism in Australia

In Australia, economic liberalism was the subsidiary tradition within the Right until the 1980s.[5] The defeat of the Free Traders by the Protectionists a century ago meant that the tradition on which the Australian Right was built was, like its British counterpart, inflected by social liberalism which allowed considerable state intervention in society. Apart from anything else, this led to the confusion that the Protectionist leader, (and Australia's second prime minister) Alfred Deakin, was regarded as a liberal and the 'true liberals' who favoured free trade and minimum state intervention were called 'conservatives'.[6] The 'Deakinite Settlement' of tariff protection, arbitration of wages, state paternalism, White Australia and imperial defence was the established framework of the Right for many decades.

The first sign of a paradigm shift occurred during the Liberal government under Malcolm Fraser (1975–83). In the wake of the expansionist Whitlam Labor government, Fraser's Liberal–Country Party Coalition called for an end to 'big government'. But the Fraser government disappointed some of its supporters. In a front-page editorial in 1978, Rupert Murdoch's *Australian* newspaper set the tone, arguing that the government 'must stop backing away from its responsibilities. It must cut expenditure—hard . . . it must give the people what they want—not what it and its bureaucracy think they should want'.[7] A writer on the same newspaper welcomed the new evangelical idealism of Thatcher and its implications 'in a world hungry for a new philosophy'.[8] Another writer argued that this new conservatism 'is little understood in Australia and indeed it is not yet become a subject of energetic ideological debate as it is in Britain'.[9]

This was to change quickly. In the period 1979–80, a small, emerging faction of Liberal Party parliamentarians began that debate. These MPs, whose most outspoken member was John Hyde, were increasingly unhappy with the direction of the Fraser government.[10] Known as the 'dries', they soon linked up with the extra-parliamentary liberal intellectual movement to form what political journalist Paul Kelly called 'the revolt against Liberal tradition'. In particular, they began to absorb the ideas of neo-liberal economics, whose guru was Hayek. Kelly notes the profound philosophical change that was involved:

> From Hayek they began to realize that they were not conservatives who merely sought to resist the socialist expansion of state power, but that they were liberals who sought a different direction—who sought to liberate the individual from state controls, direction and solution. This was a political tradition which throughout Australian history had been particularly weak.[11]

In 1980, a group of academics and economists published a key libertarian manifesto, *Australia at the Crossroads*, which, along with a national discussion network, helped build momentum and urgency for liberal economic thought.[12] Together with the 'dries', the Crossroads group and others were full of crusading zeal and moral purpose.

This zeal was also characteristic of their intellectual leader, Friedrich Hayek, who had visited Australia in late 1976. The apocalyptic and extreme tone of Hayek's speeches cast its shadow over the succeeding years. At Sydney University, his theme was 'the atavism of social justice'—that is, that notions of moral obligation to others are a hangover from humans' time as hunter-gatherers and are therefore to be rejected.[13] At a forum sponsored by the Institute of Public Affairs in Sydney, presided over by Sir David Griffin, he referred to the 'fundamental immorality of all egalitarianism', and forecast a revolt by the welfare-supported masses who would have to be 'subdued with the knout and the machine gun'.[14] Such extraordinary statements flowed from an intellectual system which was less obviously bizarre than this conclusion. Perhaps for this reason, as well as his recent Nobel prize, Hayek was welcomed by Prime Minister Malcolm Fraser, as well as by numerous businesspeople and the Chief Justice of the High Court, Sir Garfield Barwick.

A key organiser of Hayek's visit was the long-time director of the Institute of Public Affairs, Charles Kemp. Later, Hayek's speeches were published by the Centre for Independent Studies. These two institutions, now known as 'think-tanks', were part of the tide of intellectual counter-revolution of the late 1970s. The Institute of Public Affairs (IPA) was founded in 1944, and was for a long time a rather predictable policy forum for conservatism and the Liberal Party. In 1982, the IPA was reinvigorated by the appointment of Rod Kemp, Charles' son, as director. In a symbolic passing of the baton, Kemp Senior represented the old Right while Kemp Junior rode the wave of neo-liberalism.[15] The Centre for Independent

Studies (CIS) was different. A new organisation founded in 1976, it was the brainchild of a crusading school teacher, Greg Lindsay, who originally operated it from his garden shed. This changed when he convinced mining businessman Hugh Morgan and a number of others to support it. With these funds, the CIS moved into modest offices. Today, it is a multi-million dollar think-tank and a powerhouse of ideas for the Right.

Critics have consistently under-estimated the depth of the revolution on the neo-liberal Right and have rather exaggerated ideas about the power of the think-tanks, which are portrayed as influential and shadowy organisations. But damning the think-tanks has been a substitute for grappling with the ideas and policies generated by them. The most blindingly obvious (and hence most often misunderstood) fact is that the think-tanks were crucial because the Right was undergoing a genuine rethinking of its most basic philosophy and outlook.[16]

In an instinctive reflex, critics also attribute the power of think-tanks to corporate funding. But it was not money that made the real difference with the think-tanks. They were supplied with something more powerful in the long run—a radical new way of looking at the world and the energy of true believers. The critics were wrong about something else, too. To carry through a revolution—even a revolution from the Right—requires vision and daring, risk-taking and radicalism. It was this last element— radicalism—which proved to be the unexpected quality of the free-market revolution. Whereas once it was the socialists and the Left who were the radicals wanting rapid social change, the new radical visionaries who now want to overturn the established order are the neo-liberals. Setting in place market mechanisms in almost every aspect of life leads to a society which is constantly and relentlessly being transformed.

The think-tanks developed a more combative and confident new Right which challenged the tired and pragmatic intellectual framework of the postwar Right. Though often demonised, the think-tanks were only part of a broader diverse radical liberal movement, with its own political and intellectual leaders, publicists and pamphleteers, journalists and commentators, supporters in the bureaucracy and interest groups.[17] By the end of the Fraser government and the election of Labor in March 1983, the think-tanks were at the centre of these networks and had become powerhouses of ideas which translated the views of Adam Smith, Friedrich Hayek, Milton Friedman and others into a new political paradigm for Australia. What was crucial, as Hugh Morgan said, was not to change mere policies, but to reshape public opinion and the public agenda.[18]

The defeat of the Fraser government in 1983 precipitated a crisis. An early voice of neo-liberalism, Rupert Murdoch's *Australian* news-paper, argued that salvation for the defeated Liberal Party lay in producing 'a clear-cut ideological alternative to the Government'. It had to decide 'whether it is a conservative or a liberal party'— and there was no doubt that the newspaper stood for the latter.[19] Within the defeated Liberal Party of the mid-1980s, the ideas of radical liberalism increasingly took hold and offered a new direction away from staid conservatism. The rising neo-liberal consensus had its sharp critics within the party. In June 1986, Malcolm Fraser argued that 'the debate on deregulation in general in Australia has been unbalanced and unhelpful to good government, because too many people have got away with depicting deregulation as an end in itself'. Deregulation alone, he said, 'leads only to nineteenth century *laissez faire*'.[20] Later that year, a leading Liberal MP, Ian Macphee, attacked the philosophy of libertarianism, which was 'debauching' the Liberal Party. It was 'the antithesis of the just society'; it elevated selfishness and was marked by 'social heart-lessness'.[21] This intellectual sea change in the Right was accompanied by radical political action. Legal challenges by employers to trade unions had succeeded in opening them up to civil damages after strike action. Within the Liberal Party, the destruction of its social liberals ('wets' like Ian Macphee) accompanied the rise of the chosen leader of the New Right, John Howard.

Labor and the New Right

While Fraser and Macphee correctly went to the philosophical and moral heart of the matter, Labor in government saw the New Right as merely the old Right in new garb. It responded to their political threats in the short term, while in the longer term it was unable to resist the tide of ideas that flowed all around it among policy advisers and elite opinion.

Labor had won government in 1983 as the neo-liberal revolution in Australia was gathering momentum, but before it wholly transformed the paradigm of politics. Labor's commitment to redistribution of income, to welfare policies and to similar reforms was predicated on economic growth and on the ability of governments to effectively intervene in the economy to achieve this goal and other social reforms. In the short term, Hawke and Keating, were absolutely determined that Labor would be the party of good economic management, unlike its erratic predecessor. Guided by advisers deeply influenced by the intellectual ground won by free-market ideas in the preceding decades—and by the early demands of a globalising economy—Labor began to mildly deregulate the Australian economy, allowing the dollar to float and licensing foreign banks. It restrained wages through the Accord, but augmented the 'social wage'.

With hindsight, some of Labor's economic reforms were unavoidable and contributed to a more efficient and globally competitive economy. Labor had to accommodate to an increasingly globalised world economy, which had to be dealt with largely on its own terms. Fundamentally, Labor's strategy was designed to transform the economic structure of Australia from a farm and a quarry to an exporter of world-class manufactures and services. Labor adopted a cautious variant of neo-liberal economic policies, tempered by its social-democratic ethos. Initially, its free-market approach did indeed make industries more productive and efficient, and hence more internationally competitive. But greater efficiency meant fewer workers, and this meant unemployment. Labor's social policies cushioned the blow and tried to retrain the casualties of change.

But what was remarkable (and dispiriting to supporters) was the inexorable sea change as Labor absorbed the agenda of the New Right. For example, in the early period of the Labor government, Prime Minister Hawke and his ministers pledged total opposition to privatisation. It was 'ideological claptrap', said one minister, Mick Young, and it would lead to 'higher costs, charges and fares, less employment'.[22] Labor won the 1985 South Australian state election on its anti-privatisation campaign, much of which was articulated by federal leaders. In his 1985 Chifley lecture, Prime Minister Hawke asked: 'What in the name of reason is the justification for breaking up and selling off the great and efficient national assets, like the Commonwealth Bank, Telecom, TAA, Qantas? The fact is that this recipe for disaster represents the height of economic irrationality . . . it is based on a blind and mindless commitment to a narrow, dogmatic and discredited ideology.'[23] And in 1987, during a bitter industrial dispute caused by a business leader of the New Right, Hawke again attacked these 'political troglodytes and economic lunatics' of the New Right.[24]

Yet in that very year, the government was moving to privatise government aviation—a move only delayed by a decision of its national party conference. The opposition to it was not so much that social justice demanded a public airline; rather, opponents could feel that something else—often referred to as 'traditional Labor values'—was dissolving. And so it proved to be. Five years later, the impact of the neo-liberal tidal wave was washing all before it: the privatisation of the Commonwealth Bank had begun and Labor's Treasurer, Paul Keating, was moving to privatise the national telecommunications agency, Telecom. Deep down, Labor had no firm philosophical ground on which to stand against the strong current of neo-liberal ideas. Its actions encouraged the tide of neo-liberalism. Later, political scientists would analyse this as the beginning of the new phenomenon of 'convergence' of political parties.

Neo-liberal policies seemed to be in tune with a globalising economy, and they responded to real problems in the Australian economy. What was not realised at the time was that the neo-liberal package was not simply a tough-minded way of running an economy. Fundamentally, it meant a different approach to running a government and a nation. Ultimately, it meant a whole world view which was quite different from the social-democratic ethos. The social-democratic ethos was originally formed in the previous high noon of economic liberalism in the pre-1914 world. It was closer to humanist values than the narrow instrumental values of neo-liberalism. It was an ethos which saw the economy as part of society, and not the reverse. But that ethos did not prescribe a clear, comprehensive and guaranteed set of policies to run an economy. Keynesian economics came closest to embodying those values, but it had been undermined by events.

So completely did free-market ideas swamp the Labor government that, by the time Labor lost office in 1996, a full-blown crisis of belief had emerged. What did Labor believe in? 'Are there any core beliefs we would never abandon?' asked its former national president, Barry Jones.[25] Its core value of greater social equality had always been envisaged as being implemented by the state, but the basis of the new ideas was that the state was part of the problem, not the solution. Twenty years after the election of Australia's longest serving Labor government, the *Australian* newspaper commented: 'It will puzzle future generations that the most radical free market reforms in Australia's history were effected by a Labor government led by a former trade union chief.'[26]

One of the deeper reasons for this was suggested by two Labor supporters of this new direction who threw down a blunt challenge to critics of neo-liberalism:

> Critiques of the Hawke–Keating government's economic rationalism will remain deficient for as long as the critics refuse to provide a realistic and comprehensive set of alternative policies that can better address the economic problems facing Australia. The 'so-called' alternatives advocated to date ... amount to nothing more than a futile hankering for the past.[27]

One of the key challenges for today's inheritors of social liberalism, old-style conservatism and social democracy is precisely to outline just such an alternative. This challenge remains today because no new vision has been formulated which can genuinely transcend neo-liberalism. It is one of the purposes of this book to stimulate such a debate. First, though, we must understand the vision and intellectual framework which brought us to this point.

Prophet of the free market

Any understanding of neo-liberalism must grapple with the complex ideas of Friedrich Hayek, because they are foundational to the revival of neo-liberal ideas which has swept the world. It was Hayek's vast intellectual output and theoretical system which gave the revival its resilience and depth. His vision and ideas helped to provide the sustaining confidence needed by the small radical liberal movement in the years before its triumph. What follows is a description and discussion of Hayek's key ideas.

Hayek was born in Vienna in 1899 and took degrees in law and politics. But economic theory dominated his early work and in the 1930s, while he taught at the London School of Economics, he clashed with John Maynard Keynes—at that stage making little impact. The disagreement was over the correct analysis of the

Great Depression and prescriptions for avoiding such calamities in the future. In 1950, he moved to the University of Chicago—the intellectual centre for the development of neo-liberal economic and social theories, where a colleague was Milton Friedman.

Hayek was not just an economist, but an evangelist who was prepared to swim against the tide. To most people, World War II had demonstrated the enormous advantages of the state in co-ordinating workers and industrialists in a single victorious focus. By 1944, planning for postwar reconstruction assumed large state-sponsored projects of education, health and national development. At precisely this most unlikely of times, Hayek wrote his best-known polemic in favour of liberty and against the state and all its works. *The Road to Serfdom* compared state socialism, economic planning, Nazism, communism and social liberalism, and concluded that they were all very similar under the skin because they shared an opposition to the free-market order. It was dedicated 'To the socialists of all parties'.

A remarkable quality of *The Road to Serfdom* is its absolutism. Not only is central control and planning an absolute evil, but there is a rapid and slippery slope between government planning of *any* form and *total* central control. Hayek was also blithely unaware of (or dismissive of) the realities faced by many ordinary people:

> In a competitive society it is no slight to a person, no offence to his dignity, to be told by any particular firm that it has no need for his services, or that it cannot offer him a better job. It is true that in a period of prolonged mass unemployment the effect on many may be similar. But there are other and better methods to prevent that scourge than central direction.[28]

At first glance, Hayek's book was a polemic against socialism and fitted the rapidly growing anti-communism that dominated the Cold War. But, as his dedication made clear, Hayek was highly critical of anti-communists who believed in a strong state. He was far from an ivory tower-dwelling academic. As an intellectual engaged in combat, he not only helped found the Mont Pelerin Society in 1947, but also the Institute for Economic Affairs in Britain in 1957— an organisation which helped fashion what the world came to know as Thatcherism.

As the years went by, it became clearer that he represented a strand within the Right which was quite different from simple anti-communism and mainstream conservatism (which had merged with social liberalism). His aim was to revive a minority strand within liberalism, which he believed had largely been taken over by a rationalistic, Continental liberalism that aimed to guarantee a liberal society more through governments than markets.[29] Hayek's liberalism, which drew on Adam Smith and philosopher David Hume, was grounded in a view which argued that liberal institutions (such as the market) evolved slowly and spontaneously and were justified by their success, not by government. In Hayek's version of liberalism, there was little room for government modification of market forces in the name of social cohesion. In his speech accepting the Nobel Prize for Economics in 1974, Hayek congratulated the selection committee for their willingness to award the prize to someone 'whose views are as unfashionable as mine are'.[30]

Hayek believed fashions changed through the central role of ideas and intellectuals, and this had long been part of his crusade. In 1960, which many thought was the high noon of triumphant and prosperous capitalism, Hayek worried that 'the propertied class, now almost exclusively a business group, lacks intellectual leadership and even a coherent and defensible philosophy of life'.[31]

Hayek's self-appointed task was to provide this intellectual leadership, together with a coherent and defensible philosophy of life. He did this by conceiving an intellectual system covering economics, law, politics, social evolution and morality. This system was developed from first principles—in this case, Hayek's particular concept of *liberty*. This gives his ideas the attractive element of coherence but like so many ideological thinkers, including many Marxists, a foundation of simple first principles also opened the way to fundamentalism. Hayek, however, had a number of genuine insights which it would be unwise to ignore. In any case, those repelled by the market fundamentalism of his followers need to understand the intellectual challenge he threw down to his fellow liberals, to conservatives and to socialists.

Liberty

Hayek's notion of liberty, and hence of liberalism, distinguished him from most other liberal thinkers. Liberty was narrowly defined as freedom from coercion by someone else, especially the state. Each person should have a private sphere which was untouchable by others. Most significantly, of course, this was based on the ownership of private property. By contrast, the social liberals to whom he was opposed supported a 'positive' notion of liberty—that is, that freedom can only be meaningful if the individual has certain capacities or resources to exercise this freedom. Adequate income, health and education can all be seen to be necessary to allow this positive freedom to flourish. It is easy to see how these different notions of liberty grounded conceptions of government that were radically different. The trouble with the idea of 'positive liberty', as Hayek pointed out, is that in this framework the concept of 'liberty' then becomes a fairly non-specific and meaningless term, able to justify all manner of state coercion in the name of increasing 'collective power over circumstances'.[32]

Hayek therefore dismissed the social liberals' support for social equality. Instead of mealy-mouthed praise for 'equality', he argued that *inequality* was necessary to the diversity and to the division of labour on which a successful market economy was founded. He had no objection to government programs to relieve *utter* poverty, but opposed those designed to create greater social equality. The kind of equality he valued and recognised was equality before the law and in the impersonality of the rules of the market: 'Not only has liberty nothing to do with any other sort of equality, but it is even bound to produce inequality in many respects.'[33] Further, the related notion of 'social justice' was simply meaningless, since injustice concerned the deliberate actions of humans, not the operation of a system such as the market. It was the evolved institutions themselves rather than the deliberate action of human beings which, following Smith and Hume, he insisted were the guarantees of liberty.

The idea that liberty and equality were irreconcilable subsequently became—and remains—something of a mantra on the Right, as has the insistence on the incoherence of the notion of social justice.[34]

The spontaneous market order

Not surprisingly, for the key thinker in free-market economics, the market is a central notion. Liberty was valued because it allowed the market to develop 'spontaneously'. This claim of spontaneous, natural growth of the market serves a key legitimating function. It provides a plausible basis for Hayek's claim that his ideas are the modern expression of classical conservatism, building on the ideas of men like Edmund Burke, whose philosophy was grounded in the value of ancient traditions.

So what was beneficial about the market other than the fact that, being undesigned, it was also a domain of freedom? Hayek's answer to this question was surprisingly subtle and perceptive. His starting point concerned knowledge. Whereas critics of the market focused on the way in which it can magnify and entrench inequalities by allocating resources to the already powerful, Hayek pointed out that it was also a medium for the rapid sending of information via prices through a network. He likened it to the process of scientific or scholarly discovery of knowledge. By this he meant that markets were an exceptionally useful and flexible device in signalling to producers what their buyers want, and in what quantity. As well, it made it possible for people and economic enterprises to find the niche that would most productively utilise their individual abilities.

These virtues of the market are a function of the limits of our knowledge. The kind of knowledge involved in an economy is necessarily a conglomerate of the knowledge individuals have of their own abilities and preferences—a conglomerate so huge that no single mind or directing authority grasp it.

Hayek contrasted this to economic planning by the state. Of necessity, economic planning had to rely on a knowledge of a vast array of situations in the economy, and had to receive and process an equally vast and continuous flow of knowledge from economic transactions. On the basis of this, the planners had to then transmit a complex series of decisions. Central planning was a practical impossibility, Hayek concluded, because the absence of a system of market prices meant an absence of immediate and useful knowledge, quite apart from it being undesirable from the point of view of liberty. (Chapter 5 outlines how the Soviet economy demonstrated just this point.)

Hayek was quite right about this fatal flaw in completely centrally planned economies but, as always, he extended this insight to its most extreme point: *any* intervention in market forces as flawed (nay, evil) as Stalinist central planning. Starting from the fact that conscious, deliberate control over a whole economy is a practical impossibility, it does not follow that *any* modification of market forces by the state, by communities or by union action—or even by corporate monopolies—fatally undermines the power of the market to transmit the individual knowledge of consumer preferences or to create opportunities for the exercise of people's capacities. Indeed, one could make a case that restraints and modifications on markets also 'evolved spontaneously' when the amoral quality of the market became apparent. But Hayek would reject this.

To recognise the strengths of markets in certain situations is not to give a *carte blanche* in all circumstances. The desire for an ultimate conclusion that markets are a Good Thing or a Bad Thing is simply a wrong-headed insistence on simplicity where there is a messy complexity. Modern markets are always embedded in elaborate social, cultural and political frameworks, and the most powerful market economies today also happen to have the most powerful states. The question—easy to pose, hard to answer—is the mix. What Hayek succeeded in making clear, though, is that certain virtues and benefits which arise from the market cannot be replaced by government regulatory mechanisms.

Morality, reason and social evolution

In the first few lines of *The Road to Serfdom*, Hayek states that 'the essential point remains that all I shall have to say is derived from certain ultimate values'. The value which is central, of course, is liberty, and on this foundation stone he erects his system. One consequence of this is that any new political philosophy which aims to trump Hayek's vision—the ultimate inspiration for so many global changes over the last 25 years—must similarly be based on clear values.

The value of liberty rests on an account of the benefits of the market. This, in turn, depends on a general conception of humanity—of the limits of human reason and of humanity's natural and social evolution.[35] Crucially, and related to this, it depends on some unorthodox and, to many, unacceptable ideas about morality.

Hayek argues that modern societies have evolved to such a degree of individual variation that there are almost no common or shared values (i.e. ends)—with material acquisition without limit being an exception. He argues that 'believing in freedom means that we do not regard ourselves as the ultimate judges of another person's values, that we do not feel entitled to prevent him from pursuing ends which we disapprove so long as he does not infringe the equally protected sphere of others'.[36]

This variation among humans makes the market all the more necessary. But, more than that, comprehensive economic planning presupposes complete agreement on the importance of different social ends. This does not exist, however, so any planning is utterly coercive. But isn't liberty itself a common value? Hayek's answer is 'yes' and 'no'. That we value liberty is not a 'given' in the nature of human beings—like, say, the value of survival or of material comfort. Rather, it is acquired and developed in the cultural evolution of the 'institutions of liberty'. Liberty, and the discipline that it requires, is something we must learn. Liberty as a value, then, has been 'selected' by cultural evolution.

Free markets are therefore justified in a moral-historical sense because they represent the product of social-cultural evolution which, like biological evolution, 'selected' the characteristics best adapted to the environment. Societies employing the most successful cultural institutions (such as the market) prospered and their populations grew. (Population growth was one of Hayek's key measures of success.) It is at this point that his extraordinary moral views enter the equation.

Hayek *defines* morality as those attitudes that are necessary for, and developed within, the market—and thus form the basis of modern society. A market relies on rules of good conduct and fair dealing by all people towards anonymous others who are rarely met face to face. (By contrast, traditional societies exchange goods to known people in processes invested with moral-religious meaning.)

These rules of conduct concerned rules about 'several [i.e. private] property, honesty, contract, exchange, trade, competition, gain and privacy'.[37] *These* are what Hayek understands by moral rules. The unexpected (and repulsive) concomitant of his notion of cultural evolution is that feelings of altruism and obligation (usually regarded as the kernel of morality) are here seen as its antithesis as primitive instincts from earlier, hunter-gatherer societies, which have to be overcome:

> For those now living within the extended order gain from not treating one another as neighbours, and by applying ... rules of the extended order such as those of several property and contract—instead of the rules of solidarity and altruism. An order in which everyone treated his neighbour as himself would be one where comparatively few could be fruitful and multiply.[38]

Hayek turns our normal conception of morality upside down by insisting that it is 'primitive', and by claiming that untrammelled self-interest is both moral and modern. The essence of Hayek's political position—that the free market must be safeguarded at all costs—follows from this.

Socialism was therefore an atavistic response to modernisation, the re-emergence of ancient, instinctive values in the face of the impersonal market. Again, Hayek is not so far from the mark in identifying this well-known difference between traditional and modern society, but as usual his insight is taken to wild extremes. A modern society with little or no altruism would be a bleak place indeed, though his modern followers in global corporations, think-tanks and governments continue to strive mightily to take us there.

Hayek, however, reserved a place for these 'primitive feelings' of solidarity and altruism—in the family and in voluntary associations. In a vitally important admission, he argued that 'if we were always to apply the rules of the extended order [capitalism and the market] to our more intimate groupings *we would crush them* [original emphasis]'.[39] That is, if we treat parents, children, family and neighbours as we do when we are buying and selling in the market, we will destroy those relationships. Hayek is right—and one reason we know this is because this damage is increasingly happening as market relations invade formerly intimate spaces and neighbourly relations, as we saw in Chapter 2. The word for this is *commodification*—the transformation of obligations based on love and altruism into those of commodity-based economic value (i.e. money).

Hayek recognised this paradoxical inconsistency, and proposed that we must simply learn to 'live simultaneously within different kinds of orders according to different rules'—those of the market and that of the family. We must be ruthlessly self-interested in the market and sweetly caring in the family, greedy at work and selfless at home. But such a 'solution' is self-evident nonsense.

If Hayek is right about some of the virtues of the market, and also right about the value of the variety of ends among individuals, the question is whether he is also right that there is no place for our more altruistic and collective dispositions in the economy and government. Aren't altruism and caring common values, known to all societies? Is it possible to find a place for these values without, as he claims, destroying these very institutions? Can we value, as we ought, the transition from traditional to modern society without stifling our caring for other humans? Unravelling these problems and exploring how we might do this is one of the challenges for developing a new kind of philosophy beyond Right and Left.

Reason and rationality

Opponents of economic rationalism are surprised to find that Hayek was an opponent of rationalism. What he opposed were those who tried to construct a society or its important institutions on the basis of a blueprint that conformed to the ideals of Reason. Socialists were the worst offenders, but also culpable were the social liberals who saw government and law as tools for liberal goals.[40] This kind of rationalist-constructivism (broadly associated with the Enlightenment) attempted to impose rational patterns on society, and so undermined the spontaneous evolution of the market and of the common law toward order.[41] His stand against rationalism and in favour of tradition runs through his work from his early anti-planning polemics in *The Road to Serfdom* to his rebuttal of socialism in *The Fatal Conceit*. Such a position allowed Hayek to represent himself as an inheritor of aspects of conservatism that cherish evolved tradition, while simultaneously being the architect of militant liberalism, which destroys tradition.

But it is here that the most perceptive critics, including sympathetic ones like the political theorist Chandran Kukathas, see Hayek's own fatal conceit.[42] As Kukathas emphasises, Hayek attempted to avoid Enlightenment rationalism by locating himself in the tradition of the Scottish Enlightenment, whose major figures were Adam Smith and David Hume.[43] The Scottish Enlightenment was distinctive because it tried to 'use reason to whittle down the claims of reason', in Hume's words, and so gave a rational (Enlightenment) basis for the conservative commitment to tradition—and, indeed, to the conservative attack on the Enlightenment. By basing himself in the Scottish Enlightenment, Hayek could legitimately appeal to conservatives while also legitimately denying that he was a conservative. But Hayek also wanted to assert the foundational principle of liberty. In effect, he wanted to measure the worth of institutions and ideas by the yardstick of liberty (and *his* particular definition of liberty). Yet this is a rationalist project. It seeks to impose a model or template on society, so discards those institutions, values and practices which do not measure up. It is dangerous for all the reasons that the sceptics of Reason (such as David Hume) say it is.

Hayek attempts to avoid the accusation of rationalism through his distinction between 'evolved' and 'artificial', or non-evolved, social institutions. If the market is indeed a spontaneous order and all interference with it is coercive, then the neo-liberal project would not be an imposition, but the recovery of an evolved order from decades of interference and undermining. But this distinction is unsustainable, and his account of what is and what is not 'culturally evolved' is too narrow. If, as John Gray persuasively argues, the market developed only in the context of equally valuable traditions to limit it—within communities, of government and of the labour movement—then Hayek's project becomes subject to his own trenchant criticisms of rationalist-constructivism.

Thus the key flaw embedded deep in Hayek's project is similar to the key flaw we perceive in market fundamentalism today: it is a preconceived scheme to remake society according to rigid foundational principles. It undermines social cohesion, and is thus deeply opposed to conservatism itself. To the extent that it motivates the Right of politics, it reconstructs the Right as a utopian force determined to reconstruct each and every society based on its particular definition of rationality. The next chapter explores the consequences of this for the Right and for Hayek's ideological competitors such as classical conservatism and social liberalism.

Many critics of free-market liberalism hardly bother to explore Hayek's intellectual and moral framework. They criticise modern neo-liberalism for being doctrinaire, for producing inequality or for not delivering all that it promises. But, as Simon Marginson argues, the claim that free-market liberalism is untrue or unrealistic seems largely beside the point. The ideas of free-market liberalism are largely internally consistent once the premises (values) are accepted. Marginson notes: 'To tackle a hegemonic discourse it is necessary to develop a counter-hegemonic argument. Most critics of free-market liberalism have not yet taken that step.'[44] A key step in such a counter-hegemonic argument, as I outline variously in the following chapters, is to identify and build on a set of positive moral values.

4

Neo-cons, ex-cons and the death of the old Right

What might be called philosophic conservatism—a philosophy of protection, conservation and solidarity—acquires a new relevance for political radicalism today . . . Some of its key ideas, however, acquire a new relevance when removed from their original contexts. We should all become conservatives now. . . but not in the conservative way.[1]

Anthony Giddens

The desire to conserve, to protect, to safeguard, to rescue, to resist becomes the heart of a radical project. A form of conservatism—to be most sharply distinguished from its multitude of imitations, its travesties and caricatures, and scarcely known to those who carry the banners of conservatism in the modern world—becomes indispensable to this work of resistance.[2]

Trevor Blackwell and Jeremy Seabrook

One night about 30 years ago, I drove in a battered car with a comrade through the darkened streets of inner Sydney, spray cans at the ready. That night we endlessly painted a slogan on brick walls, fences and the sides of factories. The slogan read: 'Stop Work to Stop Fraser'. It was just a few days after the notorious sacking of the Whitlam Labor government by Governor-General Sir John Kerr, and the abrupt installation of the leader of the Liberal Party, Malcolm Fraser, as prime minister. The response of the Communist Party, of which I was a member, was to try our hardest to organise a general strike by trade unions to protest the assault on democracy represented by the sacking. Politically, lots of things have changed since then, but I don't regret for one minute trying to help organise that strike.

One of the things that *has* changed is Malcolm Fraser's political outlook—and therein lies a significant key to understanding the new politics beyond Right and Left. One of the trade unions which supported the strike was the metalworkers' union. Recently, the same union invited their former foe to address their national conference about the issue of the detention of asylum-seekers. Trade union delegates interrupted Fraser's speech with applause several times and, after the speech, the metalworkers' leader, Doug Cameron, commented that Fraser 'had grown in stature since his period as prime minister. He is a true statesman for this country and a great spokesperson for the issue of humanity for all people around this globe'.[3]

The wheel has turned for the former prime minister who, for seven years, headed one of the most disliked governments in Australian history. His own popularity was never high. The public saw him as 'cynical, opportunistic, dominant, conservative and confrontationist'. He established a rhetorical climate 'filled with threats and scorn, with blaming and shaming . . . his voice was grating, his speeches hectoring'.[4] Today Fraser is a changed man. Gone is the bluster and bullying of yesteryear. His government is seen to have failed according to the new orthodoxy of the Liberals and their economic rationalist philosophy. Fraser is in a philosophical no-man's land. He is no longer a reactionary conservative, nor is he an economic rationalist. He laments that 'our generation is without a political philosophy relevant to our time and circumstances. We have a theory of globalisation but, baldly stated, it is cold and technical . . . We need an idea of how our society will develop and how, in a more global society, people will relate to each other. *We need a philosophical framework*'.[5] As we shall see, Fraser's pinpointing of a crisis of political philosophy is an accurate one.

The journey Fraser made beyond the Right is not unique. From 1990 to 1997, another conservative, Robert Manne, edited Australia's premier right-wing intellectual journal, *Quadrant*. In his time, Manne penned many attacks on left-wing causes. In 1990 he celebrated the collapse of communism, but warned about the 'fashionable new orthodoxies' of 'radical environmentalism, feminism, gay liberationism, multiculturalism and animal liberationism'.[6] But soon after this he began to genuinely rethink his position, and that of the magazine, in the new post-Cold War world. This led to deepening disagreement with most of his editorial board and to his highly public resignation from *Quadrant*.[7] Today, Manne supports many causes usually described as left-wing. He supports a republic and feminism, and he has championed issues concerned with Indigenous people. He mounted the most effective attack on the Right's denial of the 'stolen generation' of indigenous children.[8] He has become an outspoken advocate for a more humane policy towards refugees. He now describes himself as someone on the Left, and is regularly (and bitterly) attacked by conservative commentators.

Fraser and Manne are two examples of what one writer on the journal *Lingua Franca* called the diaspora of the 'ex-cons'—conservatives who have cut themselves adrift from the Right. *Lingua Franca* also focused on John Gray, Professor of European Thought at the London School of Economics. Gray was once a house intellectual for Margaret Thatcher and a darling of the New Right. He wrote a book on John Stuart Mill and another on the theoretical godfather of the New Right, Friedrich Hayek. Of the latter, Hayek himself was effusive in his praise, describing it as 'the first survey of my work which not only fully understands but is able to carry on my ideas beyond the point at which I left off'.[9] Today, Gray is a savage critic of Hayek and of market-driven globalisation, which he regards as a form of fundamentalist utopia. Gray's ideas, which were touched on in the last chapter, will be examined in more detail; they represent a new kind of conservatism which has a place in the reconfiguring of a new politics beyond Right and Left in the twenty-first century.

Neo-liberalism, as we saw, is more radical than conservative. Its trajectory is corroding much of the social fabric. Genuine conservatives like Gray, therefore, become its natural and effective critics.[10] Other conservative critics emerged in the late 1980s as the tide of free-market philosophy engulfed the old Right. The Catholic ideologue B.A. Santamaria, in his later years, regularly attacked the worship of the free market and small government. Deregulation of the finance and banking system, he argued, had enriched the few at the cost of the many. It had created an explosion of credit and debt. Worse, it expressed a breakdown in moral values because deregulation fuelled 'the cult of instant gratification', 'where the volume of money flooding every nook and cranny of the Western world is corrupting everything it touches'.[11]

Another critical voice was that of Charles Kemp, the founder of the oldest think-tank, the Institute of Public Affairs. By 1991 he had had enough of the simplistic nostrums of the economic rationalists. In *Quadrant* he warned that the 'great danger of extreme market philosophies is that they enthrone profit, greed and self-interest. After the horrors of the eighties it is not surprising that the restoration of decent ethical standards is figuring high on the agenda of the nineties'.[12] His ironically titled article 'Those Terrible 80 Years?' points out that the era before market economics enjoyed full employment, low inflation and a booming economy. By that time, both of Kemp's sons—David and Rod—had rejected their father's position and become militant economic rationalists. Both became ministers in the Howard government, and the latter spent the 1980s as the head of the institute his father founded, unravelling his father's work and reconstructing right-wing philosophy.

Finally, there was the populism of Pauline Hanson and her One Nation Party—not so much a remnant of the old Right as a new force prompted by its dissolution. Part of her appeal to many country people was her attack on economic rationalism, which had closed banks, government offices and railway lines in country towns. One Nation's rural policy argued that Australia's competitors 'have continued to protect their industries and national sovereignties while Australia has exposed itself to deregulation, free trade, globalisation and economic rationalism'.[13] To One Nation's constituency (8.4 per cent of voters in 1998), a seamless connection existed between their fear of cultural globalisation and loss of national identity, and their fear of economic globalisation and the loss of national sovereignty.

Social liberalism in Australia

The old Right in Australia was often seen as a single force, labelled 'conservatism', but was actually an amalgam of different political ideas and trends, some of which now oppose the current neo-liberal and neo-conservative hegemony.[14] For example, the great icon of the Australian Right, Sir Robert Menzies, supported social justice and the welfare state. The Liberal MP who now holds Menzies' old parliamentary seat, Petro Georgiou, points out that 'pro-market purists' in the modern Liberal Party damn any notion of social justice as a 'Labor plot', when it was in fact a foundation stone for the Liberal Party.[15] Georgiou cites Menzies' colleague, Paul Hasluck, who said: 'Although a traditionalist, Menzies was not a conservative in any doctrinal sense . . . His political thinking was in accord with the liberalism of Alfred Deakin and the liberalism of late nineteenth century England.'

In a similar vein, former Liberal Party minister Peter Baume argues that 'liberals welcomed measures, and continue to welcome measures, which empower people. Free public education empowered young people. Extension of the franchise empowered adults. Home ownership and income support empowered families. Anti-discrimination legislation empowered people otherwise powerless . . .'[16] Retired Liberal Party president John Valder actively campaigned against the war in Iraq on quintessentially liberal 'human rights' grounds, while former Liberal cabinet ministers Fred Chaney and Ian McPhee, together with former leader of the Coalition John Hewson, deplore the Howard government's xenophobic attitude to race.[17]

People like Petro Georgiou, Peter Baume, Ian Macphee and others were the first victims of the neo-liberal takeover of the Liberal Party in the 1980s, described in Chapter 3. But they are more than this: the liberal tradition they inherited had been deeply affected by 'social liberalism', a radical variant of liberal thought at the turn of the last century. Strongly influential in Australia, especially at the time of the federation of colonies, social liberalism became part of the conservative amalgam, and its values and achievements are being studied anew by researchers such as Marian Sawer.[18] Her work, and that of others, emphasises the gulf between social liberalism and modern neo-liberalism. Advocates of the latter, like Hayek, claim to be the inheritors of the true tradition of liberalism, but this can be strongly contested. In my view, acknowledging a vital social-liberal tradition is important in trying to establish new philosophies beyond Right and Left, and I deal with this in the final chapter of this book.

What is social liberalism? It is the name given to an important development of liberal thinking in Britain and in Europe which placed great emphasis on what was called 'positive liberty'. In the latter half of the nineteenth century, social liberals argued that the era of liberalism as a philosophy opposed to the privilege of the aristocratic state had passed.[19] These 'New Liberals', as they were then called, believed there was an important distinction between private and public spheres. In the latter, it was possible to speak of a public good and a common interest. They argued that the abstract liberal notion of rights-bearing individuals and freedom of contract could become oppressive. 'Freedom of contract', for example, meant one-sided and unequal bargains between employers and workers. 'The social liberals', notes Sawer, 'did not seek the abolition of the market economy but believed that it must be subordinated to the democratic state which put the welfare of its citizens before the sanctity of contract and the rights of property.'[20] The 'New Liberalism' was influential in Britain and elsewhere well into the twentieth century. Discrediting it and seizing the mantle of liberalism was one of Hayek's main motivations (discussed in Chapter 3).

In Britain, its ideas can be traced back to the nineteenth-century British philosopher T.H. Green. Green saw the development of the individual taking place within a community, in the form of an 'ethical state'. The state had a duty to promote active citizenship through redressing poor health, education and housing. His ideas contributed to the reforming British Liberal governments of 1906–14. In Australia, the popularisation of Green's ideas influenced Alfred Deakin, who was prime minister of Australia in the decade after Federation, and instituted a number of reforms with the support of the young Labor Party.[21] This early Left–Right alliance between labourism and liberalism was vital in defining Australia as one of the most progressive democracies in the first half of the twentieth century.

The reforms included the establishment of a system of industrial arbitration, age pensions and, eventually, the vote for (white) women. In this context, social liberalism was expressed specifically in Justice Higgins' 1906 famous 'Harvester' judgment. This legislated a minimum wage, based not on market forces, but on a conception of workers as 'human beings living in civilised communities'.[22] (Over-turning the Harvester judgment was one of the early goals enunciated by John Howard, who said in 1983: 'The time has come when we have to turn Mr Justice Higgins on his head.'[23] According to Sawer, a similar commitment to fairness and to the obligations of a state to its citizens was behind the introduction of old-age pensions and what grew into the welfare state.[24] As well, she points out, social liberalism provided an obvious framework for early feminist ideas and activism.[25] Because it helped set an intellectual and practical agenda in Australia's formative years, social liberalism was a major element in the ideological makeup of both the non-Labor and Labor parties. As Sawer said, it was translated into the Australian notion of the 'fair go'.

Neo-conservative radicalism

The breakup of the Right is not confined to Australia. The most significant recent events in global politics—the 'war on terror' and the invasion of Iraq—have been shaped and initiated by a group of intellectuals now popularly known as the neo-conservatives, or neo-cons. Inordinately influential in the Republican administration of George W. Bush, many neo-cons travelled from Left to Right, coming originally from the Democratic Party where they had been repelled by the political and cultural radicalism of the 1960s. In the face of this, they mounted a defence of Western values and many gravitated to the Republican Party. Neo-conservatives were both cultural conservatives (liberals 'mugged by reality', in the words of an early neo-conservative, Irving Kristol) and enamoured of free-market economics.

Yet the neo-conservatives do not represent the American Right. Their assertion of US hegemony in the Middle East is not the action of conservatives. Just before the Iraq war, one leading neo-conservative, Kenneth Adelman, argued that 'conservatives are now for radical change and the progressives [i.e. the State Department] are for the status quo'. He added: 'Conservatives believe the status quo in the Middle East is pretty bad and the old conservative belief that stability is good doesn't apply to the Middle East.'[26] Some of the most scathing critics of the radical global ambitions of the neo-conservative White House are old-style conservatives allied with the former Republican nominee for president, Pat Buchanan. Their journal, *The American Conservative*, denounced the plan for a war on Iraq and now attacks the Bush presidency as a betrayal of the Right. Its executive editor had this to say in 2004:

Bush has behaved like a caricature of what a right-wing president is supposed to be and his continuation in office will discredit any sort of conservatism for generations. The launching of an invasion against a country that posed no threat to the US, the doling out of war profits and concessions to politically favoured corporations, the financing of the war by ballooning the deficit to be passed on to the nation's children, the ceaseless drive to cut taxes for those outside the middle class and working poor: it is as if Bush sought to resurrect every false 1960s-era left wing cliché about predatory imperialism and turn it into administration policy.[27]

Equally, the global free-trade economy is attacked in traditional conservative terms for its corrosive effects on communities worldwide. 'The conservative movement has been hijacked and turned into a globalist, interventionist, open borders ideology which is not the conservative movement I grew up with', said Pat Buchanan.[28] Today, Buchanan and *The American Conservative* magazine are often described as 'paleoconservatives'.

In the 1990s, this old-style conservatism of Buchanan was frozen out of the Republican Party, which was divided between the religious far Right and the economic liberals and representatives of business. The result was the reassertion of conservative populism by Buchanan. As Michael Lind, a renegade from the Right, argued: 'Patrick Buchanan exposed conservative populism as a fraud by becoming consistently populist: denouncing affirmative action *and* Wall Street; homosexuality *and* corporations 'downsizing' their work forces; feminists *and* rich country-club Republicans. He denounced [his rival] Bob Dole as "the bellhop of the Business Roundtable".'[29]

Criticism of the neo-conservatives is not confined to old-style populist conservatives like Buchanan. One of the most influential intellectual figures in Washington for many years was Owen Harries, a former Australian diplomat and editor of the conservative journal

The National Interest from 1985–2001. Harries was also alarmed by the neo-conservative thrust into Iraq:

> Under the neo-conservatives' guidance, we now have a president committed not only to nation building in Iraq but also to region building throughout the Middle East. The belief that democratic institutions, behavior and ways of thought can be exported and transplanted to societies that have no traditions of them is a profoundly unconservative, indeed a radical, belief.[30]

To many genuine conservatives, the neo-cons are reckless utopians.

The rise of the American neo-conservatives is only the most dramatic evidence of the global shift in the politics of the Right. Over the last 25 years, there has been a sea change in the Right's dominant ideas and values. The rise of economic neo-liberalism and the collapse of the Soviet Union dissolved the glue that once unified the Right. One of the key consequences within countries like Australia is that a broadly shared consensus about the public good and social cohesion has collapsed. Valuing the 'public good' and social cohesion appealed both to what we might call 'traditional' conservatism and to social liberalism. As the fragments of the Right find their respective voices, a number of them have become sources of opposition to the new order. Out of this melting pot, Malcolm Fraser's hopes for 'a new philosophical framework' could well be realised. Working against this are skilful politicians like John Howard and George W. Bush, who have built political coalitions between the contradictory forces of economic liberalism and social conservatism. A battle for the hearts and souls of conservatives is one of the features of the new era beyond Right and Left in which we live.

Classical conservatism has all kinds of weaknesses, but it offers a useful model for framing a new kind of values-based politics which has a sense of the common good and a respect for tradition, and whose opponent is amoral, neo-liberal radicalism. This may strike some people as a strange approach, but then the times we live in are new and different. However, to explore the unravelling of the Right any further, we first have to re-examine the *philosophical* roots of this dislocation.

Taking conservatism seriously

While the headline news at the turn of the century concerned 'the death of socialism', the other death—that of the old Right—has escaped deep scrutiny. This is not surprising in some ways. On the Right, most participants are too close to the action. The winners have accepted their laurels while the defeated are licking their wounds. The Left, while happy to welcome the views of Manne, Fraser and Harries, is largely uncomprehending of the deeper forces at work. In left-liberal academia, only a few take seriously the ideas and the evolution of the Right—even though it has the allegiance of at least half of the population.

The most significant feature of the evolution of the modern Right is the sudden rise of philosophical rationalism within the Right. This was embodied in the economic theory of Hayek and is expressed in the Australian-originated phrase 'economic rationalism'. In its most virulent form, it represents a kind of fundamentalism. Neo-liberals believe that their theory is relevant to the solution of many—perhaps all—social and economic problems, just as others once believed Stalinist Marxism did, and as some believe religious fundamentalism does today. On this count, Robert Manne rang the alarm bells early in the piece in his 1992 book *Shutdown*. Rationalist philosophers, he argued, want to remake the world according to a blueprint provided by Reason:

> [Rationalists] are surprisingly free of doubt about the relationship of theory to practice. They are more willing than the older style conservatives to go wherever their arguments might lead. They are untroubled by the problem of the

unintended consequences of political reform; for older-style
conservatives, the unpredictability of the outcome of radical
experiments is an axiom. Because of the rationalists' greater faith
in theory and in their capacity to control the future they are
less perturbed by the apparent short-term failure of their
policies . . . The older style conservative prejudice is in favour
of maintaining, wherever possible, established communities or
ways of life. They regard interest-based politics as normal and
inescapable. The rationalists see things quite differently. They
regard interest politics as despicable. For them the habit of
defending *what is* against *what may be* is nothing better than
cowardice or romanticism. They know they can improve the
world and shape it to their will.[31]

The rejection of this kind of rationalism was fundamental to
conservative doctrine. (Interestingly enough, it is similar to the
postmodern critique of the Enlightenment, a theoretical stance which
is widespread among the tertiary educated, cultural left.)

Classical conservatism's opposition to rationalism is grounded
in a general wariness of the role of abstract ideas in politics. This
makes conservatism an odd kind of philosophy for anyone used to
Marxism, liberalism or even anarchism, which are *systems* of ideas
integrating interpretations of history, society and economics into
a coherent whole. Rather than a system, conservatism is an organic
philosophy which arose from the earliest times in human history,
and is more a set of attitudes and values than an elaborate theoretical
schema. When conservative philosophers like Roger Scruton discuss
the foundations of conservatism, they talk about a 'conservative
attitude' and 'an attachment to values which cannot be understood
with the abstract clarity of utopian theory'.[32] The British philosopher
Michael Oakeshott talks of a conservative 'disposition', rather than
a theoretical stance. (It is this approach, based on values, which makes
classical conservatism interesting in fashioning a new political
philosophy beyond Right and Left.)

This values-based approach originates in conservatism's critique of rationalistic politics in the French Revolution, and specifically in Edmund Burke's *Reflections on the Revolution in France*, which is a touchstone of conservatism.[33]

The revolution, which helped usher in the modern world, was a triumph of the liberal ideals of liberty and reason. While the revolution involved the dramatic execution of King Louis XVI, and the disestablishment of the Church, it was preceded by a long period of intellectual ferment in which liberal ideas were developed. This period of the Enlightenment challenged the authority of the monarchy and church with two related revolutionary concepts: reason and liberty. In place of superstition and religion, which saw worldly events as ordained by God, reason (in the form of science) offered new explanations as well as the possibility of dominating nature. In place of deference to the divinely ordained power of the lord and the king, the authority of the new world would be based on the secular power of parliaments, which would protect the rights of individuals.

But the Enlightenment-style reason had two sides. Simply put, one side was the attitude that opposed superstition in the name of rational thought, and whose political aspect was a project to *persuade* people to change society. This was the 'weak' Enlightenment ideal to be contrasted with the 'strong' Enlightenment ideal. The latter aimed at *radically transforming* society and people with a view to perfection, as defined by the rational ideal—thus the reign of terror in France from 1793–94 and the schemes to change the names of the months and the calendar. The new calendar, designed by mathematicians, began time anew, similar to Pol Pot's 'Year Zero' in Cambodia.

Against the 'strong' rationalistic ambitions of the French Revolution, Burke made two points of enduring significance. First, he talked about a 'human nature' which limited the *philosophes'* utopian assumptions that human beings could be remoulded by the new society. In other words, he rejected the idea of the 'perfectibility of man'. Rather, he insisted, human nature limited what human social institutions could do.[34] While such talk had nothing in common with postmodernism, which sees human nature as entirely socially constructed, Burke's next thesis did. Projects for transforming society strictly according to a rational plan, he warned, are doomed to failure and to terror, the latter being the only way to deal with the former: 'But that sort of reason which banishes the affections is incapable of filling their place . . . power, of some kind or other, will survive the shock in which manners and opinions perish; and it will find other and worse means for its support.'[35] Postmodernists express the same thought more elusively in the idea that 'meta-narratives' (general theories of history or society) lead to the Gulag. However, while Burke located the failure of rational projects to reconstruct society in a lack of realism about human nature, postmodernists locate that failure in reason itself.

Burke's criticism went further. He also saw talk of human rights in the abstract—or, indeed, talk of any principles transcending the particularity of context—as at best an empty rationalism, and at worst as riding roughshod over the emotions which in fact constituted the weave of the social fabric.[36] You do not have to agree with Burke's dismissal of abstract rights to see that he has an insight into the weakness of policies built on ideals and principles removed from their circumstances. And one of the keys to his insights is an emphasis on what he called circumstances and traditions, and also on 'sentiments' which we would call emotions.

Conservatism and emotions

As already suggested, classical conservatism is an odd kind of philosophy for anyone used to the ideas of Marxism or of liberalism, which are *systems* of ideas or 'grand narratives' which have a clarity and purposefulness. Both arise from attempts to apply reason to human affairs, and this is both their great strength and their great weakness.

While systematic ideologies appeal to the power of reason and logic, conservatism is often very powerful because it appeals to deep emotions in the human psyche. Behind its overt political and social outlooks are emotions, instincts, intuition and passion. Until the rise of the new social movements, especially feminism and the Green movement, conservatism had a strong hold on the non-rational, moral, emotional, spiritual side of politics. These were woven together in a knot made up of patriotism, religion and moral uprightness. In the glory days when conservatism dominated the Right, this emotional–moral appeal (rather than its literal 'policies') was one of the secrets of its success. (Neo-liberals like John Howard and neo-conservatives like George W. Bush try to retain this emotional aspect of conservatism through their emphasis on 'moral values' and national identity, while abandoning the economic ideas that underpin them.)

Central to conservatism's attitudes are notions of authority, both within the family and within the clan or tribe, as well as obligations of kinship. It is an outlook borne of a society frequently at war. Loyalty to the group is at a premium, and loyalty is repaid through group protection of members. Its concomitant—group suspicion of non-kin—is one of its dark sides. As these ideas developed as a political philosophy during the last 300 years, conservatism explicitly came to value traditions, institutions and the wisdom of the past, especially as a means of group cohesion. It is sceptical of novelty, experiments and utopian plans. Promises of progress and reform, especially those based on rationalist schemes, are greeted warily. Conservative philosophers like Roger Scruton, emphasise the importance of a common heritage. This insistence on preserving a collective inheritance appeals to very different emotions than does liberalism's notion of the fulfilment of individual potential—one aspect of the difference is that between an appeal to duty and an appeal to rights.[37]

Given all of this, the conservative impulse has two sides. Its ugliest side is virulent nationalism and suspicion of foreigners. Its war-like roots predispose it to militarism and the rule of the physically strong. Its moral side condemns sexual 'deviancy', and demands that women submit to men.

But for every ugly aspect, there is another side. Love of the nation, group loyalty and valuing a common heritage merge with a belief in the common good. This is a belief that, because we share something, we all have obligations to each other, particularly the obligations of the strong or the rich to the weak or poor. *Noblesse oblige* is a quintessentially conservative notion. But it is also possible for conservatism to encompass the idea of the 'public interest' and of public institutions which are not run for commercial purposes. This was the basis on which conservatism—albeit sometimes grudgingly—supported public health care and public education, as well as a myriad of other public goods, such as protecting the environment. Conservative values can also be part of the matrix that gives rise to an ethic of care and nurturing, which is utterly antagonistic to 'user-pays' schemes of free-market economics. A conservative disposition can value citizenship, and conservative national pride can reinforce the democratic *polis* and democratic institutions. National self-interest can also resist unjust global pressures to deregulate and globalise.

Valuing the family or the clan can mean valuing the deepest possible emotional ties that humans have, and those which can give us the deepest personal satisfaction: love, as well as friendship and companionship. This may not sound like the word 'conservative!' when used as a swear word, but nevertheless it is part of its heritage and its actual appeal to many people.

One person who warned against what I regard as the positive and communal side of conservatism was Hayek, whose ideas we dealt with in Chapter 3. In a small influential article, 'Why I am Not a Conservative' (in fact the postscript to his 1960 book *The Constitution of Liberty*), Hayek spelled out, in prescient terms, why pure liberals (like himself) should carefully and decisively distinguish themselves from conservatives. The two drew from different philosophical trends which were antagonistic. They had merely made a tactical alliance in the face of a common enemy: communism. (Like all good political fundamentalists, Hayek made sure he occasionally attacked his closest allies.)

In 'Why I am Not a Conservative', Hayek criticised conservatism for many reasons. Fundamentally, it stood for nothing definite, he said, and thus it was dragged along in the wake of socialists with whom it continually compromised. It offered a brake on socialism, but not a change of direction. Conservatives also lacked courage and believed in authority: the conservative 'feels safe and content only if he is assured that some higher wisdom watches and supervises change, only if he knows that some authority is charged with keeping the change "orderly"'. Conservatives therefore have no problem with the power of government—or even coercion 'as long as it is used for what he [sic] regards as the right purposes'. Linked to this, the conservative love of the nation could lead to socialism: 'to think in terms of "our" industry or resources is only a short step away from demanding that these national assets be directed in the national interest.' Thus this 'nationalistic bias' can provide the bridge from conservatism to collectivism. While liberals stood for 'a thorough sweeping away of the obstacles to free growth', conservatism stood for an unthinking and cowardly caution toward the new and the unknown. Conservatives were also obscurantist (often resisting new scientific knowledge) and were strident nationalists rather than internationalists, like liberals. On top of this, they 'frequently supported socialist measures in agriculture'. Hayek's damning of conservatism as a competitor to liberalism and as close to socialism is very revealing, in my view.

Of course, none of these deeper philosophical trends—like liberalism or conservatism—are expressed in a pure form in the real world. The ideologies of political parties and individuals are rarely uniform in their views. But, for the sake of untangling and understanding the roots of the ideas of Left and Right, it is necessary to use some classificatory shorthand. With that in mind, let's look further into the outlook of classical conservatism.

Conservatism, human nature and social justice

Classical conservatism's component of what is now called 'communitarianism' offers protection to members of the clan, the group or nation on the basis of common heritage. But this positive idea is offset by another strand of conservative thought, which is a pessimistic acceptance of social injustice and social inequality. Here it is sharply distinct from the optimism of both liberalism and the Left, which arises from their rationalist, Enlightenment-influenced core ideas. The reasons for conservatism's acceptance of social inequality lie in what conservative American political philosopher Thomas Sowell describes as its 'constrained vision'.[38] This is a vision which 'sees the evils of the world as deriving from the limited and unhappy choices available, given the inherent moral and intellectual limitations of human beings'.[39]

In other words, conservatism's acceptance of what custom and tradition deliver rests on a pessimism about human nature. Conservatives rightly argue that human social institutions should accord with the nature we actually have (rather than utopian assumptions of perfectibility), but just what kind of nature do humans have? This is a highly controversial question, and many leftists, postmodernists and social scientists believe that human attitudes and practices are entirely socially constructed. But setting this issue aside for the moment, it is clear that conservatism's conception of the nature of human nature is bleak. For, while pointing to the obvious—that we are complex creatures with the potential for both moral and immoral behaviour—conservatism tends to emphasise the darker side of human nature—greed, selfishness, jealousy, a tendency to violence. In his recent book, *Heresies*, John

Gray argues that 'the idea that humans are an incorrigibly flawed species is taboo today but it was the Right's key tenet for much of the past 200 years', only to be ditched by the neo-liberal Right.[40]

This is the side of humans which must be kept in check at the risk of unravelling the social fabric. Attempts to radically change custom threaten to unleash these darker aspects. This makes a lot of sense when looking at events such as the Great Terror of the French and Soviet revolutions, as well as Pol Pot's Year Zero. These revolutions, having stripped away custom and tradition, solved the inevitable problems which arose from this with naked power and terror.

But are such terrible tragedies the inevitable result of *all* attempts to promote egalitarianism and social justice? There are many reasons to think not. Many societies have achieved major improvements in the material and cultural lives of people gradually over many decades, indeed centuries. These changes certainly involved social conflict— the struggle to achieve voting rights broke out into violence in a number of countries—but the conflict was such that other constraints operated and the whole of civil society was not destroyed in the process.

Although conservative thought over-emphasises the bleak side of human nature, it is realistic in acknowledging that some kind of human nature exists. As I've said, this puts it in stark contrast to the rationalist philosophies that underlie liberalism and socialism.[41] But the answer to conservatism's pessimistic view of human nature lies in modern, more sophisticated studies of human nature which show that all humans have, for example, an altruistic side which initially is expressed in love of family and kin. Much of the evidence for the existence of a human nature—both its pleasant and unpleasant sides—is emerging from the new fields of evolutionary biology and evolutionary psychology.

As I shall argue later, a modest realism about our human nature will have an important place in any new political philosophy beyond Right and Left.[42]

Conserving the globe

The displacement of what I call anti-rationalist or classical conservatism, as well as of social liberalism, from the old Right has unexpected results in contemporary politics. One is that both these strands of thinking can be part of a new politics beyond Right and Left. The rest of this chapter argues the case for this controversial proposal.

British sociologist Anthony Giddens has pointed out that the current kind of economic globalisation has a detraditionalising and disintegrative effect on many of the bases of communal life. The security associated with regular employment, stable community and family life, and social solidarity is undermined by the spread of markets into areas far beyond the economy. All this is inimical to conservative values. Giddens argues that: 'Unchecked capitalistic markets still have many of the damaging consequences to which Marx pointed, including the dominance of a growth ethic, universal commodification and economic polarization.' In this context, he adds, 'what might be called philosophic conservatism—a philosophy of protection, conservation and solidarity—acquires a new relevance for political radicalism today'. He adds provocatively that conservatism has collapsed, but: 'Some of its key ideas, however, acquire a new relevance when removed from their original contexts. We should all become conservatives now . . . but not in the conservative way.'[43] A similar argument is advanced by the left-wing Swedish philosopher Torbjorn Tannsjo in his book *Conservatism for Our Time*, where he argues that conservative arguments are some of the most important in dealing with 'problems altogether outside the traditional left/right spectrum [such as problems] raised by the nuclear threat and by the environmental situation'.[44]

These insights are vitally important and their paradoxical nature is a sign of the times. Another example is the confluence of concern by thinkers of both Left and Right around the need for strengthening of social capital and trust.[45] Social capital and trust 'do not compute' in the instrumental rationality of neo-liberalism—but they are also foreign to some leftists who tend to think that the social conflict is to be applauded and social cohesion is not important.

Let's look at two examples in which conservative attitudes and caution overlap and are mistakenly identified as largely 'left-wing'. The first concerns the social consequences of the growth of a global economy increasingly dominated by the large corporations of industrially advanced countries. In the face of the powerful winds of economic globalisation which are sweeping the planet, versions of conservatism offer one of the strongest forces of resistance. French sociologist Pierre Bourdieu pointed out that the emerging new liberalism is encased in an older social order which it is slowly dismantling. This social order is made up of old institutions and old solidarities which protect people from the excesses of rampant individualism. As such, the forces for conservation are forces of resistance and can become subversive.[46] This is hardly recognised at all by the radical elements of the 'anti-globalisation' movement, who refer to it as an 'anti-capitalist movement'—vainly hoping to revive the revolutionary socialist movement of a previous era. Rather than these chimeras, the strategy of the reform-minded majority within the anti-globalisation movement offers a better model for successful restraint on corporate globalisation. The 1998 campaign in Australia against the Multilateral Agreement on Investment (MAI) is a good example. The MAI was an attempt by the OECD to radically restrict the right of any national government to regulate global corporations and to give corporations the right to sue governments to 'protect their investment'. It would have meant a major change in the ability of nations to control what occurred on their national territory.

The campaign of opposition to the MAI was not 'left-wing' in any simple sense, but drew from a diversity of forces, including conservative political forces and instincts which favoured retaining national economic sovereignty. For some critics, any nationalist tendencies in advanced industrial countries are seen as incurably reactionary. But, in the new global era, an assertion of national interest can be a progressive force since it is only at the level of the nation-state that a framework of democratic institutions exist and that democratic decisions are made. Totally deregulated trade and foreign ownership of a nation's productive enterprises make it more likely that their operation will fit the interests of a transnational corporation and be less subject to local, democratic pressure.

More generally, conservative opposition to barely regulated globalisation is also found in a traditional conservative desire for social cohesion, order and stability. One of the most articulate conservative opponents of globalisation is the conservative political philosopher John Gray, who has already been mentioned. In his book *False Dawn: The Delusion of Global Capitalism*, he argues that the drive for unregulated globalisation is a fundamentalist striving for a utopia based on rationalist ideals of the Enlightenment. It is fundamentalist because the neo-liberal ideologues brook no opposition to their first principles. 'In their cult of reason and efficiency', says Gray, 'their ignorance of history and their contempt for the ways of life they consign to poverty or extinction, they embody the same rationalist hubris and cultural imperialism that have marked the central traditions of Enlightenment thinking throughout its history'.[47]

The neo-liberal cult of reason assumes that markets spontaneously evolve, and are thus 'natural', and that restraints on them are unnatural. 'The truth is that free markets are creatures of state power, and persist only so long as the state is able to prevent human needs for security and the control of economic risk from finding political expression', Gray says.[48] Gray also fears the collapse of cohesion in a purely market-driven society: 'The free market is most recklessly short termist in its demolition of the virtues it once relied upon. These virtues—saving, civic pride, respectability, 'family values'—are now profitless museum pieces.'[49] Neo-liberal policies such as outsourcing, combined with technological change, have meant the wholesale disappearance of entire occupations and the disappearance of career structures. Job insecurity, the growth of casual, part-time and contract work, and the end of loyalty to a single employer corrode a settled life, he says. The demand for flexibility and mobility puts strains on traditional modes of family life: 'How can families meet for meals when both parents work on shifts? What becomes of families when the job market pulls parents apart?'[50]

While Gray's critique is absolutely based on traditional conservatism, his conclusion is very close to that of 'left-wing' critics of globalisation in trade unions and non-government organisations: 'Only a framework of global regulation—of currencies, capital movements, trade and environmental conservation—can enable the creativity of the world economy to be harnessed in the service of human needs.'[51] So perhaps Hayek was right to see conservatism as too close to socialism for his liking!

Another sign of rapprochement between old-style conservatism and progressive forces can be seen in the contact between disgruntled Republican Patrick Buchanan and the left-liberal advocate Ralph Nader in 2004. Seeking support for his presidential candidacy, Nader approached Buchanan's magazine, *The American Conservative*. In an interview, Nader indicated to Buchanan areas of agreement with old-style conservatism: opposition to neo-conservative foreign policy and the invasion of Iraq; hostility to the loss of sovereignty to bodies like the World Trade Organization; and criticism of aggressive corporate marketing to children, which undermined families.[52]

Given that conservative values can provide a basis of opposition to the regressive and undemocratic aspects of globalisation, some may ask, 'so what?' There are two answers to this: first, the very simple lesson that broad coalitions which include conservatives can be stronger than narrowly based ones, and hence more likely to achieve their aims; and second, the fact that successfully appealing to conservative instincts can have the virtue of diverting some of these same instincts from other targets such as immigrants and refugees and from drifting toward the siren songs of race hatred.

Conservation and conservatism

The second example of new movements which go beyond Right and Left, and which draw on conservative instincts, is the environment movement.

Environmental concerns established themselves on the agenda of countries like Australia with two striking characteristics. The first was the speed with which they grew, and the second was the breadth of the movement, which received support from across the political spectrum, including the overtly non-political. One reason for the breadth of the movement is that it accords with traditional conservative values. Today, the environment movement, along with 'green politics', is the most significant place towards which unanchored conservative values may converge. One of the dangers to the future of green politics is that both its friends and enemies refer to it as 'left wing', hoping by this appellation either to praise or to condemn it. But the kind of politics based on environmental issues are a new form of politics 'beyond Right and Left' in which conservative values are vital. Understanding the dynamic of green conservatism means abandoning the reflex use of the term 'conservative' as a swear word and realising that we all have genuinely conservative instincts.

For those who assume the environmental movements are left-wing movements, this is heresy. The convergence between environmental and conservative values does not necessarily take the form of high-profile members of the old Right announcing their conversion (although a number of elections have shown that a Green vote normally attracts disenchanted conservative voters). Usually it is a more subtle process whereby the conservative (not radical) instincts of many ordinary people incline them sympathetically towards green ideals. This is true in the case of genetic engineering and biotechnology, one of the big issues facing humanity, and one imagined to be a new corporate gold mine. Many regard the critics of biotechnology as left-wing, but one of the most thoughtful critics is the conservative political scientist Francis Fukuyama.

His recent book *Our Posthuman Future* raises important issues about the effects of human biotechnology on human rights, human dignity and human values.[53] Unless regulated, biotechnology of humans will undermine democracy and equality in the long term, he believes. Fukuyama is disturbed by several possible scenarios. One is the development of pharmaceutical drugs tailored to suit the genetic profile of an individual and whose purpose is to alter (or to correct) personality problems. Personalities can be changed at will, and there is no longer any excuse to be depressed or unhappy. Another scenario is that stem cell research will allow new body parts to be grown at will. The age of people lifts well over 100 years, and the average age of all people grows higher and higher. It becomes an old people's world. Expectations between generations in families are destabilised. A third scenario is well known. The rich begin to design babies for themselves: 'You can increasingly tell the social background of a young person by his or her looks and intelligence.'[54] In this world, it becomes possible to cross humans and apes. Are these new creatures humans? Apes? What rights do they have? Human rights? What will happen to political rights generally? What will happen to the assumption which underpins our current world that 'we share a common humanity that allows every human being to potentially communicate with and enter moral relationships with every other human being on the planet'?

The issue underlying Fukuyama's fears is that 'biotechnology will cause us in some way to lose our humanity—that is, some essential quality that has always underpinned our sense of who we are and where we are going'.[55] This possibility that biotechnology will alter human nature will move us into what Fukuyama calls a 'posthuman' stage of history. Of central concern is the notion of the human dignity and equal worth of all humans. The genetic embedding of social elites is one fear, but a wider one is that the unhooking of human values from humans as presently constituted.

Fukuyama's criticism is not based on religious belief, nor is he an absolute opponent of biotech—there are many benefits from human biotechnology and that's part of the problem, he says. Rather, he is sceptical of radical experiments which promise utopias. In this way, he is part of an established conservative tradition, once sceptical of utopian political changes, now sceptical of the radical 'progress' of commercially driven science and technology.

This conservative tradition has intersections with green ideas at the philosophical level. Consider the words of one of the classic conservative thinkers, the British philosopher Michael Oakeshott. The general characteristics of conservatism, he says:

> ... centre on a propensity to use and enjoy what is available rather than to wish for or look for something else; to delight in what is present rather than what was or what may be ... To be conservative then is to prefer the familiar to the unknown, to prefer the tried to the untried, fact to mystery, the actual to the possible, the limited to the unbounded, the near to the distant, the sufficient to the superabundant, the convenient to the perfect, present laughter to utopian bliss.[56]

To prefer the 'sufficient to the superabundant' could well be the motto of a sustainable society which rejects consumerism and which does not seek fulfilment through ever-increasing material goods. His conservative suspicion of schemes for improvement and leaps into the unknown is the feeling shared by those who warn about genetic engineering of crops, animals and humans. Yet Oakeshott was not thinking of modern environmental problems when he wrote these words—indeed, the modern movement did not yet exist. Frugal habits, once associated with conservative thinking (and poverty), have been abandoned as a cornucopia of commodities is endlessly generated. As two British writers argue,

> ... there has always been a popular tradition of taking pride in people's ability to stretch and amplify limited resources, to make a little go a long way, to make ends meet, to make do and mend, to make a meal out of a few odds and ends, to improvise, to eke out, to share the little they had when someone dropped in at mealtime ... How remote this seems, how antiquated by the fall-apart luxury, the throwaway opulence of all that has displaced it.[57]

As we've seen, classical conservative thought values tradition because it represents the refinement of wisdom of the past. Conservative thought argues that the practices that are handed down to us are the result of many generations of trial and error. Rather than beginning by erring again, we should begin by attaching value to the tradition. As well as the traditions of humans, tradition presents itself to us through the existence of the ecology of the planet. The interdependence of living organisms—a process which has evolved through millions of years—is a tradition indeed! But tradition is one thing to which market fundamentalism attaches no value and which it aims to overturn. Humanity has built societies largely based on the manipulation of the ecology through farming. Farming communities, both in the developing world and in advanced capitalism, are deeply conservative. But today, the modern manipulations in industrialised farming, unlike the previous small-scale versions, are quite different. The results are actually unknown and incalculable, and increasingly disturb some rural conservatives.

Other conservative ideals link tradition with ideas of ecological sustainability. One is the conservative notion of stewardship of heritage, with the present generation playing steward to our ancestors and to the as yet unborn generations. An identical notion of stewardship for the past and future is found in green movements. Such conservative notions appear among the belief systems of

Indigenous and first nation people whose societies are extremely conservative. In such societies and elsewhere, respect for tradition can be a suffocating thing, but in regard to ecological stability it makes very good sense.

Scepticism towards endless 'progress' is therefore shared in environmental and conservatives outlooks. By contrast, the Enlightenment-based theories of liberalism and socialism share a notion of unending progress based on the accumulation of material goods. This version of the good life and progress is understandable, since material deprivation for masses of people is still in living memory in industrial countries and is a living reality for millions in developing countries. But endless material progress on the model of advanced industrial countries is not generalisable to the rest of the world because it is simply unsustainable on a global scale.

While it is true that the Left in Australia, earlier than most, adopted an environmental stance, this can be misleading. The image of green politics as 'left-wing' and radical drives away potential supporters as well as forcing new politics into old categories. At a less abstract level than the philosophical intersections of conservative and green thought, there are at least four other reasons to reject describing the environmental movement and green politics as being of the Left.

First, in the industrialised world, the environment movement— significantly also called the *conservation movement*—grew up to protect the natural world (or, in the case of cities, the heritage of the built world) from predatory forces which saw the existing world as a mere raw material to be exploited. It represented a *conservative* response to the dynamic of expansion which markets contain, and their tendency to constantly drive a relentless change. Whatever else they are, concepts such as sustainability and harmony with the biosphere are conservative concepts.

Second, the origins of the environment movement were not among trade unions, or socialists, or Left intellectuals. They were largely among middle-class nature lovers, many of whom were conservative in politics, such as Sir Garfield Barwick who was the first president of the Australian Conservation Foundation. An eclectic mix of social forces built the early environmental consciousness in different countries. They included hunters, aristocrats, transcendentalists and scientists.

Third, the Left was a historic force based on the organised working class, and it struggled for a just share of capitalism's wealth (while a minority strove to abolish capitalism). Green politics are not based on class and their analyses are not reducible to class. The enemy is not capitalism, but relentless expansion of an industrial system aimed at generating products to satisfy a consumerism which substitutes for other meaning and value in the lives of its adherents. Instead of the socialist logic to abolish all private ownership and markets, it makes environmental sense to use market mechanisms to raise the price of timber from native forests, of coal, of oil and of fresh water in order to reduce their depletion.[58]

Finally, both conservatism and environmental thought share values which might be termed 'spiritual', in the sense that they seek a dimension of life that contains a sense of the sacred. Classical liberalism and socialism are avowedly secular. Any movement which has a spiritual dimension appeals to deep feelings of humans. This dimension provides an alternative measure of value and meaning other than that which believes that human happiness can be achieved by the endless production and consumption of commodities.

The break up of the old Right is both a cause and effect of the deep changes in political ideas since the end of the Cold War, the rise of the global economy and the triumph of neo-liberalism. Just as these changes undermine old conceptions of the Right, they also give rise to the possibility of new ideas and philosophies. With this in mind, it is important to take seriously the strands which made up the old Right.

From classical conservatism, we can learn about the necessity for caution in social change, about the importance of emotions in politics and about the need for realism about human nature. Equally, social liberalism's insistence on the duties of the state to support social cohesion, and its support for a public sphere, as well as social justice, are worth reviving. If these ideas are to be put together in new ways, they also need an injection from another tradition. So it is time to look at what emerges from another defeat—that of socialism.

5

What was socialism?

When the union's inspiration through the workers' blood shall run,
There can be no power greater anywhere beneath the sun.
Yet what force on earth is weaker than the feeble strength of one?
But the union makes us strong.

'Solidarity Forever', *IWW Songbook*

Once upon a time leftists acted as if they could fundamentally re-organize
society. Intellectually the belief fed off a utopian vision of a different society;
psychologically, it rested on self-confidence about one's place in history;
politically it depended on real prospects. Today the vision has faltered . . . Almost
everywhere the Left contracts, not simply politically but, perhaps more
decisively, intellectually.[1]

Russell Jacoby, *The End of Utopia*

Shortly after I began working on the *Sydney Morning Herald* in the mid-1980s, I wrote a long 'summer-reading' style article on the tradition of coal miners. I spent a day on the New South Wales South Coast meeting former miners Fred Kirkwood, Jack Wright and Bob Shadlow, as well as the leader of the Miners' Women's Auxiliary, Sally Bowen. I also visited a remarkable church at Mount Kembla, which sits on a mountain flank above the lowlands and beaches around Wollongong. The Anglican Miners' and Soldiers' Church, decorated inside with miners' lamps and a stained-glass memorial window to miners, stood before a graveyard holding the bodies of over 90 men and boys. They were killed nearby in a gas explosion deep underground in what became known as the 'Mt Kembla disaster', in July 1902. The words on a headstone which recorded the burial of two sixteen-year-old brothers along with their father still had the power to move me to tears.

I had a certain fascination for coal miners. My paternal grand-father had come from Scotland around 1910 to work on the Hunter Valley coalfields, where my father was born. Years later I was surprised to hear my politically conservative father still speak with bitterness about the police shooting of striking miners during the Depression. Later I learnt of the miners' ability to conduct determined strikes which 'broke through' on issues like paid holidays and shorter hours—benefits which later spread to other workers. It was the miners who were a foundation stone of the Labor Party and of the Communist Party. Coal miners, in the jargon of those days, were the vanguard of the working class.

But by the time I had joined the Communist Party in 1972, I was puzzled to hear that the miners were the subject of a wistful regret by the industrial organisers of the party. A similar regret was expressed about the waterside workers. Both of these sections of the working class had become relatively affluent and their militancy turned inward, spurred more by self-interest than by a wider role in the shared interests of all workers.

As I researched the *Herald* article, I once again struck this wistful regret—a feeling that was a mourning for a lost ideal. Much of the tradition—the close-knit villages, the miners' bands, the regular pit-top meetings and the annual May Day picnic on the coast to which special trains brought miners from another town on the other side of the mountains—had died. The physical difficulty and danger of the work, along with the poverty, had changed. Old-timers complained that the modern coal miners were too 'hungry', eager to make money by cutting corners and caring less about the effect on others. 'There are plenty of goodies out there if you are prepared to work for it,' said a rueful Jack Wright. Fred Kirkwood summed it up: 'They've lost some of that feeling for their fellow man.'[2]

Today, miners continue to mine, to get dirty and to face death from rockfalls. Most are members of a militant trade union which bargains collectively (though some have been enticed into individual contracts). But outward appearances are deceptive. The class-consciousness of miners and many other groups of workers has been hollowed out. Social classes still exist in Australia, but the idea that membership of a class engenders a certain outlook on life, a class-consciousness, is now an article of faith, not a fact of life.

The death of a legend

This hollowing out is part of the death of 'the Australian Legend'. One of the most influential studies on the ethos on which Australian unions and the Labor Party were built appeared in 1958. The left-wing historian Russel Ward wrote a book called *The Australian Legend*. Ward was deeply influenced by Marxism, and his title referred to a 'national mystique', a 'people's idea of itself' which, although often deeply romanticised, had a basis in fact:

> According to the myth the 'typical Australian' is a practical man, rough and ready in his manners and quick to decry any appearance of affectation in others. He is a great improviser, ever willing to 'have a go' at anything but willing too to be content with a task done in a way that is 'near enough'. Though capable of great exertion in an emergency, he normally feels no impulse to work hard without good cause ... [He is] sceptical about the value of religion and of intellectual and cultural pursuits generally. He believes that Jack is not only as good as his master but, at least in principle, probably a good deal better ... he is a fiercely independent person who hates officiousness and authority ... above all he will stick by his mates through thick and thin ...[3]

This 'up country' and 'convict ethos' was refined and developed by hostility between pastoral workers and land-owning squatters in the late nineteenth century, and that in turn gave a distinctive character to the culture of the labour movement and to the Labor Party. Much of this was embodied in values such as egalitarianism and mateship, and the notion of the ordinary worker as a 'battler'. In its time, it was an insightful work of what today is called 'cultural history', and for a long while the ethos described by *The Australian Legend* was Labor territory. Political scientist Judith Brett argues that a mild revival of this ethos, with a strong nationalist flavour, occurred in the 1980s under the Hawke government. But this revival:

> . . . added an overlay of obvious cultural difference to the tensions between the ALP's historic labourist working class base and its new urban middle-class supporters excited by contemporary Australia's cosmopolitan possibilities. The legend seemed to be about Australia's past, with little to offer its multicultural present and future. So, as with the symbol of the worker, Labor in government loosened its grip on the egalitarian imagery of the Australian legend and Howard claimed it to fill out his picture of the consensual mainstream of Australian life.[4]

The success of John Howard in claiming the values and language of the Australian Legend is one of the most successful pieces of cultural politics in modern times. The ethos of the mateship of ordinary people is now used to project the world view of the Liberal–National government and to attack unions and the Labor Party. Howard's speeches are peppered with statements such as: 'Being Australian means doing the decent thing in a pragmatic and respectable society which lives up to the creed of practical mateship . . . Australians are a down-to-earth people. It is part of our virtue. Rooted deep in our psyche is a sense of fair play and a strong egalitarian streak.'[5]

In the discourse of the Howard government, the 'battlers' are those who are opposed to 'cultural elites' and 'special interests', such as trade unions, migrants or Aborigines. When discussing his government's changes to Aboriginal land rights laws, Howard said that all Australians would be treated 'equally' before the law. To some, this is merely a confidence trick, a device of political rhetoric, but unfortunately this is not so. Nor is this reversal solely an Australian phenomenon. In the United States, the Republican Party has captured support from many workers in the South and elsewhere—a process that began with people dubbed the 'Reagan Democrats'. Thatcherism too appealed to a substantial group of blue-collar workers. In Australia, the Liberal Party is making inroads into blue-collar constituencies on the basis of moral conservatism in a culture war against the values of the unions, Labor, the left and feminists—and against values of social liberals who were once part of the Liberal Party.

When conservatives seize hold of the language and ethos about 'battlers', egalitarianism and 'ordinary Australians', it is much more than skilful public relations based on appealing to the moral values, rather than economic interests, of many workers. Like all skilful public relations, it interprets and builds on actual events, rather than promoting falsity. The fact is that traditional working-class voters, whatever their economic opinions, tend to have relatively conservative views, especially on race and nation.[6] That is one of the reasons for the phenomenon noted by political scientists Clive Bean and Ian McAllister, who argue that 'One Nation support ... comes disproportionately from manual workers, trade union members and those who describe themselves as working class, the less well educated and people who never attend church'. This list of characteristics 'comes close to defining the archetypal Labor voter', they say.[7]

This culture war for the souls of workers also reflects an instinctive grasp by skilled politicians such as John Howard of the profound changes in society and in political ideas—something about which the Left is still confused.

Among the Left, there is still a residual feeling that workers and trade unions are not just important institutions, but are *central* to building a better society, even to the exclusion of other constituencies.[8] There is even a view that workers (by which is meant *blue-collar* workers) are more authentic, 'better' people. Often this is larded with a deep sentimentality and romanticisation about industrial workers and a divisive scorn for the middle class and intellectuals. This attitude is often mobilised by the most short-sighted and narrow sections of the unions when they want to vilify environmentalists who want to stop a logging project, a mine or a coastal resort development that will provide a handful of jobs. Such attacks are not based on the facts of the case, but on this romantic kind of fundamentalism, which is comforting to those who believe it, but mystifying to others—particularly to a younger generation of idealists. Even more difficult problems exist in the public sector where trade unions are the main vehicle for representing a progressive policy. In the fields of education, health, local government and the public service, trade unions are capable of representing their members' interests, but this is by no means the same as the interests of parents, patients, ratepayers and the public at large. The strategic answer adopted by unions in the public sector is to demand more funding overall but, while often necessary, this does not address certain issues and looks self-serving.

Beyond the world of class

The New Right is not the only movement whose triumph depended on a powerful political idea. In its time, the class analysis of socialism was an enormously powerful weapon. It cut through the ideologies that obscured the greed of the corporate ruling class, both locally and internationally. More importantly, it gave a confidence and inner strength to working-class movements, even in the darkest times. The idea that all workers shared a status in that they were oppressed by the same force was the basis for class-wide solidarity, the first expression of which was the formation of trade unions, on which were founded labour and socialist parties in the late nineteenth century. Today, the trade union movement is one social movement among many others. Its institutional form still means it is the biggest social movement, but it was once the sun around which other planets orbited, a reflection of the theory that 'class' was the determining reality in advanced capitalism.

Today this world view is in its death throes. In Australian suburbs today, we still have Workers' Clubs (Broken Hill even has a 'Social Democratic Club'), and in our universities intellectuals study the ideals and history of the labour and socialist movements. We still have a viable trade union movement with 1.8 million members and—even more distinctively in a global sense—we have a Labor Party. Yet these institutions are shrinking. In a mere twelve months between August 2001 and August 2002, the proportion of trade union members in the workforce dropped from 24.6 per cent to 23.1 per cent. That was down from 31 per cent in 1996 and 46 per cent in 1986.[9] The rise of part-time work, the decline of blue-collar workplaces where unionism was strong and a long campaign by the New Right to de-legitimise unions have all played their part.

Social class is still important in understanding Australia, and indeed any advanced industrial society. The social power and privilege conferred by individual wealth to a small elite is a central feature of such societies. But this is not the point. A world view based on class presumed that workers would develop a collective interest, and that this would be expressed in trade unions and labour parties. But this class-consciousness is demonstrably fading and changing. However, a crude class analysis continues to define part of the Left, partly because of a desire to cling to comforting assumptions and partly because no other framework has emerged as an analysis and guide to action for social change.

What happened to the miners of the New South Wales South Coast is the story of the Left's dreams of the working class as bearers of a new society—a more egalitarian one and a more collective one. It is the story of the decline of a world view built on material deprivation, which gave almost exclusive primacy to the *economic* facts of life as the forces that determined politics and ideas, rather than to beliefs and values.

But the story about the South Coast miners is also the story behind the Australian Labor Party's long-term crisis of vision about its purpose and political philosophy. Many have attributed this crisis to its substantial period in national office from 1983 to 1996, which saw many reversals of traditional Labor economic policy. The Commonwealth Bank and a host of other publicly owned institutions were privatised, and industry and commerce were broadly deregulated. But was this change in direction a *cause* of the crisis or an expression of an already existing one?

While many writers and participants blame the Hawke–Keating leadership for 'selling out', it is equally valid to argue that Labor's previous political philosophy had simply run out of steam. Labor's ideas, and their intellectual origin in the tradition of socialism, could not withstand the worldwide neo-liberal revolution.

If there is one thing that Labor and the Left should learn from the rise of the New Right, it is the foundational importance of ideas, philosophy and world view to political action. A necessary part of any rethinking is an unsentimental look at the contemporary ideas inherited from traditional socialism.

The death of socialism

To many, the death of the socialist movement is not news, nor even of interest. The requiem has been played, so let's leave the funeral. Indeed, many of the undoubted flaws in the socialist and Marxist frameworks were identified many years ago.

Socialist morbidity in the West has led to the slow disintegration of the radical Left or its transformation into moderate progressive parties (such as the Italian Communist Party, which has become the Democratic Party of the Left). Trade unions have shrunk, sometimes dramatically. More significantly, this has meant the floundering of labour, socialist and social-democratic parties which periodically form national governments. But all of this crystallises tendencies which have been in evidence for many decades, above all the fact that the working class in advanced capitalism—like the miners I discovered on the New South Wales South Coast—was not doing what was expected of it.

Many of today's Left actually have no investment in a concept of socialism, which is in itself revealing of the changes underway in the meaning of the Left–Right concept of politics. It also reveals that 'the Left' today is composed of at least two schools of thought: a 'cultural left' based on an educated middle class; and a socialist left, based on trade unions.

The death of socialism also arises from a long string of fallen idols—Leftist leaders or socialist regimes which have failed to overcome problems such as ethnic conflict with terrible results (Yugoslavia), or have quickly become party dictatorships of varying degrees of physical repression (Cuba, Vietnam, China, North Korea), or which have imposed barbarities that are unequalled (Cambodia). And all without Russia's excuse that it was the first to venture into the uncharted waters of making a socialist society from top to bottom.

Why then should we bother? The dogs bark and the caravan moves on. In his book *The Latin American Left After the Cold War*, Jorge Casteneda gives three reasons to be interested in the fate of socialism.[10] The first is simple historical curiosity; the second is because, on a global scale, the original causes that gave it birth have not disappeared—poverty, injustice, gaping social inequality and violence; and last, and most importantly, the socialist Left has been a weighty force for over 150 years in forcing social change and reform. Its greatest achievement, ironically, has been civilising capitalism. But its sudden eclipse poses the question of what, if anything, will replace socialism as an oppositional force to the undoubted injustices and inequalities generated by a more dynamic global capitalism.

I would add two further reasons to Castaneda's. First, we are now seeing the emergence of a youthful movement around global economic injustice, which some hail as a new 'anti-capitalist movement'.[11] It would be of some interest, then, to discuss the tragic fate of the previous anti-capitalist movement. Second, analysing a pivotal moment in history can often illuminate useful and interesting things about the past and the future—and we are certainly at such a pivotal moment. When searching the literature on this, I discovered that immediately after the collapse of the Soviet Union in 1989–90 there was a flurry of analysis, some debating the future of socialism, others attacking books like Francis Fukuyama's *End of History*, which symbolised triumphant anti-socialism.

As the 1990s unrolled, less and less was written about the demise of this 150-year-old tradition of socialism. Those most deeply affected are in denial. It is as if a shocking event has occurred (akin to the death of a loved one, or a fatal road accident on your doorstep) and those who survived cherish their memories and simply don't want to talk about the unpleasant reality. This is all the more remarkable since, in relatively recent times, it was possible to speak of a New Left, which was intellectually confident and was actively intervening in the political field to refashion it in significant ways. Less than 30 years after this high water mark, it's now clear that the socialist component of the New Left was the last gasp of an older Left, not the promise of a renewed one.[12]

Why did it happen, then—and why was it so rapid? There are a number of reasons, all of them involving cherished, core beliefs of the socialist Left which proved flawed. Understanding them takes us a long way towards understanding how a new politics of social change might evolve.

The collapse of 'actually existing socialism'

The pivotal moment for the death of modern socialism was the collapse of the Soviet Union and the liberatory revolution which swept Eastern Europe. These momentous events crystallised problems which had been accumulating in the ideas of socialism for several decades. Yet this is paradoxical, since almost no one in the modern socialist Left held any illusions about the Soviet model of 'socialism'. The repression and brutality engendered by the Soviet Union under Stalin had been exposed in the West in the 1930s and in the Soviet Union in the 1950s. The post-Stalin Soviet Union was bureaucratic, conservative and repressive. By 1989, only a minuscule group of sentimental communists still put their faith in the Soviet Union. In part, these were the ancient dreams of a generation traumatised by the Great Depression; in part, it was based on a logic that the enemy of my enemy—in this case, American capitalism—must be my friend. Yet the collapse of the Soviet Union dealt a hard blow to a much broader Left generally, and even to social democratic and Labor parties. Why was this? How could its collapse be pivotal to the collapse of a variety of other socialisms in the West?

The socialist Left had no illusions, bar one: that, under a genuine reformer like Soviet leader Mikhail Gorbachev, it might be possible to destroy the party dictatorship, introduce democracy and grassroots control—that is, create a socialism worthy of the name out of the ruins of a dysfunctional bureaucratic society which had no capitalist class. This was underpinned by a theory of history that the existence of a 'socialist base' was a progressive historical step which would inevitably be followed by another higher stage. The idea that history could go into reverse—backwards into capitalism—was barely conceivable.

In all, this represented a triumph of hope and faith over commonsense. The dream ended when it became clear that forms of democracy and freedom could not be combined with the continuation of an entirely state-owned economy, and that some form of market economy was needed. This had become clear in the final years of the Soviet Union, when the absence of markets and lack of entrepreneurial initiative were precisely the failures identified by the highest level of Soviet political leadership.[13] By the 1980s, Gorbachev was desperately trying to overcome 'inertia' and to introduce 'initiative and incentive'. The problem lay 'in the archaic nature of our economic mechanisms, in the rigid centraliz-ation of administration, in over-reliance on planning and in the lack of genuine economic incentives'.[14]

I quote Gorbachev and his advisers because they were in a good position to know what was really going on, and also had a vested interest in avoiding this conclusion—which was entirely at odds with their adherence to Marxism. Significantly, the only 'socialist' countries which avoided a sclerotic economy were those which experimented with markets, such as Hungary and Yugoslavia—and today the People's Republic of China.[15] Markets alone, of course, are no guarantee of economic success, as we have subsequently seen in Russia. They require a strong framework of law and civil society to restrain their dynamic but destructive tendencies, and the absence of these continues to be one of the key reasons for economic and social chaos in modern Russia.

I argued in Chapter 3 that, despite a harsh overall philosophy, Friedrich Hayek had an important insight into why market mechanisms can be both efficient and dynamic, and why totally planned economies can be neither. The market, he argued, acts as an information medium, rapidly signalling the response of other economic sectors, including consumers, to the production of a commodity and to its price. Similar conclusions have been reached by economists sympathetic to the ideals of socialism, such as Alec Nove. Nove points out that models of a planned economy assume that unanimity about what constitutes the general good can be reached.[16] Even granted this assumption, putting a democratic economic plan into actual operation will be just as difficult as introducing a bureaucratically devised plan: how can any plan forecast the needs and desires of a highly differentiated population?

As well, even a highly 'democratic' planned economy—for example, based on decisions of workers' cooperatives or self-managed units—depends ultimately on coercion. Why? Essentially because the price of total planning is the outlawing of any private economic enterprise. If someone wants to set up a small business to employ people and sell things, thus disregarding 'the plan', they will ultimately face a legal penalty, since such activities constitute a 'black market' and the 'exploitation of labour', and must be penalised lest planning unravel. Nor is it an answer to have a planned economy while allowing a limited sphere of small business 'on the side' with limited markets. Successful small businesses become bigger businesses and, logically, this must be prevented because at some point they will tip the society over into capitalism. In China, where very large private businesses operate in elaborate markets, the price paid for preventing this is the coercion exercised by the Chinese Communist Party through its total domination of the state.

Some Marxists, observing the Soviet disaster, conclude that a model of 'market socialism' is viable for advanced industrial countries. By this, they mean a publicly owned economy managed by cooperatives which all compete in a market. But is it really possible? Leaving aside the question of how we might arrive at this situation, it is hard to see how the existence of markets would *not* lead to the resurgence of private enterprise in fact, if not in words. As well, certain problems of capitalism would reappear. A corporation managed by its workforce which acted against the public interest would present similar legal and moral problems to the private corporations with which we are familiar today.

The conclusion that the market mechanism is necessary for any complex economy, and that in some circumstances it can be more 'democratic' than bureaucratic planning, is obviously unpalatable to many socialists. This is why the collapse of Soviet-style socialism badly wounded other kinds of socialism and non-market ideas: it suggested that planning and regulation, as mechanisms designed to replace markets, had some inherent flaws. And this synchronised with the renewal of the Right based on free-market economics in many Western countries. This tandem triumph was symbolised by the appearance of Francis Fukuyama's book, *The End of History*, which argued that human societies had reached an end-point in ideological evolution which was the acceptance that there was no alternative to the model of liberal democracy.[17] The left-wing sociologist Erik Olin Wright conveys the current state of play: 'No serious thinker on the Left still upholds the vision of comprehensive centralised planning as a viable institutional design to replace capitalism.'[18] Having said all that, it is obviously possible for society as a whole to agree on and pursue certain kinds of general interests or a common good (e.g. health and education standards), and to do so through governments. The problem arises when this government-regulated method is applied to a large part of the productive economy.

The question now is not whether markets are good or bad, nor whether non-capitalist markets are possible. Rather, a host of other questions emerge: Within what institutional and moral framework should markets operate? To what degree should market mechanisms be used in any given sphere? Which areas of human activity should largely be quarantined from markets? To what extent should the surplus generated by private enterprise be put to social uses by the state? How can value and prices be attributed to finite natural resources such as water, minerals, timber, and so on. Far-sighted Left thinkers like Eric Aarons have argued that errors within Marx's economic theory about value, price and the nature of human labour lead to the assumption that, in some future socialist society, labour and capital could become entirely social and have no private element. This in turn leads to a whole series of problems, including the elimination of consumer preference, the absence of such information for central planners and also the absence of the necessary recognition and reward that humans need for achievement and innovation.[19]

Aarons' conclusion is a radical one, given that he devoted a large part of his life to achieving a socialist society on Marxist lines. He concludes that the failure of socialism in centrally planned economies 'was not primarily due to a distortion of socialist programs and/or the evil deeds of its leaders, grievous as they were, but to the fact that the project of abolishing markets as such is impossible in conditions of widespread division of labour ... Insofar as ideological, one-sided views about the malleability of human nature sustained this project, they too were a large part of the problem.'[20]

I will return to his comment about human nature, but at this point we need to ask: if socialism needs markets—indeed, if it needs a degree of private enterprise—then what is socialism? It is certainly not a radical negation of capitalism, but perhaps a significant modification— maybe a mixed economy? Such a conclusion undermines another of the classical tenets of Marxist theory, that capitalism was a 'stage' in human history which would be surpassed by socialism, just as feudalism was by capitalism.

But there is one further, important conclusion to draw from the collapse of the world's first attempt at a post-capitalist society. This concerns the connection between the ideas of Marxism and the reality of repressive, undemocratic and stagnant life under Soviet socialism. The many disasters of post-capitalist societies have long been explained by the poverty and hostility which such societies faced at the time of their birth. Many on the Left have long refused to see a connection between Stalinism and the ideas of Marxism, because the latter is so obviously permeated by high ideals. Stalinism, they maintain, is a distortion of Marxism. While this is true, aspects of Marxist thought did lend themselves to Stalinism—if only because a fully planned economy is not viable and because an impossible project can't be attempted without increasing coercion, finding those responsible for failures, dealing with them, and so on. But a planned economy was not one poor idea among many good ones; rather, it is conceptually linked to other deeply flawed ideas.

Both the left-wing German philosopher Jürgen Habermas and the British political scientist Andrew Gamble point out that Marx's vision of a planned economy assumes a dangerous fusion of the political and the economic.[21] Andrew Gamble points out that Marx was deeply influenced by the moral critique of the early socialists. In particular, he believed that in a non-capitalist society the state and society would become one and that civil society (the sphere where the power of the private owners was located) would be abolished and thereby classes also abolished.[22] Together with Marxist economic determinism—the idea that the economy largely determines the character of social life more generally—this fusion opens the way to what, in the twentieth century, has become known as 'totalitarianism', the defining features of which are a lack of separation between politics and social life and the abolition of civil society.

In other words, Marx had no conception of the specificity of the political domain and no theory of its proper functioning. In its fundamental beliefs, his theory is unable to provide a framework in which opposition and political conflict can continue in a post-capitalist society. In the West, where the acquisition of state power was not a possibility, these flaws manifested in a contempt for liberalism and 'bourgeois' democracy, especially by many intellectual Marxists in love with theory. Believing that, one day, class conflict would be resolved, Marx was unimpressed by the question to which liberal political theory is addressed—that of the better and worse ways of dealing with such conflict. The belief that social equality (communism) was necessary for democracy, anything less being largely a sham, meant that the democratic process and liberal ideals of a public sphere in which impartiality and fairness were the desired norm could be either ignored or accorded, at best, strategic value.

In practice, many socialists and Marxists have since adopted quite different views about democracy, and it is not hard to mount an argument that their efforts have helped democratise modern society in important ways. But this contempt for 'bourgeois democracy'

survives in radical movements today which undervalue the achievement of democracy with all its flaws by comparing it with the
standards of an imagined and impossibly perfect utopia. Moreover,
the 'politically correct' mindset, which identifies with oppressed
groups to the point of abandoning the liberal ethos of fairness
toward all, is one of Marxism's more negative surviving legacies.

The moral origins of socialism

The Left was not always socialist, nor was its vision always grounded
in economics. As mentioned in Chapter I, the term 'Left' predates
socialism, originally designating those on the left-hand side of the
chamber of the National Assembly in the period of the French
Revolution. The original 'Left' in those days stood for a thorough-
going implementation of the ideals of the Revolution: emancipation
from the monarchy and the landed gentry on which it was based,
universalism, a radical concept of democracy and a fuzzier concept
of social equality. Fifty years after the French Revolution, by the
middle of the nineteenth century, 'socialism' was emerging as the
word to describe the Left's goal. This 'socialism' was quite different
from the later versions of social-democratic and Marxist socialism
emerged as globally powerful forces in the twentieth century.

In England, early socialism was a less complicated moral vision
with a strong sense of right and wrong, and was often linked to
Christian ideals. This moral socialism 'saw itself as the elevation
and pursuit of the social interest as opposed to the private interest'.[23]
In many ways, it was a heartfelt yearning for a return to the
communalism that was part of rural, pre-industrial society, which
was broken up by manufacturing, commerce and the pursuit of
individual self-interest. It was in the magazine of the movement
started by the far-sighted industrialist Robert Owen that the word
'socialism' was first used. Those who believed that the new industrial
capital should be commonly owned became known as social-ists,

as opposed to the individual-ists. This early socialism was an affirmation that humans were naturally cooperative, and some leaders of the early socialist movement set up model communities to demonstrate the superiority of cooperation over competition. They included colonies and cooperatives, mostly in rural areas of Europe and the United States. Something similar was set up in Paraguay by the defeated Australian trade union leader William Lane in 1893 but, like all the others, it soon collapsed.[24] I believe the reasons for these failures should tell us something important about human nature, just as the far more terrible failures of Soviet-style socialism can do.

Such socialist experiments based on moral examples were described as 'utopian' by Frederick Engels, in order to emphasise the distinctiveness of the doctrine that he and his intellectual partner, Karl Marx, were developing. Their doctrine was *scientific* socialism—so called because, instead of being underpinned by vaguely defined moral ideas conjured out of the heads of idealists, it was underpinned by a complex intellectual framework which they spent their lives developing.[25] Socialism would be achieved not by reasoning and appeals to ideals, as the 'utopians' suggested, but by understanding the complex inner forces driving capitalism, which in turn revealed the path of history.

The 'scientific turn' of socialism in the later half of the nineteenth century went way beyond the ideas of Marx and Engels. It was very much part of an intellectual era that believed deeply in science and rationality as answers to superstition and to traditional authority, and saw them as a way of social improvement. *Scientific socialism* became popular, partly because of the undoubted achievements of science in expanding human knowledge and the consequent awe in which science was held. It was also because scientific socialism was more practical than earlier approaches. Socialists relied increasingly on trade unions and on political parties, and this strategy was very successful: fundamentally, it forced capitalism to reform. This in itself was unexpected by most socialists, who had wildly overestimated the rigidity of the society they called capitalism and under-estimated their own ability to civilise it.

Over its 150 years of existence, socialism diversified and influenced advanced industrial societies in many ways. Apart from the ideas of radical socialism and communism, socialism manifested itself as forms of reform socialism (including labour and social-democratic parties in Germany, Britain, Australia and Scandinavia). As well, socialist ideas and struggles have influenced liberal and conservative parties by insisting on ideas of equality and in defining what is meant by progress. Nevertheless, over the course of the twentieth century, the varieties of socialism tended to share an outlook based on a number of flawed ideas which need to be confronted.

Fatal flaws

These flaws and inadequacies are most clearly seen in the ideas of Marxism itself. Marxism is important not because it was the majority current within socialism—it was not. Indeed, non-Marxist socialism and social democracy has been more successful in transforming social conditions, through governing countries like Britain, France, Sweden and Australia for significant periods. But Marxism's flaws are crucial because, until a few decades ago, Marxism acted as a kind of wellspring of ideas and intellectual strength whose influence rippled out into labour and socialist parties, into cultural and academic life and into society generally. It dynamised succeeding generations of young people, fired by the ideals of socialism. So, in this last part of the chapter, I'll refer to aspects of socialism particularly influenced by Marxism. Many of these flaws have been recognised by some Marxists and socialists for several decades, and for a long while they tried to save the patient by amputation, addition or invigoration. The whole experience of the socialist component of the New Left was dedicated to this attempt. My conclusion, however, is that the patient, in the case of Marxism, is well and truly dead and the broader doctrine of socialism, as a stand-alone theory, will never recover. The original motivations and values of socialism, however, can be reconfigured as part of a new social and political philosophy; however, this first requires us to understand why such an idealistic and hopeful doctrine failed.

Class

Analysing society in terms of class was central to socialism, not just because it seemed so useful to explain the inequalities and the wildly different life chances of so many people, but also because class struggle was central to the transformation of capitalism into socialism.

Only 150 years ago, capitalism was obviously a dramatically new kind of society in human history. Socialists quickly grasped that one of its new features was that ordinary people, instead of being tied to the land and to a feudal master, were compelled to sell their labour in a market to another class of people. They pointed out that capitalism treated this commodity called labour like other commodities in production, to be used or discarded at will. But, unlike other commodities, labour was intimately attached to the lives and wellbeing of human beings. This insight still rings true.

But even more important to socialist analysis was the view that this new class which sold its labour—the working class—was destined to develop a consciousness of its own interests which would pit it against the capitalist class. With the growing strength of the trade unions from late in the nineteenth century and for much of the twentieth century, this seemed to be coming true before the very eyes of socialists. This 'class-consciousness', once it was mobilised as a powerful political force, would usher in a new kind of society—and ultimately build a classless society in which all people were equal.

But socialist ideas of class are inadequate, and in some instances simply wrong and misleading. This is particularly so with the idea of 'class-consciousness'. Donald Sassoon, a historian of European socialism, notes that, right from the start, there was no simple relationship between the spread of industrialisation and the generation of class-consciousness. Judging the degree of class-consciousness by the creation of and support for socialist parties, Sassoon notes: 'Neither the date of creation of the socialist party, nor its electoral strength correlates with the level of industrialization or the size of the working class electorate. In fact the statistical correlation is negative . . .'[26] Some European socialist parties, he points out, often received more support in rural areas than in cities, while Britain—the home of the Industrial Revolution—hardly produced a socialist party worth the name.

Today, a working class—defined by its lack of ownership of the means of production—may indeed exist in advanced capitalism, but it is—for all its vast size (about 70 per cent of the employed)—so divided and dissected along lines of skill, education, income, gender, and so on that it is hard to find a use for that all-encompassing term. And the development of a unified class-consciousness has still largely failed to occur. Even the commonality of interest expressed in institutions like trade unions and labour parties is becoming less and less coherent. Instead, all kinds of other social divisions and differentiation have emerged, and this process will continue. There will be no return to some simple, over-arching capital-versus-labour division in society.

With its social analysis squarely based on labour and class, the socialist tradition—especially Marxism—has enormous trouble explaining the family. The reason is that, in spite of the insights which socialists had into women's oppression, the theoretical apparatus of socialism simply did not provide the tools to analyse adequately this key social formation of human existence. The categories of labour and production referred to the process of commodity production of food and objects, which disregarded the labour of women in the family. But the unpaid economic work of women—especially in caring for children and the aged, as well as domestic work—has a significant economic value. In the 1970s and 1980s, many socialist-feminists proposed all kinds of theoretical categories, such as 'domestic labour', to fill these gaps and retain the overall framework based on class and labour; in the end, none was convincing. The socialist prescription for the liberation of women was that they should all take part in 'productive labour'— that is, outside the home—and that domestic tasks should be industrialised.[27] This has since occurred to a large extent, but this simple prescription has caused a whole new set of problems (see Chapter 7). In effect, the socialist tradition tried to understand the family—a social formation which predates the rise of capitalism— within the narrow confines of an economic analysis of capitalism.

In a similar way, other social phenomena were believed to be dependent on and determined by this analysis of labour and production under capitalism. Yet some of the great issues of our time concerning race and the environment simply cannot be explained in these terms (though this hasn't stopped people attempting this reductionist kind of analysis). Moreover, class inequality within a society today has much less power to explain the causes or solutions of a range of urgent problems. Increasingly, what appears as poverty (economic inequality) is generated by the crises at the level of the family—by substance abuse, mental illness, poor education or often by a combination of these things.

Perhaps it may be argued that the one unequivocal and modern example of the importance of class might be the vast wealth and power held by the wealthy corporate elite of many countries, particularly in Europe and the United States. Such a concentration of power is indeed a massive problem, as well as being morally obscene, but acknowledging these problems does not validate or make up for all the flaws of class analysis as a world view and a prescription for social change.

Rationalism

A second flawed feature of socialism is one it has shared with many other political and social theories since the Enlightenment, including liberalism. This is an over-dependence on *rationality*, in the philosophical sense. The elevation of reason seems so sensible to us today that it is sometimes hard to understand what criticism could be made of the concept as such.

One way of thinking about reason and rationality is to contrast the ways of thinking which existed in European societies before the Enlightenment. These pre-Enlightenment societies were ruled by elders, landowners or monarchs—invariably male—whose power was based on a traditional authority, usually deemed to flow from divine legitimation. In the wider society, religion and superstition were central to the meaning and operation of everyday life. All actions by individuals or groups were seen through a moral lens and were often entangled in duty and obligation to family, to a wider clan and to authority.

They were also deeply *collective* societies, and this was expressed in the shared values which created a rigid moral core for the society. One consequence of this was that individual transgressions were punished—sometimes savagely. Such societies were deeply conservative, with the security and identity of the group bought in exchange for moral unity and the suppression of individual preferences. The feudalism of Europe still bore many of the hallmarks of such traditional societies when it was challenged by the liberating ideas of rationalism and liberalism. Aiming to build on and surpass rationalism and liberalism was socialism.

But rationalist philosophies also have their downside, as we saw in Chapter 3. They assume that society itself can be reconstructed to bring it into line with abstract principles. They sideline or tend to ignore the side of human activity and the beliefs which exist in all societies: human feelings and emotions; empathy and altruism; bonds between family and friends; obligations between children and parents involving caring; feelings of personal and social identity; a sense of the sacred and spiritual. Rationalist political philosophies assume these will go on forever, so the need to nurture them is rarely considered. Indeed, the non-rational is often seen as containing the primitive past of human beings—the backward, superstitious and reactionary.

But socialism's rationalist approach rendered it unable to identify or challenge one of the more powerful tendencies in modern society, that which German sociologist Max Weber called 'rationalisation'. He saw its expression in the shape of industrialisation, the bureaucratic state and the market economy. Rationalisation meant the progressive spread of rationality and a narrow instrumental logic into every part of private and public life, displacing other kinds of values. Initially, this challenged the central role of religion in industrialising societies. And, because religion was often the main repository of ethical or moral values, these were flattened by rationalisation. Today, the process of rationalisation continues relentlessly. Short-term economic efficiency and profits are increasingly the sole measure of value. Public institutions are privatised, education is commercialised and regulation of the economy in the interests of non-commercial goals is reduced. Activities which are properly the means to an end (efficiency, money, bureaucratic organisation) become ends in themselves. The logic of this process tends toward a profound irrationality in the best sense of the word, since it results in the suppression of human ends or values, such as the production of useful goods, an ordered, fair and safe society, and so forth. Weber's framework offers profound insights into a globalising, post-socialist world dominated by neo-liberalism.

Social constructionism

Linked to this kind of social analysis based on excessive rationalism is 'social constructionism'. This is a dogma which argues that

human beings are a product of our experience and environment—
and only of our experience and our environment. Our attitudes and desires,
our virtues and vices are socially constructed. Stated in this way, it
is a view that is widely held in society and appears in many forms.
Popularised by some branches of psychology and social science, social
constructionism decrees that we are shaped by culture alone. It is
particularly strong among intellectuals and the academy.

It follows that, if we assume that humans are constructed solely
by their social conditions, then in order to have happier and better
humans, we need only to change the social conditions. Put in this
way, it sounds unexceptional: it is certainly true that our experience
of society shapes us. Abusive parents have a deep and lasting
impact on children (as do loving parents). And poverty undoubtedly
shapes the lives and limits the possibilities of people. It is also true
that government programs and funding can make real differences
to people's lives.

Throughout history, rationalists—including Marxists—have
taken this idea further. They believed that the human possibilities
were practically limitless; that human beings, as well as society, could
be perfected. Given the right social conditions, greed and self-interest
could be eliminated. Or, as Marx put it in his 'Theses on Feuerbach',
'the human essence is no abstraction inherent in each single
individual. In its reality it is the ensemble of the social relations'.[28]

But dogmatic social constructionism—like its parent, rationalism—
is an inadequate tool of analysis and guide to social change today.
The belief in the totally plastic nature of humans, and hence their
perfectibility, is increasingly being shown to be grounded on false
assumptions about the human species. Studies of human beings and
their behaviour are strongly suggesting that some sort of basic human
nature is present among all people, regardless of their dramatic
cultural variations.[29]

To utter these words is to provoke a passionate rebuttal from
most people on the Left—from social scientists, from postmodernists
and from liberals. For over a hundred years, 'human nature' was the

underlying excuse advanced to try to prevent almost any kind of social reform. It was also a counsel of passivity and despair. For example, the supposed natural inferiority of colonised peoples was justified by 'human nature', just as votes for women were said to be 'against human nature'. For a long while, a popular version of right-wing Darwinism argued that all kinds of violent, competitive behaviour were due to 'human nature'. Only more recently have studies found that social, cooperative elements exist naturally among humans, along with competitive ones.[30]

But, rather than exploring what kind of nature humans might have, progressives have dismissed the whole idea as irretrievably reactionary and opted for social constructionism. And this occurred in spite of many liberals and leftists glibly referring to *both* nature and nurture as forces shaping human beings. Yet in practice, many have opted almost exclusively for nurture (culture). The result is, as Steven Pinker argues, that an extreme position (culture is everything) 'is often seen as moderate, and the moderate position is seen as extreme'.[31]

Bio-ethicist Peter Singer is one of a small but growing group of Left thinkers who believe that we can now be confident that some kind of nature is common to all humans.[32] While wide variation exists across cultures in many aspects of life, other aspects show little variance.

For example, humans are social beings and do not generally live completely alone.

> Equally invariant is our concern for kin. Our readiness to form cooperative relationships, and to recognise reciprocal obligations, is another universal. More controversially, I would claim that the existence of a hierarchy or system of rank is a near-universal tendency . . . Women almost always have the major role in caring for young children, while men are more likely than women to be involved in physical conflict both within the social group and in warfare between groups.[33]

Other near-universals which Singer identifies are the existence of sexual infidelity and sexual jealousy as well as ethnic identification and its converse, xenophobia and racism. Both competitive and cooperative tendencies exist among all humans.

Acknowledging some sort of human nature does not mean that every feature is unavoidable or inherently worthwhile (many human tendencies pull in opposite directions). Innate tendencies are moderated or magnified by culture. The point is that to be blind to the facts is to risk disaster. If humans naturally tend to form hierarchies and ranking systems, it is the height of naiveté to imagine that we can 'abolish' them, believing that they will not reappear in some new guise. This is a lesson which has come from attempts to enforce rigid 'equality'. But this need not mean abandoning attempts to create situations of greater rather than lesser equality. There is a world of difference between a ranking system based on a peaceful democracy and one based on brute physical force.

Defining progress

Finally, socialism has had a rather narrow definition of what constitutes *progress* in human affairs. For the kinds of reasons developed here, it has tended to see human needs almost exclusively in material terms—food, shelter, income level—and to believe that they can be satisfied in those terms. In this, socialism's origins in societies of hunger and deep poverty are evident. Obviously, satisfaction of material needs is vital, and unless they are satisfied it is difficult to see how other more subtle and more elaborate human needs can be met. The history and culture of nineteenth-century socialism is full of moving appeals for justice by those in poverty and their allies who could see the life of abundance lived by a wealthy few. Socialism therefore sets itself the task of satisfying these material human needs by its central demand for the socialising of the source of wealth—in terms of factories, mines and land. In many countries, this translated into reform programs of the social-democratic and labour parties based on laying hold of the state machinery and setting up an elaborate series of public institutions to provide public education, public banks, health services, and much more. This was a logical response to a society of relative scarcity.

But the long postwar boom took many industrial societies out of the realm of scarcity into a world of relative abundance. The economist Clive Hamilton, in his book *Growth Fetish*, argues that a larger proportion of society today is more materially wealthy than any other human beings in history.[34] Yet the socialist Left continues to ground its critique of capitalism in the assumption that the problem with capitalism is material deprivation.[35] This assumes that a large number of people in Western societies lack enough of the basic goods to live a decent and reasonable life. The 'material deprivation thesis' is thus both an analysis of what is wrong and a signpost toward the kind of social change needed. As Hamilton argues, this thesis is simply no longer true for most of the working class. More significantly, while it is true for a small number of people, this fact is not sufficient as the foundation for a movement towards social change. The moment of socialism, understood as the solution to material deprivation, has passed. The kind of material deprivation which existed for a majority of people in Western industrial countries from the nineteenth century until after World War II has been overcome. In spite of this, many ideas based on this are deeply ingrained in the socialist Left and in the neo-liberal Right. Both demand ever more material abundance and productivity, based on the unspoken assumption that this will lead to human happiness. The Left, Hamilton argues, simply demands a fairer distribution of proceeds of this growth.

Apart from a narrow definition of progress rooted in material needs, there is another even more serious problem. The demand for ever-rising living standards has great difficulty in coping with the physical limits of a world which has finite resources of energy, minerals and productive land. To generalise to all human beings the current living standards of countries like Australia, Britain and the United States is simply not possible, given the damage already done to soil, water, the atmosphere and biodiversity, let alone finite natural resources of the world. (It will be interesting and frightening to see what happens as China sets out to do this, mimicking the wasteful industrial methods of the West.) In the end, reasonably good living standards may well be compatible with the ecological balance, but this will involve an upheaval in thinking about what constitutes good living standards, as well as radical economic and technological changes designed to create an ecologically sustainable society. Contemplating what this might mean is a task so far only undertaken by ecologists, and hardly at all by traditional socialists.

The future

All of this has implications for the ideas which are embedded within the Australian Labor Party and similar parties of the working-class tradition around the world. Although it was never socialist, Labor was based on a tradition through which the ideas of socialism permeated.

Socialism has always involved more than an intellectual framework which we now know to be flawed. In its time, it inspired many millions of people to form movements which ultimately tamed— at least for a time—the creative destruction of markets and the social power of private economic wealth. Socialists refused to accept that human labour was merely another commodity to be bought and sold. Socialists were part of the forces demanding political equality and democracy—above all, the labour movement. Together they helped to achieve many of the enjoyable material conditions of modern life which today we take for granted. Socialists were a vital part of movements challenging racism and supporting rights for women. Socialists also led the opposition to colonialism and wars, and strove for land reform in under-developed countries.

Some of this was dictated by theory, some was not. At the heart of socialist movements were moral goals which asserted humanist values. These involved a desire for a society meeting human needs which included, but went beyond, the material wherewithal of life. These goals included justice, fairness, equality, caring for others, valuing of human life, and the development to the full of the potential of every individual. Although most of the intellectual architecture of socialism must now be discarded as out of date or inadequate, it is vital to recognise and retain the values on which it was all built.

Rather than the classical socialist paradigm which is based on material progress, the Left in the advanced industrial economies needs a new paradigm. It needs to reconceptualise a framework for its basic values and let go of what once seemed appropriate, but is no longer. It needs to identify the core values that were always the heart of socialism, such as egalitarianism, a common good and altruism. These need to be configured in a new philosophical vision along with values drawn from other flawed political philosophies such as liberalism and classical conservatism. Such a new vision would have both moral progress and quality of life, rather than only material progress, at its core. By moral progress I simply mean the ability to say that one social practice is better than another.

Identifying and reconfiguring the core values of socialism in new syntheses and in new political forces is the best way to pay tribute to a remarkable political movement and the people who sacrificed much for it over 150 years. Of course, such a new philosophical vision is easy to talk about, but harder to construct. Its basis in values is therefore the next challenge I wish to address.

6

The culture war and moral politics

[Apart from the Iraq war] *there is another war of values, and it is the culture war being fought within the West. This is the war between those who feel that on the whole our values and traditions are sound, and those among the intellectuals who argue that they are simply a cloak for racism and brute power.*

Editorial, *Australian*, 12 April 2003

At its heart, Howardism is about the culture war. Howard knows that Australia must change, and he has long championed economic liberalism and deregulation. But Howard sees no need for cultural reinvention driven by the urban intellectual elites.

Paul Kelly, *Australian*, 27 October 2001

In early 2004, Prime Minister John Howard sparked a brief but intense national debate about the values taught in public and private schools. Parents were increasingly sending their children to private schools because, he said, 'they feel that government schools have become too politically correct and too values-neutral'. The acting education minister, Peter McGauran, joined in, adding that too many government schools were 'hostile or apathetic to Australian heritage and values'. Treasurer Peter Costello backed his leader. Parents turned to private schools, he said, because they delivered hard work, achievement by effort, respect for other people and strong academic standards.

At first glance, these comments seem oddly misplaced. The public–private divide in education was perceived as a weak point

135

for John Howard's Coalition. In 2004, his government had given $4.7 billion to private schools, including some of the nation's most elite, doubling the $1.9 billion it gave when first elected in 1996. Moreover, school education is largely a responsibility of the states, not the federal government.

Why, then, was he intervening? His remarks made sense on two levels, and they give an insight into how a new dimension has entered Australian politics. In the short term, the values-in-education issue was good politics. Said one commentator:

> [Howard] wanted Labor to respond by engaging him on that issue because by doing so he would turn the debate on education (on which he is weak) into a debate about political correctness (on which he is strong). The unions and others bit hard . . . [Mark Latham] refused to engage the debate on Howard's terms. He knows that most people in his electorate agree with Howard.[1]

In the longer term, the values issue was part of a broader strategy. A perceptive editorial in the *Age* commented that it was difficult to discern any real difference between and state and private schools on values. It added: 'This is all about Mr Howard's view that there is an ongoing culture war. It is not that schools are values neutral but rather that he does not like the values taught in schools—public and private.'[2]

In the short term, the culture war is about shaping and mobilising certain values in the community in order to win elections. In particular, it is about dividing your opponents on the basis of issues about values. A revealing indication of this came after Labor's defeat at the 2001 election. Paul Kelly of the *Australian* had predicted that Howard 'is going to focus on social policy this term and set out to smash the post-Whitlam political alliance between the working class and the tertiary educated Left that defines modern Labor . . . [Howard] senses that the 30 year alliance of the Australian Left is collapsing because of its fundamental contradictions'.[3] Kelly rejected the idea that this strategy was merely about 'wedge politics' to win elections. Instead, it was about carving out a new policy direction on social issues which had been the preserve of the Left for many years. No doubt both statements are true.

But the culture war is also about giving the Liberal government a moral legitimacy. Just a couple of days after Howard's comments about values and education, one of the most ideological members in the government, Tony Abbott, attacked the 'chattering classes' and the 'politically correct establishment' at a conference of Young Liberals. To most of its critics, 'the Howard government is not just mistaken but morally illegitimate,' he said.[4] This taint of moral illegitimacy worried Abbott, particularly in an election year. He responded that 'moral courage is doing what's right when people who should know better declare you're wrong'. He maintained that the Howard government had demonstrated such courage on tax reform, East Timor, work for the dole, stopping refugee boats and joining the war on Iraq. On Iraq, he noted that the government 'sent Australian forces into action in the teeth of public opinion' because it was the right thing to do. Abbott concluded his moral defence of the Howard government by arguing that 'it's the Government's participation in the "culture wars" which has most put out its habitual critics. Especially in an election year, the moral case for the Howard Government ought to be made . . . because the best government since Bob Menzies deserves a fair trial.'

It's true that governments sometimes get public respect when they are perceived to be doing what's right, rather than what's advantageous. There is a new hunger for what is called 'conviction politics'. But this situation marks a change in the way governments and oppositions conduct political discourse. It is rare for politicians to openly debate their success in terms of morality. Most politicians conceive of government in terms of the material benefits, resources and policies it produces, rather than the shaping of culture and values.

In the 2004 federal election, 'culture war' and values issues were present, but not as sharply posed as in the 2001 election, where security and border protection were vital after the September 11 attack and the '*Tampa* crisis' over the arrival of asylum-seekers. But values issues were present in the choice by the Howard government to campaign on 'trust'. The strength of this powerful word was that it was capable of meaning both trust in the economic management of the Howard government (and lack of trust with the untested Labor leader, Mark Latham), but also capturing a less focused public desire for this quality in daily life.

The culture war continued after the election. In January 2005, Tony Abbott talked about the fourth term of the government. He signalled that the Howard government would increasingly set an agenda on issues that were once the home territory of the Left. It would do this by changing the 'pessimistic and narrow-minded aspects of Australian conservatism'.

Fear of Asia, mistrust of difference, obsessive concern with whether people are getting more than their share are much less part of our national makeup than they were, Abbott argued. Modern Australian conservatives seek allies among Indigenous people and take pride in their achievements. They are no less committed to a sustainable environment than the green movement—just more practical and realistic about achieving it. They no longer feel threatened by diversity.[5]

Critics often described the Right's campaign on values as a 'return the 1950s'—as a desire to return women to traditional roles and to roll back the acceptance of cultural diversity and the gains of multiculturalism. While the Right does capitalise on such sentimental desires to return to a supposedly uncomplicated past, this 'return-to-the-past' analysis seriously under-estimates what is going on.

Abbott's statements reflect a flexible and confident conservatism which looks to the future as it adapts and reframes issues which were once solely part of the Left's agenda. This can be seen especially in areas such as Indigenous policy and social welfare.

Genuine return-to-the-past issues such as abolishing abortion rights are not likely to get anywhere, given wide pro-choice sentiment in Australia, and in the Liberal Party itself.

Such an analysis is another example of the way the Left has consistently under-estimated the Right's intelligence and flexibility. Rather than mindlessly wanting to drag Australia back to the 1950s, the thinkers of the Right are addressing a series of very real and topical problems felt by many ordinary Australians, which the Left either cannot see or in some cases refuses to recognise.

To explain: over the last 30 years two upheavals occurred in Australia. One was that caused by liberal economics, the other was a libertarian cultural revolution. In the former, the working lives of people changed, respected institutions—both public and private— were transformed, and economic efficiency became the new measure of value. In the libertarian cultural revolution, the role of men and women changed, the family loosened and a less defined national identity emerged.

These changes made Australia a more tolerant, diverse society, and spurred economic dynamism so that Australians became richer. But with these changes came losses as well as gains. Family life changed and marriage became less secure. Stable identities and expectations of father, mother, husband, wife and children changed. Assumptions based on an Anglo-Celtic population with shared values could no longer be made. The history of British colonisation in Australia was reassessed, and a simple kind of pride in the past became less possible.

To many people, Australia is now a less secure place. Sociologist Michael Pusey, who studied 'middle Australia' in the late 1990s, found widespread 'moral anxiety'. Security is unfamiliar territory to the Left. The Left of politics conceives of security as economic security: it means having a job or decent income; it means reliable government services in health, education and elsewhere. This captures one aspect of security, but misses another dimension altogether: people worry about their job security, but also about quite different, less tangible things. One is cultural identity. In the case of the 'old Australians', fears about loss of identity rate very highly and can be mobilised for political gain. In the 2001 election, the Howard government did precisely this by placing 'border protection' as a central issue on the political agenda. The desire for security also drives 'law and order' campaigns for tougher gaol sentences. The Left regards these as phony issues and sees only a desire to punish rather than a desire for security. Yet, in its time, the Left has connected with and reconfigured a public desire for security and for law and order. One of the main victories of the women's movement was to massively transform the operation of the criminal law on domestic violence, violence against children and sexual assault. This was possible because the women's movement had won a 'culture war' and had changed social attitudes and values on these issues.

But too often, issues of security are left to the Right, and are automatically discounted by the Left. Grappling with them means entering a territory in which both legitimate and fanciful fears lie in wait. But skirting this territory is no longer an option in a world where globalisation is disrupting established patterns at home, at work and in the national culture. Globalisation has been seen as primarily an economic event, but its cultural impact is arguably more dramatic.

In the face of cultural insecurity, Labor and the Left have not found a way of articulating their values into a coherent and convincing popular stance. This is not a problem of 'packaging', but a much deeper problem, It is a problem of whether to recognise cultural fears as legitimate and real. It is also a philosophical confusion and incoherence about which values and which ideas constitute a progressive standpoint in Australia today. To win a culture war, a political force must exercise intellectual and moral leadership— but this is impossible without clarity on underlying issues.[6]

The culture war—declared by the Right on the Left—is a central feature of modern politics in the United States and Australia. While the clash between labour and capital was largely about material things—wages, jobs, the positive role of the state—the culture war is about post-material concerns of values and identity. In fact, both are about similar things (such as education and public schools), but expressed in different ways. And 'post-material' issues have actually been part of human existence since the beginning of time: each clan had an identity and values as well as being engaged in a struggle for material survival. What is occurring now are the political consequences of the gradual dissolution of working-class identity based around male breadwinners often doing hard physical labour and organised in trade unions.

Above all, the culture war is about mobilising political support through articulating issues which strike a chord with many people. In a sense, that is what all political rhetoric is crafted to do. But the Right's method of fighting the culture war is about framing the issues of politics as *moral* politics and setting this agenda in such a way that it isolates and divides its opponents. Hence the companion phrase to 'culture war' is 'wedge politics'. The immediate purpose of cultural politics is to drive a wedge that splits the supporters of your opponent and draws one section nearer to you.

But the culture war is more than a way of achieving short-term advantage. It is about deeply held but slippery concepts such as social cohesion in a multicultural society; it is about 'family values'; it is about the national identity of Australia and Australian values; it is about relations between the Indigenous people of Australia and the non-Indigenous settlers; and it is about Western values. Above all, the culture war is about ideas of right and wrong—both in society at large and at the personal level.

In contrast to politics seen in rationalist terms, the culture war is about emotion and how people feel. And in case such matters are regarded as vague and insubstantial, remember that 'how people feel' covers a range of emotions and includes both passionate love (e.g. for children) and intense hatred (e.g. against other ethnic groups). To this extent, playing politics as a culture war means playing with some of the most powerful ingredients in human nature.

To a significant degree, the culture war is the backlash of the Right to the rise of feminism, multiculturalism and libertarian social attitudes in the 1960s and 1970s. When these ideas emerged, they recast the political and cultural landscape and helped to create a better society. But everything has unintended consequences. Some ideas that still form the basis for a progressive outlook have turned out to be wrong or silly—for example, that moral wrongdoing should be discussed in terms of underlying *social* problems and not in terms of holding people morally responsible for their actions. But, as time went on, the inherent weaknesses of such one-sided ideas have emerged. The Left's flat-footed refusal to recognise them has laid the ground for the Right's largely successful roll-back on the cultural and values front.

The culture war in the United States

Many commentators agreed that, in the 2004 US presidential election, George W. Bush effectively mobilised fears around 'moral values'—especially gay marriage—as part of his successful campaign. In the key state of Ohio, 22 per cent of voters said the deciding issue for them was 'moral values', and they were overwhelmingly Bush voters. In exit polls in some areas, 'moral values' were placed above the issue of terrorism and national security.

The US culture war is relevant to Australia because of a number of similarities. Both are new nations in historical terms, which began as colonies of the British. Both are settled lands which were inhabited by societies of Indigenous peoples. Both developed industrially and politically without all the weight of custom and culture of tradition-bound societies in Europe. Both underwent a cultural revolution in the 1960s and 1970s which questioned the role of women, rejected authority and established cultural identity as a central political concern.

In both countries, the Right was initially put on the back foot by this turn of events. But by the 1980s a backlash was well underway in the United States. In Australia, the intellectual Right represented by *Quadrant*, the Institute of Public Affairs and other think-tanks watched developments in the United States with great interest, and a great deal of their current culture war discourse is derivative.[7]

The United States is the home of the culture war—a term derived from the German *Kulturkampf*, which originally referred to Protestant–Catholic disputes in German schools.[8] In the contemporary United States, the term began as a contest over art and cultural institutions and its meaning then spread to a generalised battle over social values in schools, universities, churches and government. The many books written about it agree that cultural politics have changed the political agenda in the United States and laid the bases for the successes of the Republican Party. The culture war is also a key part of American neo-conservatism, which at bottom sees itself as defending 'Western values'.[9]

In the United States, the culture war began in earnest in the late 1980s as the Reagan era faded. For Reaganites, the use of conservative moral issues was only one part of the armoury, and it took its place alongside anti-communism and calls for small government. The renegade writer of the US cultural Right, David Brock, dates the rise of culture war politics to 1988, the year when the radio show of shock jock Rush Limbaugh went national, reaching 450 radio stations. Unlike more buttoned-up conservatives, Limbaugh scornfully attacked the values of the radical social movements of the 1970s. He appealed to traditional family values and satirised 'feminazis', 'environmental wackos' and gays.[10] In more moderate tones, but also targeting cultural issues, was conservative Republican Patrick Buchanan, who noted in 1989 that 'while the Right has been busy winning primaries and elections, cutting taxes and funding anti-Communist guerrillas abroad, the Left has been quietly seizing all the commanding heights of American art and culture'.[11] Buchanan called for 'a cultural revolution in the 90s as sweeping as the political revolution in the 80s'. The reference to the commanding heights of art and culture arose because of *Piss Christ*, a photograph by Andres Serrano showing Jesus Christ on a crucifix submerged in a container of urine. Serrano had received grants from the National Endowment for the Arts (NEA), whose budget and personnel became the centre of a storm in Congress which lasted several years. Not surprisingly, the Right wanted to know what the Left's attitude would have been if such an artwork had caused deep offence to Blacks or feminists, rather than devout Christians. It was a legitimate question.

At the same time, the fundamentalist Christian and televangelist, Rev. Pat Robertson, founded the Christian Coalition to promote 'restoring the greatness of America through moral strength'. The Christian Coalition began to represent itself as a persecuted minority whose rights were being trampled on by a cultural elite that controlled Washington, the media and the universities: 'They argued that historic "family values" were specifically threatened, and vehemently rejected demands for rights for homosexuals or acceptance for diverse lifestyles. This new "we are victims too" theme proved highly successful [and] allowed the Coalition to link up with conservative Catholics and Jews'.[12]

By 1992, the Christian Coalition had become very influential in the Republican Party, comprising up to 42 per cent of the delegates at the party's convention in that year.[13] By that time, the Berlin Wall had fallen and cultural politics had become the key to a renewal at the convention. A challenger to Bush Senior, Patrick Buchanan, issued a call for 'a religious war for the soul of America . . . as critical to the kind of nation we will one day be as the Cold War itself'. Referring to recent rioting by Afro-Americans in Los Angeles, Buchanan said: 'As [the troops] took back the streets of L.A., block by block, so we must take back our cities and take back our culture, and take back our country.' The Establishment which the conservatives began to fight included institutions once thought of as the pillars of society, such as 'national foundations, the textbook publishers, the Hollywood studios, the professional societies, the Ivy League universities'.[14]

Under the eight years of Democrat President Bill Clinton, cultural politics was one of the main weapons of the Right. Their shrill accusations against Clinton were intended 'to caricature the opposition as immoral, even evil', according to David Brock, a one-time participant in the Right's culture war who is now a critic. In the 1990s, a vast array of controversial cultural issues arose, largely premised on the view that major institutions should embody certain moral virtues. Gay rights were elevated to a national political issue, and 'gays in the military' was an early battle of Clinton's presidency. Political correctness became a code word for the critical university studies endorsed by liberal academics. Multiculturalism and cultural diversity were successfully portrayed as conscious and zealous attacks on the values of Western civilisation. A national curriculum program for standard history was attacked for its negative portrayal of American history and a keenness to promote Black and female figures in history.[15] Throughout this, the Right's battle was articulated as a fight by the mainstream ordinary Americans against liberal 'elites'. The political effect was to drive wedges into the Democrats' support among blue-collar Americans by appealing to their values and parodying those of the liberal middle class.

After the election of Republican President George W. Bush in 2000, cultural politics continued to be the battleground. For example, in his State of the Union address in January 2004, he talked about the US war on terror, about the invasion of Iraq, about the US economy—but he added three other topics to this agenda-setting speech: drugs in sport; gay marriage; and sex education. On the last of these, he pledged to double funding for abstinence programs 'so schools can teach this fact of life: abstinence for young people is the only certain way to avoid sexually transmitted diseases'.

He warned judges not to undermine the recent *Defense of Marriage* Act that defines marriage as a union between a man and woman.[16] Gay marriage is vintage culture wars rhetoric. It aims to mobilise fears of homosexuality and to capitalise on the genuine worries surrounding relationships and marriage while being, at the same time, a complete distraction and a wedge between small (l) liberals and socially conservative workers.

The culture war in Australia

In Australia, the politics of the culture war at the national level came later than in the United States and was articulated differently. In the United States the 'class war' between labour and capital has been more completely defeated than in Australia. One result is that American progressives ('liberals' in the US lexicon) are far more strongly focused on the agendas of cultural and identity politics than Australians. Another difference is that Australia does not yet have the equivalent to the powerful Christian Coalition to drive an agenda on abortion, religious instruction at schools and opposition to sex education and to gay marriage (though many conservative Australian Christians are working hard towards this end).[17]

Labor was the first party to practise a modern form of culture war politics. In the 1990s, Prime Minister Paul Keating projected a vision—the Big Picture, he called it—drawing on national pride to project a republic, constitutional reform, environment policy, reconciliation with Indigenous peoples and progressive social policy.[18] The Big Picture tapped the new constituencies of Labor and tried to unite them with its working-class base. It inspired many people, especially Labor's middle-class and intellectual supporters. But the cultural vision of the Big Picture was rather abstract. It felt imposed from above, lacking organic connections with society, and failed to strike a wider resonance—most of all with Labor's working-class base. That base had slowly been shrinking for years, and the great success of modern Labor from Whitlam onwards had been to assemble a Grand Alliance of middle-class people, ethnic groups and women, along with its core working-class base. This alliance carried Labor to power in 1983, but by 1996 its inherent weaknesses were showing. Unlike the ideology of class politics, this alliance was not based on any underlying philosophy or a unifying set of ideas. Moreover, the alliance brought with it a patchwork of small lobby groups which reinvigorated Labor's less noble tradition of patronage and pork barrelling. The culture of jobs for friends and funding for sympathetic organisations made Labor vulnerable. Public interest competed with patronage. But, above all, Labor's Big Picture left many Australians feeling that no common *Australian* identity existed which might incorporate them.

This vulnerability was precisely what Howard targeted in the year before he won the 1996 election. His vehicle on this chosen field of battle was a series of 'headland speeches' which articulated values and took the place of policies. (A remarkably similar pattern was followed after Labor elected its new Opposition leader, Mark Latham, in December 2003—and with similar success.) In his first headland speech, Howard argued that Labor's decisions were driven by the 'noisy self-interested clamour of powerful vested interests with scant regard for the national interest'.[19] Australians in the mainstream felt 'powerless to compete with such groups who seem to have the ear of the government completely on major issues'. Australians, he said, had been exhorted to think of themselves as members of sub-groups. In another speech, he praised the strengths of supportive and stable families. Parents with young children should have 'greater freedom to choose whether one parent cares full time for their children at home, or whether both are in the paid workforce'.[20]

Signalling a further theme which became a hallmark of his prime ministerial years, he said: 'We learn from our history, and we build on it. But we should not deny it or misrepresent it. The current Prime Minister must be one of the few leaders from any era, anywhere in the world, who appears to have so little respect for his own country's history that he is attempting to rewrite it.'[21] This 'black armband' version of history (a term coined by historian Geoffrey Blainey) meant that history since 1788 was 'little more than a disgraceful story of imperialism, exploitation, racism, sexism, and other forms of discrimination. I take a very different view'. Howard's tactic was to pick up on genuine concerns and fears, as expressed in detailed polling of opinion, and turn them into political capital.

They included a widespread concern about national pride and identity. This had been a central issue in the culture war since the 1988 Bicentenary, where tension centred around whether official support would extend to a re-enactment of the landing of the First Fleet.[22] The cultural Left's ongoing concern was that European settlement meant the destruction of Indigenous societies, and that this should not be glossed over by historical triumphalism of the inheritors of that settlement. In fact, these concerns grew to have considerable weight in all kinds of official decisions about historical events, as well as having a growing research focus in the academy. This legitimate rebalancing took place (and still does) in a situation in which nearly all Australians desired some kind of national identity of which they could be proud, or which held moral truths. To the extent that they disregarded this desire in the rebalancing exercise, the left-wing intellectuals and historians sowed the seeds of the Right's cultural resurgence. Unadulterated criticism of European settlement was seen as sneering at ordinary people who simply wanted something to believe in. Howard later used this desire to engage in historical denial over the 'stolen generations' report on the removal of Aboriginal children from their parents. The controversy around the report was a copybook example of the way New Right intellectuals could mobilise a popular desire for national identity, mix it with attacks on 'elites' and set an agenda for the Howard government.[23]

The dilemma posed by the need for acknowledging good and bad in historical events was best put by Robert Manne in his assessment of the Centenary of Federation celebrations:

> A test of our maturity as a nation will be whether we can find a language equal to the complex strands of our history—a language that acknowledges the depth of the British inheritance; which celebrates the many ways in which that inheritance was enriched after its transplantation to Australian soil; but which does not flinch from the recognition that in the building of a new civilization in Australia there was, for the indigenous inhabitants of this continent, a truly terrible price to pay.[24]

John Howard's rhetoric also had a familiar ring to the ears of working Australians. He skilfully built on the American neo-conservatives' language of the culture war, which denounced the elites, political correctness and the new class, by adding inventions of his own.[25] He inveighed against 'powerful vested interests' which crushed the 'battlers' in Australia, 'the families battling to give their children a break, hardworking employees battling to get ahead, small business battling to survive, young Australians battling to get a decent start in their working lives, older Australians battling to preserve their dignity . . .' [26]

As in the United States, there was a rush to adopt the mantle of victim. By framing the conflict between 'powerful vested interests' ranged against powerless ordinary Australian 'battlers', Howard picked up and echoed a vital part of traditional working-class culture. This framing was also behind his statement in the 'children overboard' affair that 'we're not a nation that is going to be intimidated by this kind of behaviour'. What was this but a distorted echo of identification with the underdog and old-stlye Labor rhetoric against big business?

Political analyst Judith Brett argues that Howard's genius was not only to reconfigure and link his policies and values to a cultural mainstream, but to do so in a way that challenged Labor's core historic identity.[27] By 1996, the grip of class on the imagination was gone:

> Class understandings no longer framed people's day to day lives nor their understandings of political action and possibilities. The spread of suburbia and increased levels of home ownership, the increased mobility given by the motorcar, the general increase in living standards, the spread of consumerist, home-centered lifestyles . . . had made the politics of class difference seem largely irrelevant.[28]

Brett argues convincingly that, in politics, the underlying explanatory frameworks only become powerful when they 'connect with the lived experiences of people's daily lives, when they provide them with explanations of their place in the world which make sense'. And that is what Howard did. Labor's class identity was a collectivist one based on notions of economic equality. Howard used this same desire for collectivism as a *cultural* phenomenon, to denote aspirations towards a collective Australian identity (which he defines in a narrow and traditional way).

One of the intellectual sources for Howard's culture war is neo-conservative critics in the United States whose signature tune is that they characterise their opponents' beliefs as a 'culture war on Western values', and modestly portray themselves as the defenders of Western values against the barbarians. One of the best known in Australia is historian and writer Keith Windschuttle.[29] These cultural warriors of the Right make an assumption similar to that made by some extreme supporters of multiculturalism. Both assume that cultures are monolithic and fixed. 'Western culture' has a fixed meaning and debate *within* it is characterised as an attack on the whole edifice. In an equal and opposite way, extreme multiculturalists regard ethnic communities as monolithic, and any criticism of cultural practices or of individual members of a cultural community is seen as an attack on the whole community. The fact that people within ethnic communities debate and differ internally over their cultural practices is ignored.

The phrase which epitomised Howard's attack on the Left's cultural politics was 'political correctness'. It was a phrase which infuriated his enemies because of its rhetorical skill in tapping actual experience. But frustration with political correctness came not just from racists and angry white males. In 1995, Jack Waterford—a prominent journalist and long-time supporter of the Indigenous struggle—wrote presciently that 'a combination of political correctness and genuine liberal sympathy for Aborigines seems to have made no-go zones of a number of Aboriginal issues as far as many professional and sincere and very sympathetic journalists are concerned'.[30] Among other things, this meant that journalists rarely mentioned the fact that a number of male Aboriginal leaders had histories of personal violence against women and of dishonesty and fraud. This 'sympathetic' approach was actually a kind of paternalism which was recognised by at least some of those who were mobilised behind the banner of anti-political correctness.

Howard's critics tried to deny the substance behind the rhetorical shadow of this phrase. One of the first counter-attacks to the culture war of the new Howard government was a collection of essays, *The Retreat from Tolerance*, edited by broadcaster Phillip Adams.[31] In one essay, cultural commentator Ken Wark dismissed concern about 'political correctness'. It was a 'beat up' (journalistic slang for a non-story) and had no basis in fact. It was derivative of the American Right's targeting of speech codes at Ivy League universities, he said. Yet, in another part of his essay, Wark puts his finger on precisely the problem. He recalls his encounter at university with feminist students who advocated all-female communities. He was partly sympathetic to this separatism: 'But I could also see that this would lead to the creation of a kind of group-think where everyone was obliged to agree with each other, where women who didn't get with the program would be ostracized, where the beliefs and practices of the group would drift away from what women in everyday life thought and felt.'[32] A better description of the problem of political correctness and in-group thinking could hardly be found. Phillip Adams reserves most of his fire for Pauline Hanson, but he also concedes that political correctness can be irritating. He observes:

> . . . a demand for niceness could be detected in our intellectual life. We were to watch our Ps and Qs in gender issues. We were to tread lightly in areas of race . . . On many topics we were urged to conduct our arguments within approved parameters. Now, much of this was perfectly in order. Discussions could be robust without being offensive . . . yet there were times when I grew impatient with what seemed a lengthening list of rules and protocols. It was like being back at school again.[33]

What is extraordinary about these two commentators is that they recognise the moralising silliness of political correctness and its attempts to steer debate, yet somehow assume a number of other people (who voted for Howard) do not experience the same frustration.

The paradox of the culture war

The attack on political correctness as part of the culture war waged by the Right helped to radically change the political agenda, not only in Australia but in other modern industrial democracies such as Britain and the United States. The scorn for 'political correctness' was international. It powerfully undermined gains made in an earlier period by the Left through the social movements of women and gays, and through campaigns against racism.

Yet all of this presents a paradox. The culture war wasn't meant to be won by the Right; it was meant to be won by the Left. As old-style socialism faded, culture became the chosen terrain of battle of the New Left which emerged from the new social movements of gender, sexuality and ethnicity. This new Left increasingly rejected the inadequacies of class analysis and preoccupation with economic analysis. It saw that the working class was not particularly radical and seemed quite content to insist on a fairer division of the consumer spoils of capitalism. Social change was blocked not by armed force, but by comfortable beliefs and values which in sum constituted capitalist culture and ideology. By contrast, the new social movements of women, youth, ethnic groups and gays were vital and full of energy. They challenged the values and beliefs of dominant culture and ideology. Their terrain was not the factory floor but public culture. Starting from activist campaigns, demonstrations and a multitude of creative protests, the New Left set an important cultural agenda, waging a culture war with enormous success. A new cultural Left emerged alongside the old economic Left.

Soon, the advocates of cultural and social change began to people the new bureaucracies of government. Their new ideas fed into policy documents and the platforms of political parties. Rather than revolution, a 'long march through the institutions' began.[34] Its success was testimony to the power of ideas to change material circumstances. But, as time went on, the success in setting a new agenda and in holding institutional positions began to calcify. Revolution became routinised; fresh ways of looking at the world became dogmas. It became compulsory to be sensitive to gender, race and ethnicity. And, because these ideas fought their way through the bureaucracy, the language and protocols of government turned them into a new orthodoxy. The battle cries for liberation of the 1970s turned into a government-sponsored political correctness of the 1980s and 1990s. And, like all new orthodoxies, it spawned rebellion.

The backlash against the new cultural politics in the United States was insightfully observed by the editor of *Dissent* magazine, Michael Walzer. The right-wing backlash, he said, was a reaction to the very visible Left success in civil rights, affirmative action, the public emergence of gay rights, the virtual abolition of capital punishment, the legalisation of abortion and limits on police power, as well as deeper processes such as the secularisation of society and the transformation of the family.[35] In many ways, the New Left had no idea just how challenging and successful its own culture war had been. But Walzer pointed out that many of these victories had been won in the courts, the civil service or by lobbying—not in the popular vote of democratic politics:

> They reflect the leftism or liberalism of lawyers, judges, federal bureaucrats, professors, school teachers, social workers, journalists, television and screen writers—not the population at large. Those liberal 'elites' no doubt had support in the population at large; they responded to demands from organised groups of various sorts; but they were not driven by the pressure of a mass movement or a majoritarian party.[36]

So when the rebellion against this came, it automatically assumed a populist character. In Australia, the rebellion against the new orthodoxy was most strongly crystallised by the populism of the Pauline Hanson One Nation phenomenon. This populism was also expressed by a Liberal strategist who framed the 'No' campaign in the 1999 republic referendum in the following way: 'This ballot should be presented as real Australians' greatest chance ever to vote against all the politicians, journalists, radical university students, welfare rorters, academics, the arts community and the rich, that, deep down, they've always hated.'[37]

But the backlash against the Left's culture war of the 1970s and 1980s was not simply about the awkward fit of the new orthodoxy, nor about allegations of elitism. It was about the fact that, while many people experienced the cultural change of the 1970s and 1980s as liberation from religious and conservative restrictions, others experienced it quite differently—particularly as changes occurred in the family and as the effects of economic globalisation began to take hold. Rather than experiencing liberation, some began to experience disintegration. Rather than feeling free, they felt fractured. Instead of gains, many felt the loss of stable families and stable jobs and the ebbing of familiar truths. Nor was this merely imagined.

Divorce did rise, certain crimes did increase, social change occurred rapidly. And progressive ideas with their emphasis on liberation and personal change were blamed for this. Walzer puts a finger on the exposed weakness of the Left: if its entire social and cultural agenda was fulfilled—or mostly fulfilled—would the resulting society be secure? Would it be stable? Cohesive? How would it hold together?

These concerns are often dismissed with a wave of the postmodern hand. They are mere 'moral panics' and 'anxieties'. Such phrases often amount to an evasion of genuine moral issues. Unless everyone celebrated every social change, they were conservative. While intellectuals may revel in unstable identities, blurred boundaries and shifting meanings, most people don't, because when such abstractions are translated into social practices they can result in aimlessness, anger or alienation. The signature phrase of the postmodern critic Ken Wark is that 'we no longer have roots we have aerials'. But he couldn't be more wrong. People do have roots and their aerials often choose Golden Oldies, not the latest or trendiest tunes.

Today the downside of liberation is increasingly being realised. In his recent book *Crowded Lives*, Labor MP Lindsay Tanner argues for a paradigm shift in political concerns. He favours many of the social changes brought about by the politics of liberation, but argues that these have come at a price. The removal of restraints on behaviour has also contributed (over the long term) to a rise in crime, gambling, drug abuse, suicide and delinquency. For some, liberation from old structures has meant loneliness, social exclusion and alienation. The libertarian impulse has been absorbed and magnified by the materialism and consumerism of the postwar boom. Personal gratification has trumped personal obligation.

While a desire for liberation and personal freedom was a totally appropriate response to the stultifying, oppressive and discriminatory environment of that era, we've failed to notice that the world has since moved on, argues Tanner. Simplistic concepts of liberation no longer provide the answer to contemporary social problems. Our most pressing problems are a reflection of insufficient social order and security, not an absence of personal rights and freedoms.[38]

Tanner does not blame feminism and sexual liberation for the widespread social problems, but argues that 'they are parallel consequences of technological change and growing affluence'. The proponents of the 1960s revolution have a responsibility to tackle these problems which they have so far failed to take seriously. This has allowed social conservatives like John Howard to monopolise genuine community concern about these issues and to twist such concern to suit his political agenda. A rethinking is needed, based on new ideas valuing social relationships.

The moral politics of Noel Pearson

These issues of cohesion, liberation and cultural change have emerged in one of the most morally charged issues facing Australia: that of the history and present situation of Indigenous people. One of the most significant contributors to such a renewal of cultural and moral politics is the Indigenous intellectual Noel Pearson. He has forcefully insisted on rethinking the frozen positions of Left and Right on Indigenous issues. In the case of the Left, this is doubly difficult because it has legitimately seen itself as occupying the high moral ground, agitating for over 70 years for improvement in the conditions of Indigenous people. Moreover, Pearson comes from the Left. Yet, to many, Pearson's statements seem redolent of the Right because he strongly attacks what he calls 'progressivist' nostrums. Single-handedly, he has sparked what may be the first battle in the next stage of the culture war.

Pearson frames his concerns around a paradox he observes as arising from the struggle for Aboriginal rights over the last 40 years:

The question that we have to confront is this: why has a social breakdown accompanied this advancement in the formal rights of our people, not the least the restoration of our homelands to our people? Aboriginal families and communities now often live on their homelands, in very much flasher housing and infrastructure than decades ago—but with a much diminished quality of life, such that commentators familiar with these remote communities increasingly call them 'outback ghettoes'. Indeed this social breakdown afflicts with equal vehemence those Aboriginal peoples who have never been dispossessed of their lands and who retain their classical traditions, cultures and languages.[39]

Referring to his own experience and community in Hope Vale, on Cape York, he notes:

The numbers of people in prison and juvenile institutions today are unprecedented: these are statistics that started to emerge in the 1970s. There was not one Hope Vale person in prison in the early 1970s . . . Petrol sniffing amongst children and youth was unknown in Cape York Peninsula until recently. Violence against old people for money for grog was inconceivable in earlier times.[40]

His point is not just that life has become worse for some Aboriginal people over a period during which, on any fair judgment, more time, attention and resources have been directed to a social problem. More importantly, neither of the two main 'rights-based' approaches to reform seems to have been adequate. These approaches are formal rights, such as citizenship and an end to legal discrimination; and cultural rights, such as the need for traditional land and the survival of language and culture. The failure of the second approach is perhaps the harder to accept, since the claiming of land and the retention of culture and language have been core issues in the widely accepted prescription of cultural identity and self-determination as solutions to historic injustice.

Part of the reason for this paradox and failure is that one obvious expression of this breakdown—alcoholism—is misdiagnosed, says Pearson. The prevailing analysis of substance abuse is that it is a symptom of underlying issues such as ingrained trauma, trans-generational grief, racism, dispossession, unemployment, and similar things. That is, substance abuse is fitted into and 'explained' by reference to a political paradigm. But, in fact, addiction to alcohol is a condition in its own right, not merely a symptom of social injustice. His solution is founded on supporting moves for prohibition by communities with government support.

Pearson's other target is 'passive welfare'. Legal rights for remote Indigenous people to apply for a regular income if work is not available are a relatively recent thing. For most Australians, this aspect of the welfare state provides temporary help between jobs. But, in many remote communities (and elsewhere, for a minority of non-Indigenous people), this income support is a permanent feature of life, extending to succeeding generations. 'What is the exception among white fellas—almost complete dependence on cash handouts from the government—is the rule for us,' Pearson says.

This has not always been the case. Pearson makes the point that, before welfare income became generalised, many rural Aboriginal people had a place in the real economy of the bush—a poorly paid and very difficult place, but nevertheless they worked for a living. As well, prior to European colonisation, a real economy also existed which gave a living to those who worked. But the current system of passive welfare is fundamentally irrational, he says: 'Money acquired without principle is expended without principle. When people have only one means of existence the nature of that income obviously influences their whole outlook. The irrational basis of the economy has inclined us to wasteful, aimless behaviours. Like other people who can't see any connection between their actions and their circumstances, we waste our money, our time, our lives.'

This lack of meaning and purpose then compounds the effects of dispossession and trauma.

Social order and trust

Pearson counts himself as an adherent of the 'old Left' and criticises the beliefs of the 'cultural Left'.[41] An early airing of his bold views occurred when he delivered a lecture in memory of former Labor prime minister Ben Chifley in August 2000. In the speech, he lamented that class analysis was rarely used by much of the Left today.[42] Class is an important tool for understanding social structures, including the situation of Indigenous people, he said, and went on to support a materialist philosophical stance close to Marxism. His speech also paid tribute to the 'civilising achievement of the welfare state' which was 'built on the backs of working people who united through sustained industrial organisation and action in the 1890s'. Today, he observed, few Australians appreciate the contribution towards egalitarianism made by organised labour, which is now demonised.

But, while he is on the Left, Pearson insists that conventional analysis of the cultural Left, when applied to Indigenous people, is simply wrong or inadequate—and is therefore partly responsible for the terrible dysfunction of violence and poor health in many communities. Pearson demands that the Left rethink its analysis and values. The debate he has stimulated is a vital part of the culture war, and of the redefinition of Right and Left in contemporary Australia. Pearson is saying things which need to be said.

His first target, by comparison with others, seems minor. It is the reluctance to publicly acknowledge and name appalling problems of violence and drug-taking within some Indigenous communities. These problems are embarrassing, and their existence is often woven into a diatribe of crude hostility by individuals who richly deserve the title 'racists'. Until recently, many liberals and leftists abided by a politically correct speech code that refused to publicly identify widespread alcoholism, bashing of women and children and sexually transmitted diseases. Many believed that a frank acknowledgment of such problems would merely give ammunition to the 'real enemies' of the Indigenous people. It would play into the hands of 'negative stereotypes' of Indigenous people. Better to take refuge in statistics and charts about infant mortality, premature death, poor health, low literacy, and so on. The distinction about these two ways of describing essentially the same problem is interesting. The former involves elements of a moral critique in which Indigenous people themselves are moral agents. Violence and sexual abuse is perpetrated *by* some Indigenous people *on* other Indigenous people. The latter is emptied of this element and by implication the moral blame is entirely allocated to abstract forces such as racism, or to the non-Indigenous community. By blaming racism or historic dispossession for such acts of violence, one sets up a chain of reasoning which refuses to see Indigenous people as exercising (or being capable of exercising) moral agency. Yet this quality is essential to breathe life into the formal rights of citizenship and equality. Self-respect, respect for others and moral responsibility for one's actions are vital for any functioning community. Yet conventional analyses of the plight of Indigenous people rarely includes these terms.

Two other problems of the conventional progressive approach to Indigenous affairs which Pearson mentions are an implied support for libertarianism and a disregard for the value of social order. The latter touches a raw nerve for social progressives. In days gone by, those who most loudly and regularly talked about social order and its concomitant, law enforcement, were the Right. Cries for law and order have often been an excuse for police thuggery directed at legitimate protests and dissent. That was certainly the experience of my generation of radicals in the 1970s. Partly because of this, a kind of pop sociology grew up among progressives that discounted the acts of criminals because of a belief that criminal acts (especially mere 'property crimes') resulted from the injustices of capitalist society. One slogan was 'the prisons are the crime'. Indeed, prisons were often barbaric places where real crimes were committed against vulnerable prisoners and the brutal culture of prisons badly needed reform. But the slogan 'the prisons are the crime' is merely a slogan, and when rhetorically counterposed to real crimes such has assault, rape, robbery, and so on, this represents a moral evasion.

Not surprisingly, therefore, progressives rarely talk about the value of social order. Rather, it is social order which must be challenged for social change to occur. Yet social order—though often invisible to many people—is vital. Social order is underpinned by a social trust. The ability to walk freely without fearing assault or to live in a house without fearing theft from your neighbours are examples of the kind of basic trust needed for a functioning community. Children who grow up unable to trust adults because they are abused by them carry these problems into their own adulthood. In some cases, they go on to perpetuate the cycle of abuse. On the social level, people need to feel a trust that, if they are unemployed or sick, they can receive support or treatment—in other words, that they live in a civilised society which values all its members. Social order and trust are increasingly important in modern politics today because the New Capitalism devalues trust and social order in favour of utilitarian, commercial and commodified relations between citizens. The notion of social order, then—once a defining characteristic of the Right—must be revitalised and embraced by the critics of neo-liberalism and integrated into new visions of social change beyond Right and Left.

Suspicion of social order and law enforcement leads to disaster in some communities, according to Noel Pearson. He points to the concern at the rates of imprisonment of Aboriginal people. For many years, people have been shocked by the fact that 2 per cent of Australians comprise 30 per cent of prisoners. Part of the response to this situation is to provide legal aid to Indigenous people charged with offences. But this then compounds the existing problem of social disorder in Indigenous communities. 'To this day however, Aboriginal victims of crime—particularly women—have no support; so whilst the needs of offenders are addressed, the situation of victims and the families remain vulnerable.'[43] On top of this, legal aid to Indigenous people accused of crimes has done little to lower the imprisonment rate. According to Pearson:

> What is needed is the restoration of social order and the enforcement of law . . . What happens in communities when the only thing that happens when crimes are committed is the offenders are described as victims? Is it any wonder that there will soon develop a sense that people should not take responsibility for their actions . . . Is it any wonder that the statistics have never improved . . . What societies prosper in the absence of social order?

Indigenous academic Marcia Langton supports Pearson's general approach. Like him, she points to the need for Indigenous people to take part in the real economy, and praises the work of companies like Rio Tinto in providing jobs and training.[44] She also praises Liberal cabinet member Tony Abbott for his preparedness to take up the challenge of providing real jobs for Indigenous people. Both Rio Tinto and Abbott are an anathema to many people because of their record in union-bashing. Like so many other phenomena in the new world of politics beyond Right and Left, it is better to judge by results than by assuming self-fulfilling prophecies.

Other Indigenous leaders have opposed Pearson's approach. Former Democrats Senator Aden Ridgeway claimed Pearson believed that 'Aborigines are to blame for their present day circumstances'— a distorted interpretation of his stance.[45] In contrast to Pearson, Ridgeway counterposed what he called a 'rights agenda'. After acknowledging a 'new approach' was needed, he argued: 'It is questionable whether new social policy should become a substitute for the absence of any national rights-based agenda. The facts of failure and the reasons for them rest with a country that is not prepared to give a rights agenda a fair go.' Another leader, Terry O'Shane, argues that Pearson is 'catering to the redneck elements who believe that all Aboriginal people are lazy bastards and should get off their butts and work. You can't go around calling your own mob parasites'.[46] Labor member for the Northern Territory, Warren Snowdon, also see Pearson's views as 'blaming Aboriginal Australians for the failings of past and present government policies'.[47]

To agree with Pearson's critique, one does not have to accept everything he says. Some of his critique of the Left is far too sweeping in my view because he seems to presume that the Left's obtuseness is a core characteristic. Precisely because of its commitment to social justice, people on the Left can be persuaded to seize an agenda which includes moral responsibility, opposition to passive welfare and a valuing of social order. This agenda comes more easily to some on the Right—but only a few, in my view, will have the deeper, genuine commitment to follow through with support over the long and tortuous path which Pearson's new policy direction will traverse. In the end, Pearson may be proved wrong on some points (to the extent that any final proof is possible), but his greatest achievement will be that he forcefully detonated a badly needed debate.

Beyond Right and Left: The wider relevance of Pearson's moral politics

My main purpose in discussing Pearson's views and the reaction to them is not primarily to suggest solutions in the difficult field of Indigenous policy. Rather, I believe that the kind of debate about progress and reform which Noel Pearson has initiated needs to take place in quite separate fields. His ideas have a wider relevance and his insights apply far beyond Indigenous communities. He is challenging a paradigm of politics which appears in many places and in many guises. In so doing, he is helping to make it possible for those who seek a way beyond Right and Left to fight the culture war and regain the initiative. In the next two chapters, I look at the implications of this for the family and feminism, and for national identity and multiculturalism.

The first lesson from Pearson is that any broader renewal must boldly acknowledge unpleasant facts rather than attempting to rationalise them.[48] George Orwell called it 'telling people what they don't want to hear'. Acknowledging unpleasant facts should be combined with genuinely trying to rethink the intellectual foundations of a world view rather than just fiddling with policy settings.

A second lesson is that he implicitly challenges the assumptions that reform comes about largely through government action and that, conversely, if failure exists, it must be a fault of government. This is an unspoken assumption of much political action which is oriented to occupying government benches and implementing an official policy. It is not that it is entirely wrong—just that it involves the major omission of individuals and civil society from the picture. Related to this is a third lesson about social change: that poverty is not just a matter of material goods. Indeed, the spiritual poverty in some Aboriginal communities has increased in spite of improved material conditions. This has parallels for people living in Australia and other industrialised countries. These societies operate on the basis that increased production of commodities and their consumption form the basis of a good life. But, increasingly, we are aware that happiness and meaning in life is not necessarily the result of this consumerism—a point made strongly by Clive Hamilton in his recent book *Growth Fetish*. Rather than a focus on improving material goods, Pearson points to the centrality of civil society—that is, networks involving families, communities and business which do not derive from bureaucratic power. This is an important point made widely by sociologist Eva Cox.[49]

A fourth lesson about social change derived from Pearson is that focusing on rights is not enough. Social change conceived of as the spreading and advancement of abstract 'rights' neglects the plain truth that, in real communities and societies, rights crucially involve obligations—such as the obligation to do something in exchange for support. This lesson applies to many industrialised countries, as well as other communities where the extreme exercise of individual rights is destroying the bonds with and respect towards others on which communities depend.

Next, there is Pearson's overt moral stance. This is in contrast to many social reformers who have tended to explain what happens in the world by looking for rational, scientific or quasi-scientific explanations. They are often sceptical of the moral language of good and evil, and of any 'solutions' which include blaming individuals. Because of their strong Enlightenment heritage, such reformers see the world of good and bad as wholly the domain of traditional conservatism, with its emphasis on the virtues necessary to sustain social order, or of 'pure' liberalism and its emphasis on individual responsibility. In rejecting this today, social reformers sometimes go to the other extreme, endorsing what is called 'social construction-ism'. This is the view—discussed previously—which denies that there is a human nature, and therefore a human condition, which establishes the moral domain within which we all function.

There are some big problems with social constructionism when such an over-arching social theory is applied directly to specific social issues. The main one is that there is no space to understand where the domain of individual moral responsibility begins and where that of social responsibility ends. As well, social constructionism discounts the ability of people to learn from experience and change their behaviour. It discounts the actions and moral choices which individuals can make in given circumstances. It concedes little or no autonomy to individuals and families, since they are seen as mere products of the wider society.

In the wider world of global politics, social constructionism is often wheeled out to 'explain' issues which have a moral dimension— for example, when people try to explain Islamic terrorism purely in terms of world poverty, globalisation or the evil actions of the US government. Almost invariably, such 'explanations' soon begin to sound like excuses.[50]

A final wider lesson: Pearson focuses on the family as the crucial institution of social wellbeing. He does this by highlighting the violence in some communities against women and children and the breakdown of respect for elders in a culture dominated by alcohol and welfare. He points out that a stable and functioning family is a crucial element of social order, and provides a moral core to a wider community. Families and family values are central to the culture war, and in the remainder of this chapter and in the next, I argue why any new political philosophy beyond Right and Left must include a positive notion of family values.

Are 'family values' the property of the Right?

It is no accident that the phrase 'family values' is a code word for the social conservatives and their notion of moral politics. Indeed, the term 'morality' has got a bad press because it is most frequently used to impose a uniform and narrow standard of behaviour in sexual and personal spheres. A notion of the family in both real and metaphorical terms is central to the socially conservative world view in politics and life. When the Right fights the culture war, its chosen ground is the family. When the cultural Left fights the culture war, it talks about the rights of gays and women and about everything *but* the family as an entity (except to denounce 'family values').

But what are family values and why are they crucial to the culture war? According to one analyst of conservatism, George Lakoff, the idea of family values is *not* simply another aspect of the politics of conservatism. An understanding of the family is absolutely central, both actually and symbolically. It is the rock on which conservative politics is built, and not just the topic for another government policy.

Lakoff argues that the conservative world view is built on what he calls the Strict Father model of the family. This model of family provides the moral framework of conservative thinking. By contrast, he says, liberals (in the US sense) believe in the Nurturant Parent model. Both are conceptual metaphors used to express views about actual families, as well as about wider political ideas.

The Strict Father model of the family assumes the world is a dangerous place.[51] A central part of the father's role is to provide protection and security for family members, and this in turn means that he assumes an authority for overall family policy. He teaches children right from wrong by setting strict rules for their behaviour and enforcing them through punishment. He also loves them, but is aware of the danger of spoiling them. A mother has day-to-day responsibility for the care of the house, raising the children and upholding the father's authority. Key tasks of the family involve developing character, self-reliance and self-discipline. Put in this way, the conservative political world view becomes more comprehensible. It clearly develops from a certain experience of the world—moreover, an experience that is not entirely wrong. The world *can* be a dangerous place, and self-reliance and self-discipline are important values.

The Strict Father metaphor is then joined to another, argues Lakoff. This is the Nation as Family, with the government or the head of government representing an older male authority figure, with citizens as children. 'This metaphor allows us to reason about the nation on the basis of what we know about a family', says Lakoff.[52] The Strict Father model of the family and the Nation as Family are a powerful basis for a political philosophy. Such a philosophy has deep cultural roots, and it resonates with people's lived experience. It has an emotional truth and it also involves a moral idealism, concludes Lakoff.[53] Nor is this moral world view limited to card-carrying conservatives. To some degree, it makes sense to a far wider group of people.

By contrast, the progressive world view—especially that of the cultural Left—draws little from this aspect of people's lives and tends to lack such an holistic approach. Its moral idealism is oriented to abstract rights, which often fail to resonate with lived experience. It offers little practical support to the family as such. Most of its family views are views about the equal status of women and about the terrible things that sometimes occur within families. The family is a territory where the Right roams at will.

But this need not be. To effectively practise cultural politics, it is important to work with, rather than against, the grain of such deeply held beliefs—that is, if you want to engender broad popular support. This involves a hegemonic contest over key cultural notions such as family values, rather than a blanket rejection of them. This is why the campaign for an *inclusive* notion of families, including those with gay parents and their children, is so valuable. It highlights the fine and loving qualities of gay parents, rather than the demonised caricatures in many conservatives' minds.

In the next two chapters, I will examine the values and strategy of the culture war in two ways: first, in terms of the problems of families, involving parents, the raising of children and work; and second, in terms of the Australian 'family', dealing with issues of cultural difference and national identity. In both areas, some hard rethinking needs to be done about assumptions which have been taken for granted for a long while.

Rethinking family values

The invisible hand represents the forces of supply and demand in competitive markets. The invisible heart represent family values of love, obligation and reciprocity. The invisible hand is about acheivement. The invisible heart is about care for others. The hand and heart are interdependent but they are also in conflict. The only way to balance them successfully is to find fair ways of rewarding those who care for other people.

This is not a problem that economists—or business people—have taken seriously. They have generally assumed that God, nature, the family and 'Super Mom'... would automatically provide whatever care was needed.

Nancy Folbre, The Invisible Heart

Being a mother is simply uneconomic. In this sense the market denies motherhood and love. It might exploit it, work with it, try to mould it... but it cannot explain the non-economic decision to mother and to nurture. Indeed the market runs counter to this care... Most mothers can make more money off paid work than mothering... Thus the only way that mothers in the labour market can persist with the loving care they want to give is by super-exploitation of themselves and even lower paid women workers, or a greater contribution from their partners, or other social contributors like the extended family or the state.

Barbara Pocock, The Work/Life Collision

I have only ever experienced one truly life-transforming event. It was being a house-father for six months soon after the birth of my daughter in 1981. It was transforming because it revealed a side of everyday life of which I was utterly unaware; it revealed a side of myself of which I was utterly unaware; it transformed my relationship with my daughter for many years; and it permanently changed my way of looking at the world. Years later, I was asked: 'If you had one wish to make a better world, what would it be?' I responded: 'That every father cares for their child at home for at least six months.'

Ilse was born in February 1981 after a longish labour at the birth centre at the old Crown Street Women's Hospital in Sydney.[1] After Ilse's mother was trollied away for some stitches, the midwife departed and I was left alone with Ilse, whom I cradled in my arms. As the minutes ticked by I became alarmed. Being supportive during labour was one thing, but now I was on my own with an hour-old baby—where was the manual, the instruction kit? Apprehension combined with elation. My experience of her complete vulnerability and dependence on my care was repeated many times in the coming months. Meanwhile, Ilse gurgled and reflexively sucked the tip of my finger. Two weeks later, she attended her first political demonstration, International Women's Day, along with her Mum and Dad.

The following six months resembled a kind of normalcy for me. I left each morning to work on a small left-wing weekly newspaper. Our small collective wrote, sub-edited, laid out and printed the paper—as well as cleaned and swept the offices. I'd come home fairly tired and at the door Ilse's mother would greet me and then immediately put Ilse into my arms. She *too* was tired. How come? She had been *at home* all day, while I had been *at work*. I didn't fully understand until months later when I became a house-father.

When Ilse was six months old, her mother returned to work and I took over at home for the next six months. Nothing prepared me for the surprise that parenting could be so demanding, both physically and psychologically. Nappies needed constant washing and drying on the line. Bottle feeding was an elaborate ritual which began with a search of inner-city health shops every few days for goat's milk. This simple trip involved taking Ilse in a carry-basket along with a spare nappy, bottle and spare clothes. Then came boiling the milk (but not too long), bottling it, checking its warmth (not too warm) and feeding Ilse. At all times, I had to be constantly aware—to develop a sixth sense—about where she was and what she was doing. How did mothers cope with two, let alone three or four children? At the back of my mind during all this time was my nightmare fantasy that she would one day pull a saucepan of hot water down over herself or eat something toxic as she crawled quickly around the house.

During that time and later, I became aware of unexpected emotional and psychological changes in myself. I had become more vulnerable. My sense of wellbeing was profoundly attached to that of another, utterly dependent, small human being. She was, after all, the most stunning and precious thing that had ever come into my life. This vulnerability and sense of caring extended to unrelated parts of my life. A year or so later, I realised that I was no longer taking pleasure in risky stunts while bushwalking or in eating lunch with my legs dangling over the edge of a 40-metre cliff face. My walking mates thought I had become a little neurotic.

My 'world view' changed too. Most mornings by 9.00 a.m., the people from our terrace share-house and those from our street had all left for work in offices and factories. Left behind was another workforce, which I had unwittingly joined. After 9.00 a.m. I'd push the stroller with Ilse up to the shops. I noticed other people pushing strollers with small children—my fellow workers, all women. As the first weeks ticked by, it gradually dawned on me that I was observing, and had entered, a parallel world that had been hidden in plain view all the time that I was self-importantly writing articles, discussing politics and working on our little newspaper. It was the parallel world of mothers and very young children, the world of home-work, the world of social reproduction which parallels the public world of production and paid work.

In this chapter I want to examine the pressures of work and family, as well as what we mean by equality between women and men and by the culture war over 'family values'.

The flowering of feminism

History is littered with the sudden emergence of movements for social change which begin with a very small but radical core of people committed to a vision that soon strikes a profound chord among a broader number of people and then spreads rapidly throughout the society.

The sweeping revolution initiated by what was once called the women's liberation movement has not only affected the texture of our everyday lives, it is reflected in changes in the positions of authority once occupied almost entirely by men. In 1970, when feminism emerged from the universities and from left-wing circles, there were three women in the Australian parliament; at the time of writing (2004) there are 56. The first presenter on a significant Australian television program, Caroline Jones on *Four Corners*, was appointed in 1972. Today there are many women presenters, including those in 'voice of authority' news broadcasting. The first woman to pilot a passenger aircraft, Christine Davy, did so in 1974, while Deborah Wardley became the first pilot for a major commercial airline in 1980, after a battle at the Equal Opportunities Commission. The first female judge in the High Court, Mary Gaudron, was appointed in 1987. The first female state premier, Carmen Lawrence, was elected in 1990. In 2001, Christine Nixon was appointed first Police Commissioner in Australia. The revolution in the education of women is striking. Women students at universities now make up 56 per cent of the total and are roughly half in many medical and law faculties, once largely the preserve of male students.

In the mid-1960s, women who married had to resign their permanent positions in the Commonwealth Public Service—a practice known as the 'marriage bar', which passed into history in 1966. In 1969 and 1972, forms of equal pay decisions led to increases in the earnings of some women workers. In 1977, the first state *Sex Discrimination* Act was passed, and in 1984 its federal counterpart came into operation. Shortly afterwards, the Human Rights and Equal Opportunity Commission began its work. By the late 1980s, equal opportunity programs, aimed at tackling deeper structural issues of discrimination in jobs, were widespread in major institutions. Beneath these headline events, deep cultural changes affected ordinary people no less profoundly. Established ideas and prejudices about women's 'proper role' were criticised, cast aside or radically reformed on the basis of the insights of a reinvigorated feminism.

The women's movement also detonated a revolution in intellectual frameworks, challenging the ways we saw the world. Until the late 1960s, feminism was seen as an interesting but old-fashioned movement largely concerned with female voting rights.[2] After the 1960s, a new kind of feminism revived notions of equality and individual rights in the most dramatic way possible. These were central ideas of the 300-year-old doctrine of liberalism. Many other intellectual frameworks flourished in the early days of the women's movement, including socialism—which linked social class to women's oppression—and feminist separatism—which argued for all-female institutions and practices based on the celebration of women-centred values. But the main way in which the goals of feminism were socially validated and translated into public policy was through an argument about equal rights which was based ultimately on liberalism. The appeal of liberalism was wide, and thus the ideals which began on the streets with a radical women's liberation movement were soon taken up by broader layers of women in established political parties, in trade unions, in business and in the professions.

So completely have feminism's aims diffused into broader society that there is today no longer a definable 'women's movement' with a single view on what constitutes feminism. Elements of feminism have been absorbed into the legal framework, into social policy, into everyday conversation, into TV sitcoms—into the whole culture. Everyday life has been transformed, overwhelmingly for the better.

But, 35 years after the first whispers of what became a roar of social change, the movement for women's equality and women's rights has run into a roadblock. Feminist academic Professor Belinda Probert notes that 'progress towards gender equity appears to have stalled'.[3] Writer Anne Summers, in her book *The End of Equality*, argues: 'although the language of equality is still used, and despite the successes of so many individual women, the actual experience of far too many women in Australia suggests that the promise of equality has to been met. Sadly, we are actually going in the opposite direction.'[4] The steady drift towards social conservatism has been going on for some time, summed up in the phrase 'family values'.

Some of the awkward facts which constitute the roadblock include:

- Women have *not* flooded into full-time employment. In spite of growing levels of tertiary education, higher pay, an end to social disapproval (and legal barriers) of married women working, 'the proportion of women 15 to 59 years employed full time is much the same today as it was 35 years ago', notes economist Bob Gregory with puzzlement.[5] Also surprising is the fact that full-time employment has increased among married women and fallen among single women.

- Women have, however, moved into part-time work in large numbers. Forty-four per cent of women in paid jobs work part-time. While paid work offers a degree of financial independence, it is often not the first step towards a full-time job—in part because many women appear to seek work that allows them to continue to do housework and raise children.

- Child-raising was one of those things that the New Age Man would share with the New Liberated Woman. But it has not happened. The gender of primary caregivers for children has not changed much at all. And when paid leave is available to fathers, it is not always taken up.

- Housework is still overwhelmingly done by women. The apparent small increase in men's share of housework is largely because the number of hours done by women has decreased.
- Families with two wage-earning parents find it increasingly hard to find adequate and unpressured time to spend with their children, let alone with each other. In the past three years, both major parties have acknowledged this largely hidden family crisis as a national problem and promised to do something about it.
- A substantial number of married women with children continue *not* to work outside the home. Even when the youngest child is teenaged, one in four mothers are not in paid work; when the youngest is aged four to five years, it's 41 per cent.[6] If the road to women's emancipation lies through work outside the home, then this substantial number of mothers are a stubborn part of the roadblock.

Shadowing all discussions on women and the family is the transition from the baby boom to the baby bust—the 'fertility crisis' which increasingly preoccupies demographers and government policy-makers. Its dimensions can quickly be sketched. In 1960, the number of children an Australian woman would bear in her lifetime was an average of 3.5. By 1980, it had reached 1.9 and by 2000, it was 1.75, and still heading south. To replace a population, an average of about 2.1 is needed. Without this level of replacement, the natural tendency of the population is towards a society with far more older people and far fewer younger (taxpaying) people. In the long term, this trend would mean the radical dwindling of the population. This future faces nearly all industrialised countries, with Spain and Italy, for example, having rates of around 1.2. The consequences of such low rates are viewed seriously by conservatives. A study by the Liberal Party think-tank, the Menzies Research

Centre, even warned of 'a cultural death wish' and the 'prospects of social collapse and even extinction within a century or two'.[7] But there are other, less exaggerated reasons for concern. In old age, the quality of life of most parents depends to a considerable degree on the care their children show towards them. Those with one child will get less support then those with two children. People with no children face a more difficult time, and will depend more heavily on friends, relatives and commodified care services.

The 'fertility strike' has also reignited debate about women and the family. In April 2002, Commissioner for Sex Discrimination Pru Goward launched a discussion paper proposing in principle a system for paid maternity leave for women workers.[8] Goward's argument took the 'fertility strike' by women as its jumping-off point, but also argued that maternity leave would alleviate the 'family cram' when women hastily return to work after the physical exhaustion of childbirth and its aftermath. Her plan was greeted with hostility from many in the Howard government, and by May 2004 it had rejected maternity leave in favour of a payment to all mothers.[9]

Both the family crisis around work and care and the fertility crisis are somehow linked to the rise of second-wave feminism—the most important and valuable social change we have seen in recent times. If we take the long view, this *impasse* at the beginning of the twenty-first century should not surprise us. History has a lesson, and it concerns how social reformers over the last few hundred years have vainly tried to envisage the role of mothers and children in an imagined future society. These utopian writings often prefigured a more equal society and a more materially rich life for ordinary people—much of which has come to pass in the wealthy West. But when it came to childbirth and rearing children, social reformers imagined the most fantastic solutions, often involving the magic of spontaneous conception in *Herland* (a visionary work in 1915 by American feminist Charlotte Perkins Gilman) or through laboratory fixes as in Marg Piercy's *Woman on the Edge of Time* and Shulamith Firestone's *The Dialectic of Sex*. Socialist writers also envisaged less fantastic but quite unreal schemes for the complete communal (or government) rearing of children, virtually breaking the bond between parent and child. Needless to say, such schemes have come to nought.

Both in history and in modern times, in spite of important advances, the movement for gender equality has stalled and the roadblock has something to do with the complex connectedness of caring for children, gender roles and paid work. Moreover, in many major industrial countries, the issues of care for children, care for the aged and declining fertility have shot to the top of the political agenda. It seems like the right time to intervene on family policy with progressive and feminist ideas, but that's the problem. What exactly constitutes a progressive and feminist response, given the experience of the last 35 years? That's what lies behind the 'mother wars' so bitterly fought out in newspaper columns in Australia and overseas. At its most positive (and this is rare), the 'mother wars' debate is about how to renew the feminist vision, and in this chapter I'll try to describe the parameters of that debate and make some suggestions.

The price of motherhood

Ann Crittenden is an American feminist who could be the prototype for the generation of women fashioned by feminism. Until the early 1980s, she was a reporter on the *New York Times*, living a lifestyle built around a deep and satisfying commitment to her job. Ready to travel at a moment's notice, she and her husband often ate out and employed a cleaner. In 1982, Crittenden gave birth to a boy and she recounts the consequences for her life—and the wider consequences for modern motherhood—in her book *The Price of Motherhood*.

Before she gave birth, Crittenden admits to feeling 'superior' to housewives. She wondered: 'Why aren't they making something of themselves? What's wrong with them? They're letting our side down.' She goes on:

> I imagined that domestic drudgery was going to be swept into the dustbin of history as men and women linked arms and marched off to run the world on a new egalitarian alliance. It never occurred to me that women might be at home because there were children there; that housewives might become extinct, but mothers and fathers never would.[10]

In her account of her experience, Crittenden concludes that, in spite of the rhetoric of 'family values', the central work of most families—that of child-rearing—is systematically devalued by society. Crittenden illustrates this by translating the cost of motherhood into dollars and cents. For herself, as a well-paid journalist, she estimates the cost of her decision to have a child and forgo income and superannuation was between $600 000 and $700 000—a cost she describes as 'the mommy tax'. For a woman on an average wage, the price is smaller but relatively just as high. The point of this was not to suggest that the value and meaning of having a child can be equated with a monetary calculation, but to highlight the unreasonable penalty which women bear when they choose to have a child.

In spite of 30 years of struggle for equality, it is still women who make adjustments for the sake of having children and, thinks Crittenden, it is likely to continue to be that way. Given this *impasse* for mothers, Crittenden concludes:

> As the twenty-first century begins, women may be approaching equality, but mothers are still far behind. Changing the status of mothers, by gaining real recognition of their work, is the great unfinished business of the women's movement . . . But revaluing motherhood will not be easy. Even feminists are often reluctant to admit that many women's lives revolve around their children . . . the standard feminist response to the fact that

child-rearing marginalises women is not to raise its status but to urge men to do more of it. Though this has been the cry for thirty years, almost 100 per cent of the primary caregivers of young children are still women. *This suggests feminism needs a fresh strategy* [emphasis added].[11]

Questions of strategy

The women's liberation movement discussed strategy passionately when it first emerged—in the United States, the United Kingdom and Australia—and one of the first and most fundamental questions it faced was the 'wages for housework' or 'mothers' wage' debate. Should the new movement demand that full-time housewives and mothers be paid a wage in recognition of the value of their work? In 1974, just a few years after the first meetings of the women's liberation movement, an article in the new journal *Refractory Girl* discussed this issue. Its author was one of the early activists of Australian feminism, Liz Windschuttle, who discussed a proposal for a 'mothers' allowance' floated by the Department of Social Security under its Labor minister, Bill Hayden. While rejecting the idea that 'all women's problems will be solved if they join the workforce', she concluded that 'the woman who stays at home, isolated from her sisters, financially dependent on a man, her ideas very largely determined by advertising agents and the other trivia merchants of the mass media, is least likely to be a force for any sort of social change'.[12]

She posed the key question: would a mother's wage raise the consciousness of housewives 'by allowing them to see that their jobs are socially necessary and worthy of a wage', or would it enforce 'the idea that a woman's natural role is that of a housewife/mother?' She added: 'What should be the attitude of feminists to women remaining housewives/mothers? Are there any circumstances where this is desirable or should we encourage all women to work outside the home?' To the two questions in the last sentence, Windschuttle answered, respectively, no and yes, and in this she spoke for nearly all of the women's movement. While isolated feminist groups took up the fight for 'wages for house work', the most convincing argument to the majority was that the road to equality lay through paid work for all. This would lead to a wider public world where women would take their place in politics, the professions, the church, corporations, trade unions—in every male-dominated institution. The article and the movement posed the choice as between paid work or housewife-mother—that is, between women who stayed at home and those who worked. It seemed a simple choice.

Windschuttle's article was written in the middle of what was, on the face of it, a dramatic shift into the workforce away from the housewife-mother role. In 1966, 36 per cent of women were in the labour force, and by 2002 this had risen to 55 per cent. As a result, the traditional male breadwinner family has now been overtaken by the dual-income family. But this is not a family of two identical income earners—it is more complicated than that. Women flooded into part-time jobs, three-quarters of which are now held by women. Women working in these part-time jobs constitute 44 per cent of working women.[13] These changes have had a major impact on the working and family lives of Australians, and are the subject of a study by someone who is supportive of feminism, but prepared to ask some hard questions.

The work/life collision in Australia

Apart from producing one of the best studies of work–family issues, Barbara Pocock has the distinction of creating a new phrase in the language: 'the work/life collision'. It's the title of her book, published in 2003. Using extensive social science data and nearly 200 interviews, Pocock investigates the transformation of work and care in

Australia over the last 40 years. The transformation has not been easy, nor has it turned out the way it was expected to.

Paid work, Pocock argues, was not the only goal of feminism, but it was a key goal for women's entry into public life and much progress has been made towards it. But 'this goal has found its happy co-conspirator in a market greedy for women's labour, its "flexibility", and enthusiastic for the spending power of women's earnings. Of all of feminism's goals, entry to paid work has been the most compatible with the globalising market'.

But, at the time more women were entering paid work, the workforce was undergoing a transformation. Gains made in previous decades were being rolled back. The price of efficiency and competitiveness meant that Australians started to work longer and longer hours, often including unpaid overtime. Significantly, women's share of these longer hours grew and is still growing.[14] The proportion of workers spending more than 45 hours a week at work increased from 18 per cent in 1985 to 26 per cent in 2001. In many workplaces, work has intensified and working hours now often cover weekends and unsocial times of the day. Australians, says Pocock, have a 'long hours culture'. [15]

All of this has consequences for the 2 million couple families with children and the more than 750 000 single-parent families, most juggling work and care responsibilities. As Pocock points out: 'Changes in workplaces have reduced the number of hours we have available to spend on our homes, communities and care. Activities that were once mostly the province of women at home—cooking and care of small children for example—are increasingly provided by the market.'[16] Spending on child care increased fourfold between 1984 and 1998–99, and between 1993 and 1996 the proportion of children under the age of three who were in formal child care rose by 27 per cent.[17]

Within the home, women still do far more housework than their partners. Women on average do 33 hours a week of housework, child care and shopping, compared with men's seventeen hours a week. The surveys which suggest that the gender gap in housework is decreasing largely rely on the fact that women are now doing less housework, rather than men doing more.[18] While much has been written about the super mum who can 'have it all', Pocock discovered this belies angst and unhappiness. Working mothers are often full of guilt at not being a 'proper mother'. There is enormous pressure to be a 'super mum' and to develop an intensive style of 'super mothering' alongside paid work: 'Most women spoke of the remorse they felt at not being able to do it all—be there for the kids and meeting the family's financial needs, the expectations of motherhood and their own ambitions or experience.'[19]

Moreover, women are divided: 'Interestingly, women with jobs feel criticised for being working mothers (called selfish and 'money hungry'), while on the other hand, women at home feel criticised for being lazy, incompetent or unable to "get a job".' Despite the sentimental valorisation of motherhood in society, the mother at home is often regarded as a 'non-person'. Comments Pocock: 'Those who respect full-time mothering and those who do it, work against the grain of society where so much of personal worth, value and self is shaped by a worker identity established through the market.'[20]

This taps into a wider paradigm in which the family is functioning. One of the answers for many families is commodified, market-supplied care, and some of us prefer this rather than engaging in the more complex emotional exchanges with grandparents or friends which non-market care involves. The market sets a clear rate for the job, free of this kind of reciprocity. But the long-term social problem is that non-market exchanges—reciprocal favours, donations, help, care—are what build personal and community relationships: 'Mutual non-monetary exchanges have embedded within them—indeed *create*—personal and community relationships. These obligations are the stuff of community and generalized reciprocity. They create trust and long term witnesses to one's life.'[21] One of the deeper processes occurring in the work/life collision is a competition between two kinds of life-world: 'While the market hungrily offers its commodified supports (food and all kinds of services delivered to the door) where the prospect of profit exists, the engine for non-monetary community creation . . . is a weaker machine, one that is starved in the face of time pressures in streets where work sucks both time and place.'[22]

This collision between the demands of work and home is quite historically unprecedented, and the crisis created—which might have once been regarded as a private matter—has become a matter for national political debate. Prime Minister John Howard referred to the problem as the 'barbecue stopper'—the sensitive discussion which dramatically brings to halt the normal small talk of that most ordinary of social occasions. Women, it seems, can be anything: high-flying lawyers, corporate chiefs, government ministers, but they are finding it much harder to be mothers these days.

The idea of equality

Another contributor to the debate around women, the family and work is Anne Summers, whose latest book, *The End of Equality*, was published in 2003. A leading figure in Australian feminism and a former adviser on women's affairs to a Labor prime minister, Summers' book rang the alarm bells at the erosion of the gains made by women in the 1970s and 1980s. She discussed the persistence of domestic violence and of violence towards women more generally. Her book comprehensively exposes the Liberal–National Coalition government's downgrading and dismantling of advisory bodies for women in the federal public service. In particular, she attacks a number of measures of the Howard government, especially its family policy—which, she says, is designed to force women back into traditional roles.

The once powerful belief in equality for women has been usurped, according to Summers, by the new doctrine which she dubs 'the breeding creed': '[It] is a powerful new ideology that defines women first and foremost as mothers. It aims to subsume all of women's other choices and ambitions into a motherhood mentality . . . The intention is, apparently, to make it financially attractive for women to become full time mothers in the hope that this will encourage more women to have children.'[23] Summers quite rightly points out that: 'As a society we ask women, to give up too much when they have children and we give them far too little in return.' She attacks the hypocrisy of a society which claims to value motherhood, but which devalues both mothers who want to stay at home and those who want to keep on working.[24]

Like Barbara Pocock, Anne Summers reports on the anguish and hard work experienced by so many mothers. Women report that they are 'exhausted all of the time', and racked by guilt for the choices they have made—whether it was to be a full-time mother or to combine mothering with paid work: 'We are probably quite equal until we have children,' commented one perceptive woman interviewed by Summers. Using federal government figures, Summers notes that 'when a double income family, both on average weekly earnings, moves to a single income, they suffer a 38 percent fall in income that government payments do not come close to redressing'.[25]

Anne Summers and Barbara Pocock share some common ground. Both used surveys of women to provide important raw material on the actual experiences of women at the grassroots. Both point to the crisis of overwork and exhaustion among women in families with children. Both see the dramatic fall in the birthrate as due to the unacceptable price women have to pay in order to become mothers. Both point out that men continue to do only a small share of housework.

But there are significant differences. Pocock examines the experience of women with the aim of being guided by the facts rather than by a preconceived framework. By contrast, Summers operates within a preconceived notion of the meaning of equality. The core of Summers' vision is that equality for women means identical participation in paid work for women and men. It is an employment-focused feminism. On this basis, equality tends to be defined as sameness, and any significant variation from this must be avoided. She therefore assumes that any break from paid work should be as brief as possible. Government support for child care to allow women to remain in paid work must *on principle* take priority over government support for full-time mothers to care for their children. This is not an argument for decent funding for child care, which many—including this writer—would support, but an argument for funding child care in preference to mothers at home. This narrow focus also substitutes for the goal of radically transforming workplaces in the interests of parents. But Summers misses the point, as Labor MP Tanya Plibersek notes: 'If you offered the average parent 80 hours [of] free, top quality child care a week they wouldn't take it. There is an additional factor, which Summers touches on but does not explore adequately: we want time with our families.'[26] Another feminist writer, Katherine Wilson, argues against her 'equality-equals-sameness' approach: 'Summers discusses children solely in terms of being an interruption to a woman's career', which reduces their value to a work expense for which women should be compensated.[27]

Even though Summers demonstrates and sympathises with the difficult financial circumstances of couples with young children, she is critical of financial support to mothers who choose to stay out of the workforce for a number of years to raise children. Summers' own figures show that this choice involves a very big financial sacrifice—which many can ill afford. Many continue to make that sacrifice for a considerable period of time—well after the few months that paid maternity leave or other government benefits might compensate for. Rather than 'enticing' women to stay at home because of a Machiavellian desire to return to the 1950s, government's compensation to mothers is miserly, considering the public good involved in child-rearing.

Summers' ideal of equality is inordinately focused on paid employment, which means she values a high participation rate of women in the workforce and hence worries that Australia (66.1 per cent women's participation) is lagging behind the United States with 71.8 per cent and the United Kingdom with 67.7 per cent. She suspects that the situation of Australian women in regard to work may be 'the result of political interference'.[28] The possibility that some mothers might prefer to care for their children but are compelled to work by financial circumstances is hardly discussed.

Summers points to the fact that, compared with men, Australian women tend to work part time. Summers' own evidence suggests that the choices made by women at least partly explain the bias towards part-time rather than full-time work. She points to an ABS survey which shows that '22 per cent of women working part time said they would prefer to work more hours, with one fifth of these women wanting full time work'.[29] One-fifth of 22 per cent is just over 4 per cent, which is hardly a strong demand by women for full-time work. And the fact that only one-fifth overall would like more hours means that many more do not want an increase in the hours. One likely meaning of these figures is that most women work part time by choice because it suits them, rather than because of 'political interference'. But Summers constantly invokes government policies which, she claims, deliberately try to force women out of the workforce and back into the home. They are constantly 'shoehorning them all into options that suit the ideological preferences of the government'.

Yet women make choices, and sometimes those choices do not accord with employment-focused definitions of equality. So is the problem with the women? Or with the particular definition of equality? Ann Crittenden puts her finger on the underlying fears of many feminists:

> [Feminists] measure progress by the distance women have travelled from *Kinder* and *Kuche* and worry that if child-rearing is made a more tempting choice, many women—those natural nurturers—will drift back to domestic subservience. They fear

that if women are seen to be mothers first, the very real gains that women have made in the workplace could be jeopardized.[30]

This is a legitimate fear, but it surely cannot override support for the choices which women make—particularly now that previous legal and social barriers have been overcome. What do women want? Clearly many want different things at different times of their lives. To what extent are their preferences freely chosen? Do they freely choose to return to work quickly after birth? Do they freely choose to remain with babies and young children for several years? Do they freely choose part-time work? Are they compelled to return to work by financial necessity, or are they bribed to stay at home by a conservative government?

What do women want?

One of the most influential figures in the debate is Canberra demographer Peter McDonald, who characterises this debate as dealing with the transition from the 'male breadwinner' model of the family to the 'gender equity' model. He defines 'gender equity' as a situation in which 'there is income earning work, household maintenance work, and caring and nurturing work, but gender has no specific relationship to who does which type of work'. Like others in this debate, McDonald states that his definition of 'gender equity' does not 'imply exact equality' between the man and the woman, but then defines it in terms of 'equality of resources and capabilities' of men and women. Yet men and women are *not* equal in one vital capability—that of giving birth to children. McDonald believes we are on the road to a gender equity family, and that 'a large majority of Australians have adopted the gender equity model'.[31]

His evidence for this is a survey which shows that 95 per cent of men and women agree that 'if both the husband and wife work, they should share equally in the housework and care of the children'. When asked about the statement 'It is better for the family if the husband is the principal breadwinner and the wife has primary responsibility for the home and the children', 34 per cent of men and 31 per cent of women agree. Around one-third agreeing with a 'traditional' family is not inconsiderable, but McDonald seems to believe this is a temporary situation and that the tide will continue to run the way of 'gender equity' as he defines it. He argues that the problem lies in the fact that social institutions have been subjected to the goals of feminism, but the family is lagging behind: 'The core change required is the one which is the most difficult. Gender equity needs to be promoted within the family itself. Changes in cultural values are slow and idealised family morality is resistant to change.' McDonald suggests that 'a different socialization of children can lead to change in the next generation', perhaps with more gender equity content in school curricula.[32] McDonald's statement should give us pause. He says the institutions have changed *but the people are lagging behind*. One could ask, on whose behalf and in whose interest have the institutions changed? No wonder the ideologues of the Right talk about feminists and the Left as 'cultural elites' engaged in social engineering.

But McDonald's view that we are on the way to a family model in which work in done regardless of gender is contested by contrary results from other surveys. Two other researchers, Mariah Evans and Jonathan Kelley, have written a series of articles based on large-scale surveys reporting that the overwhelming majority of mothers (71 per cent) think that mothers should not work when their children are of pre-school age.[33] A substantial minority (27 per cent) think part-time employment with young children is good, while a tiny 2 per cent favour full-time work.

Another critic is feminist writer Anne Manne, who has often written about the dilemmas thrown up by employment-defined equality. She points to one of the most sensitive issues of all, which is research that suggests that certain kinds of institutional child care may have detrimental effects on children, especially on the very young and on children who spend long hours in care.[34] In particular, 'children in over 30 hours of care in all ranges of care and including father care, showed three times as many aggressive behavioural problems as children in care for less than ten hours'. The research— some of the most sophisticated and extensive ever carried out— usually brings the response from some feminist critics that the detriment is due to poor-quality care but, as Manne points out, all variables such as 'quality of care, type of care, mother attributes and stability of care were carefully taken into account. Quantity not quality was the issue'. Perhaps reservations about child care explain women's preference for caring for their child themselves in the child's early years, she suggests. Manne may well be right, but the problem for many people committed to extensive child care to underpin their work choices is that it is difficult to discuss such results in a detached and calm way. This research simply cannot be true because its implications are alarming.

Anne Manne also points to the work of British sociologist Catherine Hakim, who has been demonised as if she is a rabid moral conservative. But this is misleading and simplistic. The basis for this attack began with her outspoken criticism of what she called 'feminist myths' in sociological research.[35] Hakim criticised the denial of certain facts because they were assumed to undermine employment-oriented feminism. Hakim is best known for what she calls 'preference theory'. She uses opinion surveys to ask men and women to express their personal preferences for one of three different family models.[36] The first, the egalitarian, was a family where 'two partners have an equally demanding job and where housework and care of children are shared equally'. The second model, the 'compromise', was one where 'the wife has a less demanding job than the husband and where she does the larger share of the housework and caring for the children'. The third is the 'separate roles' family where 'only the husband has a job and the wife runs the home'. She argues that none of these options has overwhelming support, although the traditional 'separate roles' model has clearly lost its dominance.[37]

On the basis of her analysis of men and women's expressed preferences and other data, Hakim concludes that government policies should be neutral, supporting a diversity of preferences on how to arrange the work/life balance. Ultimately, she says, part of this diversity involves paying 'all full time mothers a wage for their time and efforts while their children are small'.[38] Where such a policy has been tried, the allowance could also be used to pay for child-care services, but most mothers take the allowance for themselves. Apart from anything else, Manne argues, this is a good anti-poverty measure.

By contrast, analysts influenced by employment-oriented feminism look at the rise in the number of women working part time and see the positives—a chance to broaden their outlook, be financially independent, participate in the public world and essentially take steps towards equality. They conclude that more steps along the road to equality could be achieved if only more women could work full time, and they conclude that this depends on government policies supporting child care, maternity leave and similar supports. But they rule out financial support for full-time mothers.

Hakim can be criticised because her categories of preference are drawn too rigidly, whereas the lived reality is blurred as many women make transitions in their life from full-time work, to full-time care, then back to part-time or full-time work. What this means is that most women value the benefits of a paid job and also recognise the value of caring. Their preferences vary at different times. Barbara Pocock points to such a 'three-stage transition [which] is common for women', but warns that this is only an 'average pattern of the majority. There are many variations around the mean. Many women spend extended periods at home, especially with multiple children. On the other hand, a third return to paid work relatively quickly after having their last baby'.

All commentators agree that the popularity of the traditional male breadwinner family with dependants has been overtaken by the dual-income family. But this conceals as well as reveals. Today's traditional family is tomorrow's dual-earner family, and vice versa. As well, most dual-income families are 'modified traditional households with one and a half workers in many cases'.[39] And in any case, about 30 per cent of families with children still fit the traditional mould of working father and home-based mother.

Recognition and support for diversity should surely be the foundation of family support policies, yet this conflicts with the definition of equality centred largely around full-time paid work. One of the great achievements of modern feminism was the struggle to broaden women's choices by breaking down legal and cultural barriers to wider fields of employment and to authoritative positions in society. But having achieved much of this, and having expanded choice, somehow we are reluctant to accept that women who *choose* to stay at home for extended periods after the birth of their child are in fact freely choosing. We blame only ideological blinkers or structural impediments such as lack of child care. Lack of affordable child care is indeed a problem preventing some women from working, but it does not wholly explain the choice by many women to care for their child(ren) themselves. Some feminists may feel privately, as Ann Crittenden did, that such women were also 'letting the side down'. But perhaps we should look again at the meaning of equality and choice.

Separating motherhood from patriarchal values

The paradigm of feminism which assumes the equality (and liberation) of women mostly depends on long-term, full-time participation in the paid workforce is not succeeding for two reasons. First, it cannot explain the actual behaviour and diverse choices made by many women who become mothers. Second, philosophically, it is an expression of a kind of liberalism which, while it has many virtues, imposes an inflexible model that fails to capture the major ethical and emotional dimensions of human lives. It also fails to cope with the felt needs of many women centred around the notions of love and caring. Prizing these qualities has been a submerged current of feminist thought which has recently re-emerged in the work of a number of feminist writers who cannot be dismissed as mere 'conservatives' or enemies of feminism.

One such is Germaine Greer, who describes her 1999 book, *The Whole Woman*, as the sequel to her feminist classic *The Female Eunuch*, first published in 1970. Greer says she was driven to write *The Whole Woman* because of her alarm at the fate of feminism and her rejection of what was being claimed in the name of feminism. Women might well have broken barriers to join male institutions but, rather than transforming them, they simply accepted their values and practices. The renaming of the women's movement from its original title, Women's Liberation, to feminism masked a deeper change.

> What none of us noticed was that the ideal of liberation was fading out with the word. We were settling for equality. Liberation struggles are not about assimilation but asserting difference, endowing that difference with dignity and prestige and insisting on it as a condition of self-definition and self-determination . . . Seekers after equality clamoured to be admitted to smoke-filled male haunts. Liberationists sought the world over for clues to what women's lives could be like if they were free to define their own values, order their own priorities and decide their own fate.[40]

Motherhood is a central concern for Greer. Where once the social ideal of motherhood acted as a straitjacket for women's potential and identity, today motherhood is scarcely understood and sometimes reviled. Breastfeeding mothers cause a panic and children are regarded as a 'personal indulgence'. The ideal of feminine beauty has become 'boyishly slim and hipless, the broad hips and full bosom of maternity as monstrous as motherhood itself'. Mothers' experience of raising children is intense, and unlike that of most fathers: 'The experience of falling desperately in love with one's baby is by no means universal but it is an occupational hazard for any women giving birth.'[41]

Germaine Greer acknowledges that her views on motherhood have changed. She disentangled the experience of motherhood from the oppressive practices which devalued it and which forced women to limit their horizons to it. In *The Female Eunuch*, she had argued that motherhood should not be treated as a 'substitute career'. She now believes that motherhood should be regarded as a genuine career and as paid work:

> What this would mean is that every woman who decides to have a child would be paid enough money to raise that child in decent circumstances. The choice, whether to continue in her employment outside the home and use the money to pay for professional help in raising her child or stay at home and devote her time to doing it herself, should be hers.[42]

In her conclusion, she says—with characteristic over-statement: 'Women's liberation must be mothers' liberation or it is nothing.'

Greer does not have the last word on the meaning of feminism, but she is an important participant in a growing debate which is rediscussing women, employment and the family. With a healthy contempt for politically correct restraints on debate, she reminds us that an original component of feminism challenged not just the overwhelming institutional power of males, but also the patriarchal values which pervaded the culture. Underlying much of *The Whole Woman* is a concern with how different women are from men—not only physically, but psychologically and in the values which they tend to express. She is aware that, to many feminists (particularly in academia), this commits the crime of 'essentialism'—in other words, believing that men and women are born with different psychological qualities as well as physical characteristics. On the basis of essentialist ideas, it is said, women have been regarded as inferior. But in order to reach that conclusion, you have to assume that the 'female' qualities are of less value.

The politics of care

Behind the 'work/life collision' and the fertility crisis lie a series of knotty problems around motherhood, the family, equality for women and women's values that have been debated within feminism for many years. Greer's recent work reminds us that, in the mid-1970s, a strong tendency existed within feminism which valued women's special attributes, including the ability to give birth and a nurturing temperament. This 'cultural feminism' prized traits that might be described as maternal, 'a certain consciousness of care for others, flexibility, non-competitiveness, cooperation.'[43] As a tendency within feminism, cultural feminism subsided partly because it became associated with an inward-turning separatism, and partly because—whether this had occurred or not—it could not operationalise its aims into a practical political strategy around work and mothering.[44] The latter required linking the abstract and ideal aims of the movement with the practical reality of many other women, through a series of campaigns to improve their lives. The only attempt at such a strategic demand was 'wages for housework' or 'a mothers' wage', but at that time this demand struck a resonance with neither the young feminists nor with the mass of women and was largely rejected, as we saw earlier. By contrast, different currents within feminism, which aimed at equality within the framework of paid work, became very successful. This coincided with a pre-existing tendency for women to enter paid work; it appealed to the ideals of fairness and equality; and it offered women financial independence. Traditional 'women's work' such as child-raising and housework, it was envisaged, would be shared equally between the two employed parents.

Philosophically, these currents of feminism which were employment-focused represented a form of liberalism and were part of the re-energising of liberalism that occurred from the late 1960s onwards. Like all liberalism, their great strength was a recognition of equality in the face of backward-looking, ancient prejudices. They assert a common humanity between men and women which gives these currents within feminism a continuing relevance. Their weakness was that they tended to ignore difference, and leaned toward an identicality between men and women. Moreover, their rise coincided with the rise of another kind of liberalism—neo-liberal economic thinking—which assumed the supremacy of the market and the public economy of production, and which deepened the devaluation of the world of care and reproduction. Both this neo-liberal devaluation of care and the limitations of liberalism are among the reasons that this interpretation of feminism has reached the roadblock acknowledged earlier.

But cultural feminism which identified women's special attributes was not quite dead. For some time, it has been enjoying a rebirth in the wake of research by feminist psychologist Carol Gilligan.[45] In 1982, Gilligan wrote a book, *In a Different Voice*, based on research on people facing difficult moral conflicts or choices (one conflict concerned abortion). Gilligan argued that she had found a 'different moral voice', which she called an 'ethic of care' and which she contrasted with the traditional ethic of rights in political philosophy. The former was found largely among women and the latter among men. The naming of caring as a vital human activity based on attentiveness to needs and to sustaining relationships was an important conceptual advance which crystallised a widely recognised but 'invisible' social phenomenon.

Arising from Gilligan's original research has been an ongoing debate about the meaning of 'an ethic of care', largely applied to the fields of nursing, education and welfare. It has not yet been articulated in a political vision in the wider society.[46] Critics of the 'ethic of care' fear that it will undermine the advances by women by reinforcing the idea that women are naturally disposed to caring. This is seen to entail the risk that women will revert to denial of self, will lose financial independence and will continue to overwork. But what if women are biologically inclined to be empathetic and to value relationships more than men? This is, first of all, a question of fact—in the sense that either it is the case or it is not. Eventually, knowledge of the makeup of humans will settle this question. If it proves to be the case, then it needs to be faced and discussed. To persist with a political theory based on identicality in the face of facts is to court defeat. We are not talking here, by the way, of a rigid template of emotions and behaviour, but rather of tendencies which are magnified or minimised by culture and circumstances. Second, the devaluation of caring and the assumption of male norms is surely a significant part of the cause of women's oppression and, if this is so, then the struggle is to initiate major social and legal reforms which value caring and empathy.

Is it possible to use an 'ethic of care' as part of a political philosophy without risking all the gains for women and plunging them back into performing compulsory care? Is it possible to spread the values embodied in nurturing and caring to men—indeed further, so that they imbue social structures, politics and our culture? This is indeed possible (though it will not be easy) and, in my view, represents a vital element in fashioning new ideas beyond Right and Left. Many creative and valuable ideas in this direction are now emerging from feminists who have confronted the problem.

Part of the answer lies in tackling those awkward questions: in the wake of women's entry to paid work, why have men not stepped in to do their share of caring work? There are many possible answers to this question. Some are about the structure of jobs and careers; others concern the values and privileges of men who refuse to do caring work.

One of the clues comes from what Ann Crittenden said earlier in this chapter: 'The standard feminist response to the fact that child-rearing marginalises women is not to raise its status but to urge men to do more of it.' Only a few men have responded, and it is unlikely that the majority will do so unless changes are made to entrench the value of caring more generally in our culture and laws. Like a growing number of people, Crittenden argues that child-rearing is an extremely valuable—but under-valued—human activity. It is the foundation on which sits 'human capital'.[47] But even economists who recognise that the skills and knowledge of a workforce have a major value often do not recognise that the formation of this 'capital' begins in the first years of a child's life, and not simply through learning skills at school or university—which is mostly what is meant by the term. Most countries do not collect statistics about the labour of women in the home and with children. Where they do, such as in Australia, it is found to constitute roughly half of the gross domestic product.

In spite of its actual value, the raising of children is largely unvalued by the New Capitalism, and is done at a cost to mothers. One of the major reasons why men still dominate the upper rungs of many institutions and organisations is not because they discrim-inate against women in some crude sense, but because these organisations assume that their employees are care-less, and because most men act as if they are care-free (even though many are fathers). This prejudice against care means that those women and few men who give priority to care are penalised when they try to assume positions of institutional authority.

Nevertheless, many mothers care full time for their children when they are young. In so doing, they make a 'huge gift of unreimbursed time and labor', argues Crittenden—and this is a major reason why adult women are so much poorer than men, even though they work longer hours than men in almost every country in the world:

In economics, a 'free rider' is someone who benefits from a good without contributing to its provision: in other words, someone who gets something for nothing. By that definition, both the family and the global economy are classic examples of free riding. Both are dependent on female caregivers who offer their labor in return for little or no compensation.[48]

Barbara Pocock, who analysed the work/life collision, agrees and points out that neo-liberal economists barely recognise this with their myopic focus on market relations. In fact, 'the paid workforce and its entire product actually swims unconsciously atop, and wholly dependent upon, an unrecognized world of the unpaid—where workers, and their managers and employers are reproduced and sustained'.[49]

Crittenden also identifies this large sea of unvalued labour, and points out that it also has another characteristic: it is largely selfless, and forms a reservoir of altruism in the world. This is not an economic fact, but a social fact of the greatest importance. If we want to shift the unfair burden of care from being largely a female responsibility, how can we do this without simply decreasing the overall amount of altruism in the world? More than that, how can we ensure that care for our children, our aged parents and our friends remains genuine loving care and is not wholly supplanted by marketised and commodified care?

One of the most exciting thinkers in the new politics of care is the feminist economist Nancy Folbre, whom we met in Chapter 2.[50] Like Crittenden, she believes care is massively under-valued in contemporary society. And that goes not only for the devaluation of maternal care for young children, but also for caring labour in the paid workforce. Child-care workers, nurses in hospitals, in aged care and other personal service jobs often bring a dimension of genuine care to their job that is qualitatively different from the instrumental and rational functions which exist on the surface. In my own experience, I recall the last two years of my father's life in a nursing home were materially and emotionally improved by a dimension of warmth given freely by nurses and nursing aides. They could have adequately fulfilled their tasks without such involvement, but they did not. As Folbre says: 'Just because care is paid by a wage doesn't mean that it isn't motivated by love as well as money.' But caring jobs, of course, are poorly paid.

However, this caring labour works against the grain of a market-oriented society in which all values are increasingly reduced to commercial values. This insight that an economy based on self-interest tends to corrode the virtues of altruism is not a modern discovery. Conservatives have worried about it for the last 200 years and have romanticised mothers and their selfless labour. But, as Folbre says, the conservative argument which idealises motherhood depends crucially on an argument about the 'separate spheres'. Men were fitted for the public world of production, and women for the private sphere of reproduction. But the separate spheres of home and work have radically changed forever.

New directions

The conservative desire to return to a past of happy families based on quite separate gender roles will never be achieved. But neither has the vision of employment-focused feminism, because men have not stepped into caring work as women stepped into work and the public world. The consequence is the 'work/life collision', especially for women.

Trying to resolve this dilemma has led me to two conclusions which I did not expect when I began researching feminism and the culture war. The first is that caring must now be foregrounded as a vital quality in society, but not in the way conservatives have usually seen it—as largely the contribution of women. Rather, caring is a vital human activity in which men should engage far more deeply. But this will not occur until the value of care is radically raised in society generally. To achieve this, a massive transformation of the structure of work is needed. Shorter working hours and parental leave are needed, along with flexible working hours and financial support for carers at home. Underpinning this, a cultural revolution in values is required to ensure that caring is genuinely held in much higher esteem by society.

This relates to the second conclusion, which is that protecting the family from the inroads of the market should now be seen as a vital progressive cause. The family is part of a parallel world of social reproduction characterised by altruism, trust and non-rational (but not irrational) values vital to human wellbeing. The family is now the focal point of social and cultural contradictions precipitated by the New Capitalism. It is becoming more apparent that 'family values' can be a rallying cry against the instrumental logic of an increasingly commercially driven society. And this involves both protecting individual families and ensuring that social supports are available.

For too long the Left and supporters of feminism have damned the phrase 'family values' as simply a code for intolerance and discrimination. Rather than challenging the meaning of 'family values', we have allowed ourselves to be positioned as opponents of something with which most people sympathise. Ceding the terrain of 'the family' to the Right allows it to speak in the names of many millions of people who are themselves not necessarily prejudiced or intolerant, but who are worried by rapid social change and dislocation. Yet the real forces undermining families are the forces of the market, of rampant consumerism, of low pay and of long and inflexible working hours. Rethinking family values means focusing on the private and the social meaning of care.

Is a new strategy possible which asserts that women can do more than 'care' and which values care much more highly *and* spreads it to men? I believe this is possible. It will not be an easy struggle, since powerful vested interests benefit from the current arrangement— not just many men, but also all major private and public institutions.

This involves waging a culture war to regain the initiative for the original ideals embedded in feminism. The foundation of such a culture war is the development of a new set of ideas and values grounded in the problems of the 'work/life collision', which are convincing to many people and which project social change for a better future. This involves reconstituting what is usually meant by 'family values'. It also involves reconfiguring what we mean by equality so that it is not largely defined by full-time, long-term paid employment. A crucial issue is collective financial support for full-time parenting for the early years of childhood.

Almost 40 years ago, British feminist Juliet Mitchell wrote a pioneering article entitled 'Women: The longest revolution'—and so it has proved to be, in twists and turns and ways unseen even by many supporters of that revolution.

8

We're all in the same boat

Multiculturalism has not valued integration enough. Retreating to ethnic enclaves—demanding our own share of recognition and resources as Gujeratis, Somalis, Bangladeshis and so on—is a dead end. We need a shared society. Integration is a two-way street. We should demand allegiance and loyalty from citizens—and tackle the racism in employment which prevents the promise of integration from being kept.

Sunder Katwala

As man advances in civilisation, and small tribes are united into larger communities, the simplest reason would tell each individual that he ought to extend his social instincts and sympathies to all members of the same nation, though personally unknown to him. This point being once reached, there is only an artificial barrier to prevent his sympathies extending to the men of all nations and races.

Charles Darwin

In the dark pre-dawn hours of Sunday 6 October 2001, on the high seas of the Indian Ocean near Christmas Island, a standoff was taking place between the *Olong*, a leaky wooden fishing boat with 223 asylum-seekers on board, and the HMAS *Adelaide*.[1] In spite of being told to change course, the fishing boat continued to plough towards the island. Around 4.00 a.m., the *Adelaide* suddenly fired four warning shots '50 to 75 feet ahead of the vessel. A searchlight was used to illuminate the weapon firer and the area in the water ahead of the vessel where the rounds were to land'.[2] A loudspeaker message in Bahasa and Arabic warned the boat to turn around, but the boat ignored this; more shots boomed out and the boat was then boarded by a crew of Australian sailors. At one point, a man held his child over the rail, intent on lowering her to an inflatable boat below. The sailors motioned to him to put the child back, which he did. Though partly obscured, this scene was witnessed by the *Adelaide*'s commander, Norman Banks, who thought the man was threatening to throw the child overboard. In the midst of this chaos, Banks was rung by his superior, Brigadier Mike Silverstone. After that conversation, Silverstone reported that the asylum-seekers had actually thrown children into the water. This statement was not true, but was judged by Liberal ministers to be extremely useful at the start of a federal election campaign. It was so useful, in fact, that—in spite of the best efforts of Defence officials over many days to correct it—the lie was repeated and then compounded by the release of photos allegedly supporting the 'children thrown overboard' myth, but actually taken on the following day.

That day's events became dramatic as the sea and the wind rose after the *Olong* was forcibly put under tow by the *Adelaide*. Its crew worked hard to keep the *Olong*'s pumps working as waves were breaking over the side of the boat. Late on the afternoon of Monday 7 October, the *Olong* suddenly began to sink. As the bow went under the waves, its passengers began entering the water. The *Adelaide* dispatched life rafts and, with women and children floundering in the heaving seas, several of the *Adelaide*'s sailors spontaneously dived into the water to help save them. As the asylum-seekers were brought on board, their children were hugged by the sailors:

> In the few hours since the rescue, Banks had seen a surprising change in his ship's company. Many whom he thought were 'white Australia' types were some of the most compassionate and humane toward the survivors. As he told his sailors, 'These

people are indeed human beings first [and] whilst we could not understand their plight, we had to treat them as refugees.'[3]

These events, and the political use of asylum-seekers which followed them, have been the subject of many articles, passionate public debate and a Senate inquiry. But before discussing these, it is worth studying the incident itself, because it is a microcosm of something deeper. For two days, the nameless asylum-seekers were seen as virtual enemies penetrating Australia's border security and were subject to hostility by the *Adelaide*'s crew. Yet, in the space of a couple of hours, the crew became compassionate and began to see the asylum-seekers as human beings. The incident showed the tantalising possibilities of change, but in wider Australian society the asylum-seekers were transformed into symbols in a culture war which is now central to the way in which Australian politics is carried on.

And at the heart of this particular skirmish in that culture war was a simple question: Did Australia owe them anything? They were not citizens, they were not invited guests—they were not like us. But did we owe them anything?

The answer is often framed as a legal question about international conventions, but the issue is a moral one beset by the visceral politics of cultural difference. The first taste of this came within hours of the garbled message from the HMAS *Adelaide*. Minister for Immigration Phillip Ruddock told a media conference that the asylum-seekers had thrown their children overboard and piously added: 'I regard these as some of the most disturbing practices I've come across in public life.' Shortly after this, Howard intoned: 'I want to make that very clear, we are a humane nation but we're not a nation that is going to be intimidated by this kind of behaviour.' Later that day, he added: 'I don't want people like that in Australia. Genuine refugees don't do that . . . they hang on to their children.'[4] Howard, a much under-estimated cultural politician, has a remarkable ability to ride the currents of supportive popular sentiment.

And it is these popular sentiments which are important. For, in spite of the lies told, the events were still capable of different interpretations. While a few looked at the heaving boat that day and saw desperate people and felt empathy, a far larger number saw the same scene and felt the asylum-seekers had deliberately tried to exploit pity for children and parlay that human emotion into residency in Australia.

The key word here is empathy. Human beings are probably born with some innate capacity for compassion, but they develop this compassion in their family and in a community. Love and its cousin, empathy, are learned in families, and those families are usually part of a larger ethnic culture. We feel first for those closest to us. That is why news stories of overseas disasters often focus on whether Australians died, not in order to demean the non-Australian dead, but to respond to feelings of connection in their audience.

To empathise with, and even love, those from another ethnic culture requires compassion of a high order. It means recognising that someone who initially appears unlike yourself nevertheless shares something with you which evokes empathy. That is why the Christian parable of the Good Samaritan is so radical—both for its own time and now.

The same kind of sentiment—that we share a common humanity—has also been the basis for radical egalitarianism. While opposing the gross injustices of English feudal lords, the leader of the English peasants' revolt of 1381, John Ball, cried out: 'Are we not all descended from Adam and Eve?' His logic was that, if we are, then we are connected—we are family, and 'family values' such as respect, sharing and love are appropriate. Such stories reveal the universalist element in Christianity, but a recognition of a thread of sameness and commonality also exists in the diversity and inconsistency to be found in the tapestry of humanity. While such universalism in Christianity was more honoured in the breach in the age of colonial expansion, it nevertheless existed and in a country like Australia provides a source for a social renewal based on human values.

But in a notionally Christian society, it seems that only a minority of us looked on the terrified people flailing in the water and recognised that we shared a common humanity. To put it another way, only a minority believe that, as humans, we are all in the same boat.

The Pauline Hanson effect

Against a background of arrivals by boat people and the terrorist attacks of September 11, Howard won the 2001 election by invoking some of the deepest passions known to human societies. Though often described as racism, these passions are better described by the terms 'ethnocentrism' and 'xenophobia', which give a more grounded and usefully explanatory meaning.

In the context of the culture war, the purpose of this chapter is to discuss how to promote human values in opposition to racism, ethnocentrism and xenophobia. Against prevailing wisdom, I want to argue that it is not by the policy normally described as multiculturalism, which aims to convince people to respect their cultural differences. Rather, I argue that the way forward lies first through convincing people to acknowledge their *similarities* with all other human beings. On the basis of a common humanity, they may then respect cultural differences.

To achieve this is a difficult process, and it is partly an argument about how ideas and beliefs can best be popularised in a modern society (if you like, about how to win the cultural war). It is also partly about asserting a scientific truth: that we *are* first and foremost all from the same species, all connected, all humans. And finally, it is about moral beliefs which can be developed on the basis of these simple facts.

The rise in the number of people seeking asylum by sea in 2000–01, and the xenophobic response to them, followed a period conditioned by the rise and fall of the populist politician Pauline Hanson and her One Nation Party. The period began one September evening in 1996 with the new Member for Oxley's maiden speech:

> We now have a situation where a type of reverse racism is applied to mainstream Australians by those who promote political correctness and those who control the various taxpayer funded industries that flourish in our society servicing Aboriginals, multiculturalists and a host of other minority groups . . . Present governments are encouraging separatism in Australia . . . I am fed up with being told 'This is our land'. Well where the hell do I go? I was born here and so were my parents and children . . .

Her thin emotional voice then said the words which reverberated around Australia:

> I and most Australians want our immigration policy radically reviewed and that of multiculturalism abolished. I believe we are in danger of being swamped by Asians. Between 1984 and 1995, 40 per cent of all migrants coming into this country were of Asian origin. They have their own culture and religion, form ghettoes and do not assimilate . . . A truly multicultural society can never be strong or united.

Shortly after she finished speaking, the switchboard at Parliament House lit up with calls, largely congratulatory. In the succeeding days, especially after an appearance on the Nine Network's *The Midday Show*, an outpouring of support emerged across Australia.

For others, Hanson evoked disbelief and contempt, and some attempted to frame the response to Hanson as largely media-generated sensationalism. When the genuine and popular resonance of her remarks became apparent, her opponents began to mobilise a wave of opposition. Both Right and Left joined forces to damn Hanson, and this was symbolised by the Joint Parliamentary

Statement of October 1996. The banner around which they coalesced was a defence of cultural diversity. The statement was a reaffirmation of 'the commitment to maintain Australia as a culturally diverse, tolerant and open society, united by an overriding commitment to our nation and its democratic institutions and values'. It was an important stance in repelling raw intolerance. But it masked radical changes in the outlooks of Right and Left in the preceding 30 years.

Right, Left and multiculturalism

One of the themes of this book is that trying to understand politics through a traditional Right-to-Left spectrum is increasingly misleading. What is meant by Right and Left has undergone a radical shift. For example, today it is the ideas of the cultural Left which are founded on cultural identity, and which champion diversity as a basis for politics. On the other hand, the dominant neo-liberal Right trumpets a world of globalised commodities purchased in an anonymous market by peoples whose cultural identity is giving away to a universal consumer identity.

This is a reversal of the traditional philosophical positions of Right and Left, which today occupy positions opposite to those of their historical forebears. The traditional Left's theoretical and practical adherence to social justice, equality and socialism in various forms was based on a philosophical universalism. It saw all people as equal without significant difference. The Left's world view was based on the universality of labour rather than on the value of diversity of ethnic minorities, women, gays, and so on. American leftist Todd Gitlin notes this reversal, and argues that the traditional Left believed that 'the overwhelming majority of human beings were united by their participation in labor. That was their "identity". But unlike the race, gender, sexual and other birthright identities of today, this membership was ecumenical. Open to anyone who migrated, or fell, into the proletariat.'[5]

It was *within* this universalistic world view that the traditional socialist Left once championed the equality and rights of ethnic minorities and women. Part of this world view stemmed from the rational ideals of the Enlightenment, while another part sprang from Marxism's opposition to imperialism and colonialism. For example, in Australia it was the traditional Left, together with a number of Christians, who were the practical champions of Indigenous people from the 1930s onwards. Overseas, it was the Left which welcomed and often led the anti-colonial revolts—driven by nationalism—in Africa and Asia from the 1950s to the 1970s.

While the old Left supported forms of nationalism and minority rights, it did not adequately comprehend that all too often what lay beneath nationalism was ethnocentrism. For a long time, the labour movement and the Left were blind to ethnic identity as central to the human experience. Apart from seeing the mobilisation of ethnicity and nationalism as useful tools to fight colonialism, the traditional Left regarded it as a diversion from the 'real' struggle against capitalism. Indeed, colonial rulers were skilled at using ethnic differences in a divide-and-rule strategy. (The British used Indian and Chinese minorities in their colonies in Southeast Asia and the Pacific.) Ethnicity was not only difficult to 'fit' into a socialist analysis which insisted that class was the 'real' social division of importance, but it was also a weapon of the enemy. (The early Australian labour movement, which demanded a 'white' Australia, mostly did so on the basis of a threat to working conditions rather than acknowledging its own ethnocentrism.)

By contrast, it was the classical Right which was fundamentally founded on *ethnos*, and believed in the differences and particularism of race and nation. The deep foundations of the Right of Europe (as we saw in Chapter 4) lay in the pillars of the nation: the church; the mandarins of the state and the law; the landed aristocracy; the military officer caste; the monarchy; and, above all, the propertied middle class which both symbolically and actually owned a large chunk of the nation. The classical conservative Right was an 'ethnic Right', with its reflex posture being xenophobic nationalism and suspicion of other nations. While this outlook was modified in countries like Australia and the United States, which lacked the local traditions that gave rise to it, it remained an important strand within the broad Right of those countries.

This classical conservative component of the Right tended not to believe in such abstractions as the universal rights of man. An intellectual precursor of the Right was French aristocrat Joseph de Maistre. In the wake of the French Revolution and its ringing declaration about the 'Rights of Man', de Maistre argued: 'In the course of my life I have seen Frenchmen, Italians, Russians. I even know, thanks to Montesquieu, that one can be a Persian: but *Man*, I declare, I have never met in my life; if he exists he is unknown to me.' In other words, humans as some abstract entity or essence do not exist outside their culture. They are entirely, as some say today, 'culturally constructed', and this was classically defined in mystical terms such as 'blood'.

By the 1990s, however, this Right–Left spectrum had swung on its axis. The Left was the first to change. Young intellectual leftists of the 1970s, faced with the inadequacy of socialism to explain society, made the 'cultural turn' by rightly acknowledging cultural identity as central to human experience and rightly accusing the old Left of being so utterly in love with Enlightenment rationality and the capital–labour contradiction that it failed to recognise this and other significant dimensions of life, politics and social change.

But this recognition came at a price. The new cultural Left combined its insights with a philosophical opposition to universalism, and made a fetish of cultural identity. It celebrated the variety of cultures, tended to romanticise such feelings, and saw them as laudably 'oppositional' to the dominant culture. The consequence of this has been a deep alienation of the cultural Left from the mainstream culture—not surprisingly, since this is seen to be the oppressive norm—and the cultivation of marginality. In turn, this has meant that much of the cultural Left not only finds it hard to communicate with the bulk of people of Anglo-Celtic-origin in Australia, but sees no role for such people in shaping the kind of cultural transformation it would like to see occur. The role of the Anglo-Celtic majority is simply to smile, step aside and be passive. The main message to this group is: you must celebrate *other people's* cultures. In the 1980s and 1990s, the cultural Left often promoted well-intended government programs favouring cultural diversity, which contributed to the populist, anti-government revolt against what it calls 'multiculturalism'.

This loss of the universalist component of the Left has meant that the cultural Left often finds it hard to talk about politics in terms of an overall vision, a national interest or a common good. It has little to say to society as a whole, but in its own fragmentation addresses a series of separate constituencies. Yet it is on the broad, national field that cultural changes are played out. The cultural Left positions itself on the sidelines and is then frustrated by its inability to change society as a whole.

By contrast, from the 1990s onwards, the intellectual Right in the Liberal Party increasingly began to articulate its politics in terms of a *culturally defined* common good and national identity of Australianness. This meant that John Howard and the Liberal Party talked about egalitarianism and the 'battlers'—which is a bold form of cultural politics, since it is code for making an ethnic appeal to the Anglo-Celtic Australians. (All the while, their economic policies continue to destroy the institutional bases of the egalitarianism of 'old Australia'.)

This appeal to a cultural identity neatly turns the tables on the old Left.[6] In the 1950s, left-wing intellectuals such as historian Russel Ward began to construct a vital definition of Australian national identity. In an Anglophile society, they insisted that Australians should be proud, not ashamed, of their convict origins and of Australia's pastoral working-class pioneers. They argued that the convicts, shearers and drovers embodied a spirit of rebellion and egalitarianism. Thus it was the Left which associated the common man, the battlers and mateship with the 'true spirit' of Australia. Though it had never heard of Antonio Gramsci and his concept of hegemony—that the Left advanced through its moral and intellectual leadership in a battle of ideas—this part of the old Left practised hegemonic cultural politics and practised it so well that it helped define a national identity of 'battlers' in spite of being defeated in other contests.

John Howard, that master of cultural politics, consciously cultivates this very ethos to win the allegiance of part of the Labor Party's base. One of the strengths of Labor's former leader Mark Latham was to recognise this, and to skilfully try to recapture this allegiance by a more nationalist foreign policy and by framing his policies as an appeal to ordinary Australians.

One of the events that grabbed at my heart during the Hanson upsurge in 1998 was a news report that, such was her popularity among coalminers in the Hunter Valley, their trade union, the CFMEU, was asking (or rather begging) its members to give Labor their second preference votes. To anyone acquainted with the struggle of coal miners and their role in the working class, this was tragic—although not entirely unexpected. The bitter paradox today is that the once progressive notion of an Australian identity rooted in equality and mateship is now most regularly articulated by John Howard and, in a cruder way before him, by Pauline Hanson.

The clearest victim of this was the Australian Labor Party. After the 2001 national election and the refugee crisis, the Coalition drove a wedge into Labor's heartland, splitting off part of its culturally conservative social base. Wedge politics succeeds in this situation because Labor is now a coalition of social forces rather than being largely a workers' party. Its simple and unifying ideas of class and equality have lost the power to inspire because they no longer correspond to reality, nor to the felt needs of what was once called the working class.

Labor's vulnerability to wedge politics is partly due to its own response to the new social movements. In effect, it has tried to crudely stitch together a coalition of social groups around a core of unionised workers. The result has been 'interest group' tribalism—a patchwork coalition that is an alliance of convenience, not one based on genuine common beliefs and an intellectual framework. Each group simply relies on advancing its own interests. The over-arching vision of Australia or of a national interest is thin, and this is one reason why wedge politics succeeds. The best example of this is the clash between Labor supporters over the future of forestry, with 'greenies' and loggers bitterly opposed. Rather than trying to develop a common vision over the long term, this clash is usually resolved by quick pre-election deals.

Without some kind of progressive national identity and unifying sense of the common good, the support base of Labor will continue to corrode and be drawn to the new Right. This is the *realpolitik* of the culture war which the Right is winning.

The identity of 'old Australia' has been eroding for many years, not only because of immigration, but because the nature of work itself has changed. To respond to such a change, it is necessary to actively project a new kind of culturally synthetic nationalism, and not merely to expect people to be happy with an abstract 'cultural diversity' which is seen to legitimise competing nationalisms within Australia.

A positive projection of a new hybridised Australian culture would tap a deeply rooted capacity for empathy among all people. Such a 'common humanity' is not a commonness of sameness, but of respect for others both because of and despite differences. Such respect is a two-way thing—it not only flows from the mainstream to the margins, but vice versa. In creatively projecting a hybridised new Australia, it is legitimate to expect newcomers and their children to absorb and accept existing cultural values, as well as expecting 'old Australians' to change and to accept a greater degree of cultural pluralism. In fact, this development of a new 'common core' is happening in a rough and ready way, regardless of the hand wringing of the cultural warriors of the Right and the diversity dogmatists of the Left. This emerging hybrid Australia will be 'multicultural'—but of a very particular kind, as we shall see.

Hodgepodge versus mosaic multiculturalism

What do most people mean by multiculturalism? How do these meanings differ from official definitions and policies? How many different kinds of multiculturalism are there? Before proceeding, let's examine what positive motives are behind these concepts. What's positive is a deep desire to oppose racism. Support for multiculturalism expresses a desire for a world in which people from different cultural backgrounds will respect each other, and in which the inevitable disagreements within any society do not lead to violence based on ethnic or cultural difference. It also represents a rejoicing in diversity and variety. It can represent a rejection of being confined to the narrowness of one's own culture, and a desire to share aspects of cultures which are not one's own. Multiculturalism is also motivated by a desire for equality—expressed as an equality between groups.

On a more abstract level, some people support multiculturalism because they rightly see the limitations of formal civil equality when discrimination based on cultural groups exists. They argue that identical formal treatment can sometimes mean very unequal treatment in practice. These feelings and aspirations are very positive, but the concept of multiculturalism which is used to articulate them has problems, some of which undercut these very aspirations and ideals.

One of the main problems is that multiculturalism is a rather fuzzy concept. It is not clear what intellectual roots it has or what its moral content is. It appears to be a repackaged form of old-fashioned liberalism and pluralism—albeit one which extends those concepts. More practically, it is not explicit what ultimate social arrangements it favours. What would a thoroughly multicultural society look like? Two academics, Christian Joppke and Steven Lukes, point out that multiculturalism is easily capable of a spectrum of meanings.[7] They range from what they call 'hodgepodge multiculturalism' to 'mosaic multiculturalism'.

'Hodgepodge' multiculturalism is a celebration of the mixing of cultures in which people and cultural practices begin to blend, and in which ultimately the boundaries blur and new syntheses emerge. This hybridisation threatens some and is celebrated by others. One of the latter is the writer Salman Rushdie, whose life was threatened and who had to live in hiding for many years for supposedly 'offending a culture' in his book *The Satanic Verses*. The other version of multiculturalism is one which resembles a celebration of separatism. Instead of blending and hybridisation, there is a mosaic—a richly patterned society, but one in which each tile of the mosaic is a sharply defined and self-contained cultural group. It advocates virtually no shared values other than absolute respect for difference.

From a distance, 'hodgepodge' and 'mosaic' may look the same, but there is a world of difference, to coin a phrase.

Before delving deeper into the implications of this, one crucial consequence must be noted which is not apparent at first, but which deeply affects how multiculturalism is defined in both local and national politics. 'Hodgepodge' multiculturalism has no natural political base to mobilise and fight for it. In contrast, 'mosaic' multiculturalism has an immediate base of ethnic groups, each of whom will mobilise and fight for its group rights under the banner of the larger cause: multiculturalism. No political leader that I am aware of has ever publicly championed hybridising multiculturalism and the creation of a new hybrid Australian national identity. But hundreds of minor political leaders have traded on the mobilisation of group loyalty of ethnic minorities in return for favours. Ethnic branch-stacking in the ALP is the most notorious and corrupt example of a practice used by all parties. In turn, such practices strengthen the 'mosaic' version of multiculturalism.

Mosaic multiculturalism has big problems. The most obvious of these is that it encourages what we could call 'group thinking'. Instead of treating individuals as having individual characteristics, we see individuals as representatives of categories or cultures. This is understandable at one level. Ethnic minorities can suffer discrimination as a group and members of that group usually share some common interests. But building a politics based on 'group thinking' can be a dangerous practice. This is because 'group thinking' is not so far removed from the stereotypes in which generalised judgments are made about particular groups (Aborigines are lazy, Jews are greedy, the English are snobs, Asians are hard-working, etc.). Preserving the authenticity and integrity of a culture is not far removed from notions of racial purity.

Mosaic multiculturalism elevates the rights of the group over the rights of the individual within the group. In the case of women, this can be very oppressive, since those who define the interests of the group are often older and male. The (rare) practice of female genital mutilation is an issue on which authorities still tread carefully.[8] More common are a series of assumptions and expectations about women, marriage and family honour. Research evidence suggests that murder is more frequent among overseas-born couples as part of a pattern of domestic violence. The report which discovered this, *Shattered Dreams* by Patricia Easteal, documents many other indications which suggest a disproportionate amount of domestic violence among overseas-born couples.[9] Easteal is painfully cautious in revealing this fact because it might fuel racism. But the contrary is also true: tiptoeing around such issues also fuels opposition to multiculturalism, because it is seen to justify a double standard towards the local and overseas born.

Part of its fuzziness is that, in the way it is often publicly articulated, multiculturalism appears to be a concept without limits. If a little bit of diversity is good, why not a huge amount of it?

Multiculturalism is often articulated on the Left as an 'oppositional' concept, undermining the constraints of the dominant culture. Because of this, those espousing a multicultural stance rarely qualify or make conditional the application of the concept. If a group insists on a demand in the name of cultural diversity or respect, who can say whether the limits of acceptable diversity have been reached, and on what basis? Multiculturalism therefore poses, but does not answer, the highly charged question about how to resolve competing and antagonistic cultural values, particularly in relation to families, marriage and the treatment of women and children. In practice, such questions are usually settled by reference to Australian law, which favours individual over group rights. But the *public* debate over the limits of cultural diversity is not 'settled' so easily. The pressure to legitimise group rights over the rights of individual women and children is one little-recognised source of hostility to multiculturalism.

Mosaic multiculturalism also has the problem that emphasising the rights and particularities of groups usually comes at the expense of emphasising what all groups share, whether that is expressed in terms of the national interest, or social cohesion and trust. One high profile supporter of multiculturalism who recognised this some time ago was the West Australian academic Laksiri Jayasuriya. He argued for a 'paradigm shift' from what he called 'cultural pluralism to democratic pluralism'.[10] He argued that the official recognition of cultural diversity in the early 1970s rested on a 'largely hidden belief in eventual integration'. One of the critical problems for this approach 'has been to demarcate with any degree of consensus the precise limits of cultural pluralism in relation to policy initiatives such as ethnic media, schools and services'. That is, the idea was fuzzy. Nevertheless, the policy worked especially in catering to the needs of first-generation migrants. But other research, he has argued, showed that in the second and third generations, inter-ethnic marriage meant that ethnic boundaries were becoming more fluid and a 'mixed' cultural society was developing, rather than a multi-cultural one. In this situation, a more symbolic ethnic identity developed which involved 'a loose nostalgia for one's historic origins but no compelling sense of identification or group loyalty'.[11]

A similar notion is expressed by the secretary of the British Fabian Society, Sunder Katwala, in an article titled 'Why I'm Proud to be a Mongrel Brit'. The son of an Indian father and Irish mother, he argues that:

> . . . multiculturalism has not valued integration enough. Retreating to ethnic enclaves—demanding our own share of recognition and resources as Gujeratis, Somalis, Bangladeshis and so on—is a dead end. We need a shared society. Integration is a two-way street. We should demand allegiance and loyalty from citizens—and tackle the racism in employment which prevents the promise of integration from being kept.[12]

Both these writers anticipate the need to promote an evolving, hybrid-ised cultural identity which can accommodate both cultural blending and the persistence of diverse cultures, but which should occur within the framework of the values of an evolving common culture.

In the absence of such a set of shared values, multiculturalism and cultural diversity are invoked by all sides as a national self-definition. They form part of the language of official statements about Australia. They are also animating forces behind a great deal of public policy. They are translated into day-to-day decisions which affect the lives of many people. The fuzziness and the 'group thinking' which allow multiculturalism to be interpreted as unlimited diversity can and did become the object of intense dislike by a section of the population by the late 1990s. In other words, when considering events such as the rise of One Nation, it is not good enough to blame solely an ill-defined 'racism' of Anglo-Celts. Part of the problem also lies with a well-intentioned but fuzzy concept. Taking seriously the views of multiculturalism's critics is an important first step to preserving the positive values embedded in the idea.

The post-Hanson debate

In 1997, in the heat of the upsurge created by Pauline Hanson and the One Nation Party, the Howard government commissioned the National Multicultural Advisory Council to undertake a report 'aimed at ensuring that cultural diversity is a unifying force for Australia'. It was also asked whether the word 'multiculturalism' should be continued as an official description for certain government policies. Over the two years during which the council was deliberating, Howard never used the word 'multiculturalism' in public. Howard had been inclined to look backwards for some time. In 1992 he had written to someone from his electorate: 'My own view on this issue is that Australia made an error in abandoning its former policy of encouraging assimilation and integration in favour of multiculturalism.' When he became prime minister in 1996, he abolished the Office of Multicultural Affairs and the Bureau of Immigration, Multiculturalism and Population Research.

The national inquiry spanned the high water mark of Hansonism. When it reported, in April 1999, the inquiry found that, while few people disagreed with 'multicultural' as a neutral description of the actual diversity of cultures in Australia, many had a problem with 'multiculturalism' as a public policy directed towards accommodating and promoting this diversity.

The council's report, *Australian Multiculturalism for a New Century*, described the attitudes of people which were critical of multiculturalism. They believed, among other things, that 'multiculturalism applies only to migrants from a non-English-speaking background and seems to deny Australian culture'. The report guardedly acknowledged that past practices had tended to focus on rights rather than obligations, but solved this by a simple assertion that this imbalance would now change, in accordance with the document's new emphasis on inclusiveness and obligation.

But the council rejected the idea that changing the term 'multiculturalism' would have any good effect. Those who opposed multiculturalism would probably oppose it under a different name, it said. In any case, argued the council, most people supported multiculturalism. This was based on an AGB McNair survey in June 1996 (before the snowball of Hansonism really got rolling) which showed that 61 per cent agreed with multiculturalism—which McNair defined in an ambiguous way as 'encouraging migrants to become Australians without having to give up their own culture'. The council also wanted to *correct the misconception* that multiculturalism is concerned mainly with immigration and minority ethnic communities' [my emphasis].

In the face of hostility to multiculturalism, the council recommended two particular changes. One was that, rather than speaking about multiculturalism, the term 'Australian multiculturalism' should now be used. The second was a broadening of the scope of the multicultural buzz word 'inclusiveness'. Previously, this word had been intended as an injunction to Anglo-Celts to be inclusive by having regard to non-Anglo cultures. Now 'inclusive' was to mean that multiculturalism would henceforth 'include' the Anglo-Celtic culture.

Inclusiveness should now be 'a major focus' of multiculturalism. 'It should emphasise the things that unite us as people—our common membership of the Australian community; our shared desire for social harmony; the benefits of diversity; our evolving national character and identity.' Just what the latter might be, the report does not spell out.

The critics of multiculturalism

Though it didn't answer them adequately, the inquiry succinctly summed up its critics' views. I'd like to examine them more closely. According to the report, such people believe that multiculturalism applies only to migrants from a non-English-speaking background and seems to deny Australian culture. A number criticised what they perceived to be an over-emphasis on the rights of particular groups without stressing their corresponding obligations. A few went so far as to say that multiculturalism influenced the scale of the immigration program and the ethnic origins of migrants and was threatening community harmony in Australia. There was also a perception that certain people were able to escape criticism about their views or behaviour because of their ethnicity or background.[13]

That seems to me to be a good summary of the kind of feelings that are currently fairly widespread and which also provided fertile ground for the Hanson cause. The description is perhaps expressed in over-polite language and, apart from the claim about a conspiracy to manipulate the immigration program, the concerns should be taken seriously, rather than summarily dismissed as 'racism'.

Yet, at first glance, a number of the claims are also obviously false or illogical. Multiculturalism can't apply 'only to migrants', since it necessarily involves the relationship between the dominant culture and migrant cultures. Similarly, the claim about the denial of Australian culture is contradicted by virtually, every single official statement about multiculturalism. All have emphasised that cultural diversity must occur within the framework of Australian law. For example, the 1989 *National Agenda for a Multicultural Australia* defines three limits, one of which is to 'accept the basic structures and principles of Australian society—the Constitution and rule of law, tolerance and equality, parliamentary democracy, freedom of speech and religion, English as the national language and equality of the sexes'.[14] Every official statement defining multiculturalism has strictly defined its limits. The report, *Australian Multiculturalism for a New Century* published in 1999, says explicitly that it is *not* an 'anything goes' concept since 'it is built on core societal values of mutual respect, tolerance and harmony, the rule of law and our democratic principles and institutions'.[15]

But fears about multiculturalism cannot be answered by quoting official definitions. The reason is that the official definition of multiculturalism is quite different from the way that the concept is deployed in public debate, including by its advocates. It parallels the council's belief that the problem is all about 'misperceptions'. This does not really come anywhere close to the essence of the hostility toward multiculturalism. Hostility or incomprehension towards multiculturalism is about feelings, not about rationality. An infinite number of reassurances about the framework of Australian law will not reassure people if the feeling they experience is one of loss or siege. And feelings, as difficult as they are to pin down, do not come from nowhere. Let's examine the possible sources of some of these feelings.

'Denying Australian culture'

In the wake of the rise of One Nation, many people simply condemned Pauline Hanson and her supporters as mere racists. Others, however, tried to understand the phenomenon more deeply. One was anthropologist and writer Ghassan Hage, who argues that it is more useful to see the basis for Hanson's support as a form of nationalism (within which racist thinking is deployed), rather than simply expressing a rather abstract notion of 'racism'. On the basis of extensive research and interviews with 'old Australians' who express 'racist' views, Hage shows that much of it is related to concepts such as 'home' and territoriality; it is a 'discourse of undesirability, not of inferiority', he says, as well as a presumption of 'managerial capacity over this national space'.[16] The use of nationalism as a concept is also helpful in overcoming some of the highly moralistic terms of debate when racism is the only guiding concept. (When analysing Hanson, Hage confesses to oscillating between 'deep sympathy and absolute detestation'.)[17]

It also makes sense in other ways. Hage argues that, while academics and politicians talk about the *gains* of multiculturalism, no one talks about the *losses*. As a result of this omission, the prevailing discourse of multiculturalism 'leaves those White people who experience the loss with no mainstream political language with which to express it'.[18] And these losses are real, in the sense that Australia actually is becoming more culturally diverse and that a number of taken-for-granted Anglo-Celtic cultural assumptions are no longer possible or realistic.

Hage argues that there is a need for 'rethinking a new cultural politics capable of recognising and dealing realistically with the sense of cultural loss from which neo-fascism is being fed'. And, although much of his analysis is imbued with rather convoluted psychoanalytic theory, Hage correctly argues that 'the answer lies in the direction of a deeper commitment to a more far-reaching multiculturalism'. Dealing with this sense of loss rather than merely demonising those who express it seems to me to be the beginning of a better strategy to succeed in the culture war.

A more controversial (and also psychoanalytic) interpretation of cultural change comes from Miriam Dixson, author of *The Imaginary Australian*.[19] She argues that many social analysts have under-estimated the attachment to the nation by its inhabitants in countries like Australia and that, given that the nation had an Anglo-Celtic 'core culture', many Anglo-Celtic Australians are mourning its loss. But, she says, this is complicated by intellectuals and theorists whose scathing critique of Anglo-Celtic Australia forbids such mourning—why should one mourn for an unworthy object, she asks rhetorically: 'In being exhorted to welcome the new, its necessities and benefits, they were, and are, not given space to mourn the old and its loss . . . It is a truism that failure to mourn the past sabotages the future.' [20]

In strategic terms, Dixson favours the evolution of a new identity, but while this evolves, the existing Anglo-Celtic 'core culture' must continue to play a role in holding society together.

Such an idea is heretical, partly because progressive intellectuals are preoccupied with exploring cultural diversity and few ever pause to think about social cohesion—and certainly not in terms of a positive role for 'Anglo-Celtic culture'. In a phrase made pungent by the experience of Hansonism, she argues that, because of such attitudes: 'By and large we have, in effect, left populists in charge of the cohesion issue.'[21] Figures like Pauline Hanson clearly respond to deep-seated changes and fears in the population at large. The Left does itself no favours by ignoring the positives in the culture of 'old Australia' and seeing the Hanson phenomenon solely in terms of its racist dimension.

Dixson is unapologetically positive about aspects of the inherited Anglo-Celtic political culture:

> We have inherited many of the best aspects of British and Continental European traditions. This inheritance is reflected in workable government, sophisticated science, reliable legal and industrial frameworks; reflected, too in an ethos and institutional structure that, comparatively speaking, still retains a remarkable (if fast shrinking) degree of respect for ordinary people.
>
> It's reflected in the fact that we still possess an unusual degree of social cohesiveness. Representative institutions, division of powers, free speech and press, women's rights, the egalitarian thrust in society and family—these are all part of Australia's Western and Enlightenment heritage, even though their enactment in everyday life falls well short of the ideals informing them. The very existence of such ideals is reason for defending and extending them in the process of rigorous critique, not for off-hand scorn.[22]

'Off-hand scorn'—the phrase well captures the stance of some passionate, radical opponents of racism who see no value at all in British or European democratic traditions. Her warning that we must not leave right-wing populists in charge of the cohesion issue echoes a comment by the left-wing British musician Billy Bragg. In the United

Kingdom, people of various political persuasions—often on the Right—urge the celebration of St George's Day, a day for the celebration of Englishness. Others are horrified by the idea of such a celebration because it glorifies an oppressive mainstream. But Bragg disagrees: 'I do worry that reticence about St George's Day is symptomatic of a refusal by the Left to engage with notions of Englishness. This creates a vacuum, allowing the reactionary Right to define who is and is not English.'[23] Similarly, in Australia the cultural Left has declined to celebrate aspects of the mainstream Anglo-Australian tradition. Yet a vital aspect of the 'culture war' is to articulate a values-based agenda of what constitutes an 'Australian way'.

The author of a recent history of multiculturalism, Mark Lopez, acknowledges that new attempts to define a multicultural political agenda are starting to grapple with Australia's total heritage, 'which included the heritages from Great Britain and Ireland, perceived to have previously been neglected'.[24] But when Dixson made a similar point, it brought the usual debate-stopping accusation of racism. Queensland cultural studies academic John Frow simply dismissed her book as 'a call for a return to White Australia', even though she explicitly talks of the creation of a new consensual culture based on integration of Anglo and non-Anglo cultures.[25]

In very different ways, Dixson and Hage are asking about the role of the majority or dominant culture at a time when cultural diversity is a fact and a new identity is slowly evolving. Should members of the dominant culture go about their business as if nothing is happening? Stand on the sidelines and cheer? Undergo self-criticism and re-education? Hage warns that some Anglo supporters of multiculturalism perceive the more insular white working-class and middle-class people as 'unable, by definition, to appreciate and value otherness, let alone govern it. Indeed deprived of the capacity of appreciating other ethnic cultures, and with Anglo culture decreed as uninteresting and provincial by the multicultural order, those possessors of Anglo-ness are left without even a stall at the multicultural fair'.[26]

While Dixson and Hage talk about Anglo loss, the anonymous voices of populist critics tell a government inquiry about their feelings of 'denial' of Australian culture. They are clearly referring to the same thing. Acknowledging cultural diversity does indeed mean a loss, and perhaps even a 'denial'. And, rather than a flat-footed defence of a fuzzy 'multiculturalism', this political reality must be dealt with in order to avoid further and even more dangerous Hanson outbreaks—let alone to make progress toward the ideals buried within 'multiculturalism'.

Universalism and cultural relativism

The debate around multiculturalism has deeper roots than simply government policies and its critics in the Australian polity. Major philosophical issues are involved, and to these I now turn. One of the reasons Dixson's emphasis on the positive side of Anglo-Celtic culture is regarded as heretical is that intellectuals from the cultural Left have scorned what are often called Enlightenment values (as we saw in Chapter 4). In part, this scorn has its roots in Marxism's rejection of liberalism. A great deal of Marxist ink was spilled showing, for instance, that the formal, legal equality in Western nations is hollowed out by massive social inequalities of wealth. Such analyses entailed an important truth. Unfortunately, they also entailed a lofty dismissal of 'bourgeois rights' and the traditions of liberal democracy—a dismissal which, as we have seen, contributed to the phenomenon of Stalinism (see Chapter 5).

Other influential ideas emerged from the Left's support for anti-colonial struggles and wars of national liberation throughout the decades from the 1950s to the 1970s. Many came to believe that the basis for colonialism and racism lay in the universalist philosophies of Enlightenment Europe. These philosophies encouraged a view that the glories of Europe were what constituted a civilised society, and other societies should be judged against this measure. Western judgments of non-Western cultures were usually deeply flawed because of this Eurocentrism. This was accompanied by the view that there was no distinction between attributing differences in cultures to nature (as did Nazism and colonialism) and ascribing them to general developmental stages of knowledge, freedom and technologies. No society was therefore 'better' than another, or more 'advanced'.

This relativist approach was one method of explaining racism, but it achieved this by way of undermining another framework of thought which also opposed racism—that is, universalism and notions of a common humanity. Democracy and human rights were therefore not universal goods, but could be portrayed as just another ethnocentric set of values in danger of colonising the world as surely as the British, Dutch and Spanish navies. The popularity of relativist interpretations grew rapidly in the 1970s in the wake of the new social movements. As movements for women's and gay liberation blossomed, their opponents often denounced them by using pseudo-universal notions which decreed what was 'normal' and 'natural'.[27] That is, local prejudices masqueraded as universal truths. Rather than distinguishing the falseness of these universalist claims, the whole notion of universalism was denounced, and a 'politics of difference' emerged.

'Difference' became both a buzzword and, in a more elaborate form, a theoretical foundation. Universalist humanism, it was argued, necessarily produced oppressed 'others'—those who did not fit the assumed mould of universal humanity and were thus lesser beings. But the politics of relativism are a shaky basis for anyone who is genuinely opposed to injustice and wants progressive social change. Taken to its logical conclusion, relativism tends to lock all of us up in our own separate cultures. The strong cultural relativist position undermines the notion of human empathy or solidarity across cultures because it argues that you cannot apply the same standards to one culture as another. They are, as they say, 'incommensurable'. Not all relativistic thinking is so extreme, but some popular versions tend to discourage criticism of various actions because they are (supposedly) 'cultural practices'.

British psychologist and philosopher Kenan Malik is one of many thinkers who argues that the claim for respect and equal recognition of all cultures (and all practices justified by culture) is very poorly based. In fact, it is illogical if it is supposed to represent an opposite to universalism.

> The demand for equal recognition is, however, at odds with the claim that cultures are incommensurate. To treat different cultures with equal respect (indeed, to treat them with any kind of respect at all), we have to be able to compare one with the other. If values are incommensurate, such comparisons are simply not possible. The principle of difference cannot provide any standards that oblige us to respect the 'difference' of others. At best, it invites our indifference to the fate of the 'other'. At worst, it licenses us to hate and abuse those who are different. Why, after all, should we not abuse and hate them? On what basis can they demand our respect or we demand theirs? It is very difficult to support respect for difference without appealing to some universalistic principles of equality or social justice.[28]

In part, the motivation for cultural relativism is a desire not to judge. We have all seen the enormous damage that has been done by those keen to judge and to impose their cultural and moral standards willy nilly on people from other cultures. Histories of missionaries, colonisers and military conquerors are replete with such examples. The latter might be called the 'extreme universalists', who see only one universal way—the right way, their way, and usually a Christian and European way. The answer is not to eschew cross-cultural judgment of all kinds, but rather to be cautious and careful about applying universal criteria and to have respect for other people. Malik then gets to the root of the problem:

The idea of the equality of cultures (as opposed to the equality of human beings) denies one of the critical features of human life and human history: our capacity for social, moral and technological progress. What distinguishes humans from other creatures is the capacity for innovation and transformation, for making ideas and artefacts that are not simply different but also often better, than those of a previous generation or another culture. It is no coincidence that the modern world has been shaped by the ideas and technologies that have emerged from the Renaissance and Enlightenment. The scientific method, democratic politics, the concept of universal values—these are palpably better concepts than those that existed previously. Not because Europeans are a superior people, but because many of the ideas and philosophies that came out of the European Renaissance and Enlightenment are superior.[29]

He adds pointedly that: 'To argue this today is, of course, to invite the charge of "Eurocentrism", or even racism.'

To respect a culture *as such* and make no judgment of it would entail, for example, opposition to satirical criticism of a religion— such as Rushdie's *The Satanic Verses*. There is no doubt that this book genuinely offended many Muslims, and may even be said to have offended that culture as whole (protests all over the world indicate that). Discussing Rushdie's case and the case of women subject to extreme cultural pressure and violence which is justified on cultural-religious grounds, writer and art critic Robert Hughes commented acerbically: 'Oppression is what we do in the West. What they do in the Middle East is "their culture". Such multicultural double standards rival the hypocrisy of Western "universalism" when its precepts said "all men" but it really meant all white men, and men only.'[30]

Universal values have a central place in opposing racism and in justifying the central moral idea embedded in multiculturalism— which is empathy and respect towards other human beings. But on what basis should we empathise with other human beings? In a more religious age, the answer would be couched in terms of all peoples being God's children. That is the meaning behind the Good Samaritan parable. Is there some basis in this secular age for a universalist outlook? I believe there is, but it is a basis which has been very unpopular with many people.

A common humanity?

Throughout this chapter, I have suggested that in opposing racism it may be better to begin by emphasising the similarities between peoples—the idea of a common humanity—rather than beginning with cultural differences and calling for all sides to respect these differences. This is not an argument opposed to valuing and celebrating cultural differences, but one about the best foundations on which to build. We need to cultivate, not simply respect, empathy across the divide of cultures. Empathy is valuable because it is a deeper commitment than mere respect, and involves a level of emotional identification with other people. Out of empathy, I believe, we are more likely to develop new, hybrid core values for our society.

As well, in several chapters of this book I discussed the idea of human nature and how it related to political philosophies. I'd now like to return to this discussion because it relates to the central concept behind the idea of a common humanity: what it means to be human. Most would agree that, at the very least, to be human means that people from diverse cultures share a common biological constitution as human beings. Acknowledging this scientific fact is important in dismissing pseudo-scientific ideas of supposedly superior and inferior races. As they say, there is one race: the human race.

Most would also agree that humanity's biological constitution is the result of a process of evolution. But, as well as evolved *physical*

characteristics, humans have other common qualities. Writer Robert
Wright points this out in his book, *The Moral Animal*:

> We take for granted such bedrock elements of life as gratitude,
> shame, remorse, pride, honour, retribution, empathy, love and
> so on—just as we take the air we breathe, the tendency of
> dropped objects to fall, and other standard features of living
> on this planet. But things didn't have to be this way. We could
> live in a planet where social life featured none of the above.
> We could live on a planet where some ethnic groups felt some
> of the above and others felt others. But we don't. The more
> closely Darwinian anthropologists look at the world's peoples,
> the more they are struck by the dense and intricate web of human
> nature by which we are all bound.[31]

A growing scientific literature exists which gives good grounds
for thinking that some form of human nature exists.[32] This research
has not settled the question, however, and the idea remains
controversial. Many believe that any acknowledgment of a human
nature implies acceptance of a rigid set of qualities which must
exist in all humans in all times. But the kind of human nature which
those who have researched it talk about is rather a set of innate
tendencies whose expression is tempered by historical and cultural,
as well as individual, circumstance. Critics, however, see only the
changing circumstances reflecting the dominance of what might be
called the 'social science world view', which looks only for social
and cultural reasons for the way we are.

Nevertheless, even among social scientists, there is widespread
agreement that humans are *social* creatures, meaning that they prefer
to live in groups and are not naturally solitary. It is here that we
return to the main preoccupation of the chapter. These social
groups are, specifically, families and local communities. For much
of human history, these communities often consisted of a number
of extended families which intermarried. Today, what we call ethnic
groups are very large groups of extended families, as the Harvard

psychologist Steven Pinker argues. Ultimately, these ethnic groups grow and sometimes become nations, who are bonded by a common feeling of identity and loyalty. Pinker believes, along with others, that there is a good deal of evidence to suggest that the human mind evolved over a million years in the context of survival in small clan groups, and that as a result ethnocentrism is a human universal.[33] One aspect of this ethnic identification seems to be a preparedness to engage in conflict with other groups, and the long history of interethnic conflict from ancient to modern times—seen most recently after the collapse of the Soviet Union—seems to bear this out. (In Australia, this occurred between the conquering tribes of 1788 and the Indigenous people.)

Acknowledging that a disposition to ethnic identification is one element of a human nature has implications for political visions and philosophies. Basically, it means that we must accept limits on such ideas and visions. I have already argued that a fatal weakness of reforming visionaries (especially Marxists) was the misconception that humans are completely malleable and that traits such as self-interest can disappear with the 'right' kind of social structure. For similar reasons, we cannot imagine that ethnic identification will one day disappear. Social conditions will greatly shape its intensity and its expression, but it will remain in some form.

This raises a problem. Surely if we acknowledge that ethnic identification is a human universal, we are condemning as hopelessly impractical the idea that we can appeal to a common humanity as a basis for opposing racism? For instance, an Australian theorist of multi-culturalism, Stephen Castles, summarily dismisses theories of human nature.[34] He caricatures theories which indicate that all humans show a tendency to prefer kin and to develop group loyalty. He then transforms this position into the most extreme interpretation that racism is 'in our genes', and hence ineradicable and not tempered by other tendencies. If this is true, he concludes, 'then the only way to prevent it is to keep the "tribes" apart. This is not a practicable nor desirable strategy in an increasingly integrated world'.

A different view is taken by another theorist of multiculturalism, Ien Ang. She argues that: 'The main long-term goal of anti-racist educational programs should be the gradual development of a general culture of what I want to call interracial trust. It may be the case that some fundamental form of racism—associated with ethnocentrism and intolerance against those who are different—is part and parcel of human nature: it is deeply embedded in the very culture of human society.'[35] It is likely that she is right. It is impossible to find a society which is not ethnocentric to some degree, but it is quite possible to find societies that display a wide variety of behaviours towards people of other ethnicities, from a murderous suspicion to a peaceful trust or even better. And societies can display both qualities at different stages in their history.

Australian philosopher Peter Singer, in his book *A Darwinian Left*, agrees that ethnic identification is a human universal, although societies differ greatly in their degree of tolerance or their degree of racism. 'Racism can be learned and unlearned, but racist demagogues hold their torches over highly flammable material', Singer argues.

But if a disposition to ethnic identification seems to be innate, so are other dispositions and capacities which moderate such feelings. Most importantly, there is accumulating evidence that altruism or caring for others is biologically based.[36] Perhaps not surprisingly, like ethnic identification, these capacities are also believed to be founded in humans' oldest social structure: families. Family members will routinely make sacrifices for each other to a degree that they will not repeat for non-family members.

That is to say that empathy and compassion begin as a local phenomenon. American philosopher Martha Nussbaum made this point when reflecting on the events of September 11, 2001. She pointed out that, in the days and weeks afterwards, 'the world has come to a stop—in a way it never has for Americans, when disaster befalls human beings in other places. The genocide in Rwanda didn't even work up enough emotion in us to prompt humanitarian intervention'.[37] Nussbaum's point was about the nature of compassion (which she argues is an emotion that is probably rooted in our biological heritage). Humans experience compassion most strongly when it affects people like themselves, and they often fail to experience it when tragedy is culturally distant. Such tendencies 'are likely to be built into the nature of compassion as it develops in childhood and then adulthood: we form intense attachments to the local first and only gradually learn to have compassion for people who are outside our own immediate circle'. Hence the tendency for compassion to stop at national borders: 'Most of us are brought up to believe that all human beings have equal worth. At least the world's major religions and secular philosophies tell us so. But our emotions don't believe it.'

But Nussbaum's point is that compassion also has a reasoned element and can be educated. Compassion can move outwards from its local, family base. When it does, it begins to assume the characteristics of altruism, of empathy with others just because they are human.

This also happens to have been the view of the discoverer of evolution, Charles Darwin, whose words I quoted at the start of this chapter. In the language of his time he foresaw a growing tendency for compassion to expand outwards, building on a foundation of local empathy. If the people within one nation can sympathise with the other, anonymous, members of the nation, only an 'artificial barrier' is preventing the expansion of those sympathies to the people of all nations and races. This 'artificial barrier' has proved much harder to surmount than Darwin thought, although advances have been achieved by different nations and peoples since his time. Perhaps the best-known formal expression of this is the Universal Declaration of Human Rights.

The attempt to surmount this barrier by the policy of multi-culturalism was important in its day, whatever flaws it had. In order to preserve the best values which it represented, I believe it is necessary to recognise its weaknesses and fashion new ideas embodying its strengths. In terms of fighting a culture war, it means we must project a vision about what constitutes national identity and 'Australian values', rather than denouncing such ideas and focusing on smaller cultural and identity groups. A progressive definition of national identity and values would necessarily be a synthesis of cultural values. We need a synthesis because the alternative is some version of monocultural assimilation that is neither desirable nor possible. Such a new synthesis would inevitably draw heavily on valuable things in the existing British-originated national culture, but it would also draw traditions and values from other cultures. It would involve a set of core values and practices to which loyalty was expected, but in other areas a diversity of values would exist. To demand loyalty and to work towards social cohesion is a valuable and necessary thing when a society's core values are just and fair. Such a synthesis would be more than the formal requirements of citizenship, since citizenship alone, I believe, is too bloodless a concept. It would resemble the hybrid Australian identity which is actually slowly developing of its own accord, and it would be an identity of which we could be proud. It would be inclusive in the fullest sense of the term because it would be based on the belief that we are all part of a common humanity, all in the same boat.

9

A new humanism

Our generation is without a political philosophy relevant to our time and circumstances. We have a theory of globalization but, baldly stated, it is cold and technical . . . We need an idea of how our society will develop and how, in a more global society, people will relate to each other. We need a philosophical framework.[1]

Malcolm Fraser

Conservative thought may well not be alone in suffering obsolescence and redundancy at this juncture in history, since it is plausible that both socialist thought and the standard forms of liberalism face a similar superannuation. In each of these traditions of thought there are insights that can and should be salvaged from the wreckage.[2]

John Gray

The death of the old ideas of Right and Left may be mourned, but it offers space and hope because it makes way for new ideas. In the last twenty years, advanced industrial countries have seen the disintegration of the intellectual foundations of both the old Right and the old Left. The end of the Cold War, the rise of neo-liberalism, the decline of social liberalism on the Right, the collapse of socialism on the Left—these represent the end of an historic era and clear the ground for new possibilities. In spite of a nostalgia for an old world of certainty, we can now be optimistic about the opportunities for weaving novel and unorthodox ideas together in new ways.

The Right has already undergone its own transformation, and the result has been the combination of militant economic liberalism with a new kind of cultural politics based on values. This has given its political agenda an ascendancy over the disparate movements and ideas of the Left. In response, the Left must undergo its own renewal. As I have outlined in previous chapters, this involves reconfiguring some ideas of the Left and discarding others. Until this occurs it is hard to see how the decline in progressive politics can be stopped.

In this final chapter, I want to broadly sketch the framework of ideas and values which could form the basis of a positive vision beyond Right and Left. None of this pretends to be the last word on the latter topic—the ideas in this chapter are very much 'first words' on issues which need further debate.

The use of ideas

Ideas and philosophies evolve to address problems. For this reason, in the long term quite abstract ideas can have very practical consequences. Liberalism evolved as a response to European religious conflict and intolerance of the seventeenth and eighteenth centuries. Socialism evolved to address the dislocation, inequality and deprivation which accompanied industrialising capitalism. Conservatism responded to the social upheavals initiated by liberalism and socialism by defending the social order. In our own time, the collapse of the ideas of Right and Left marks a historic turning point because it signals that the old ideas are less and less capable of responding to the emerging problems. This does not mean that all the old ideas of Right and Left should be wholly discarded. In searching for a new vision beyond Right and Left, we should first identify what was valuable in the old ideas.

So what can legitimately and usefully be retained from old philosophies of Right and Left?

Liberalism

Liberalism is the source of ideals which value the human capacity for autonomy of the individual and of self-expression. These ideals are articulated in terms of political equality and of political freedoms which underpin representative democracy. The rule of law, in which each person is equal before the law and faces the same set of laws, is another vital part of the liberal heritage. The principle that governments are obliged to follow the law and that their power must be separate from judicial powers must be part of any new political vision. This heritage of the Enlightenment, expressed in liberalism, retains its relevance not only because despotic and theocratic regimes still exist at the global level, but also because all governments are tempted to employ arbitrary coercion to achieve their goals. Of particular importance is the strand of liberalism which emphasises that the individual realises their capacity within a supportive community. The combination of the *public good* with individual liberty is the great strength of 'social liberalism'.

Although I am critical of extreme neo-liberalism, it serves no useful purpose to ignore the usefulness and dynamism of economic markets in many circumstances. As American feminist philosopher Martha Nussbaum argues, liberalism and its insights, when combined with humanist and feminist values, are vital for social justice.[3]

Socialism

Socialism embodied certain values and ideals which are essential to any new political vision. Over its 150-year history, socialism became a diverse and broad school of thought, encompassing not just radical and evolutionary wings, but also support for women's rights and for anti-colonial struggles. Its central belief is an ideal of collectivism and the common good, which today means that a strong sense of the public interest is vital to a good society. This is linked to another ideal: that of social equality (as distinct from political equality) and social solidarity. On the basis of these moral values, socialists—through the workers' movement—struggled for decent health-care, education, employment, income support and the other building blocks of a civilised way of life with which we are all familiar.

Central to socialism's core belief in the common good is its critique of the social and political power that comes from concentrated wealth. Historically, this led socialists to believe that all social evils stemmed from the private ownership of wealth, and that it was possible to create a society without private wealth, markets or self-interest. We now know that abolishing these things—even if it were possible—would not solve most social evils, but rather create new ones. Nevertheless, a valuable part of the socialist heritage is its preparedness to challenge commercial self-interest which places profit before the public interest. Private wealth has a long history of opposing progressive social reforms, particularly those which require a greater contribution from the wealthy. Contemporary social changes such as a better work/life balance, a sustainable economy and a less commercially driven public policy are strongly opposed by the corporate and business elite. A new vision should build a moral critique of greed and self-interest, and design policies to restrict the power of this elite. The New Capitalism, however, will not be supplanted by the New Socialism. We face a future composed of a choice of different kinds of capitalism, including those which have not yet evolved.

Conservatism

Conservative attitudes in a new context can make a useful contribution to a new political vision on several counts, some of which I have already mentioned in connection with ecological conservation. These arise because conservatism is philosophically sceptical about notions of never-ending progress based on reason alone. Radical experiments in genetic engineering, like adventurism in foreign policy, rightly disturb conservative instincts. Conservative attitudes value social cohesion and the common good, in contrast to economic libertarianism and the lack of security which it generates.

This regulatory aspect of conservatism, expressed in terms of social obligation and security, can be a valuable ally in protecting society from radical economic liberalism. Depending on how it is projected, a vision which wants to protect society and the environment from the endless expansion of the New Capitalism can mobilise conservative instincts and attitudes.

Conservatism also insists that plans for social reform take account of the limitations presented by human nature. As remarkable as human diversity and capacity are, they are not unlimited. Any new political vision which assumes we can create societies without conflict or without self-interest is doomed to fail. Attempts at perfection, in politics or religion, have proven disastrous.

I am not, however, suggesting that the mere blending of the existing positive qualities of liberalism, socialism and conservatism constitutes a positive vision. Additional elements are needed, and these emerge when we examine a series of contemporary problems associated with the New Capitalism.

The terrain of the New Capitalism

The New Capitalism is one way of describing the form of economy which is evolving in the most industrially advanced countries. It is dynamic, productive, innovative and, for many people—though not all—it provides a materially comfortable life. But this comes at an unsuitable cost.

If the old Capitalism was a simple system built on class and on economic inequality, the New Capitalism is far more complex. The price of its productivity can be calculated in the consequences on families and on social cohesion; on the global environment; and on the values and ethos with which society is imbued. Importantly, each of these areas reveals the vulnerability on the neo-liberal Right.

The New Capitalism is not a friend of the family, nor of the values which families embody at their best: caring, altruism and love. Such relations do not make any sense to a system whose logic insists that the truly valuable things are those that can be commodified—that is, bought and sold in a market. Capitalism, old and New, has been stripping the family of its functions for many years, putting a price on those functions and selling them back. This has been very much a two-edged sword. For example, meals prepared outside the family home and child care have been important benefits, but the problem is that there is no end in sight to this process of commodification of personal and family life. Left to the logic of New Capitalism, it is inexorable and unstoppable.

The New Capitalism induces families and communities to mimic its values. Thus parents outsource their needs and commodify care; they emotionally downsize, telling themselves they can get by with less intimate personal contact; civic life becomes lean and mean and self-interest displaces a common good. Life resembles a work–spend treadmill which leaves little time for unhurried, non-market relations between people. Yet these kinds of activities create personal and community bonds which are quite different from market relations.

The economic theorist of the New Capitalism was perfectly aware of this problem. Friedrich Hayek regarded the 'primitive feelings' of solidarity and altruism as the instinctive products of traditional society. They were an echo of our ancestry as family-clans of hunter-gatherers who shared food and depended on such solidarity for survival. The Great Society or Extended Order, as he termed modern capitalism, depended on the adherence to abstract rules of the market which, for example, meant rejecting the ancient urge to share equally.

But Hayek reserved a legitimate place for these urges in the family and in voluntary associations. He admitted that 'if we were always to apply the rules of the extended order to our more intimate groupings *we would crush them* [emphasis in original].[4] That is, if we treat parents, children, family, friends and neighbours as we do when we buy and sell in the market, we would destroy those relationships. Hayek's solution was that we must simply learn to 'live simultaneously within different kinds of orders according to different rules'—that of the market and that of the family. The impractical and—let's face it—absurd, nature of this proposition is becoming more obvious in the social laboratory of Anglo-American New Capitalism.

Rather than the two worlds existing simultaneously, one world is slowly crushing the other. Hayek's intellectual paradigm has turbo-charged the privatised, marketised economy, which is relentlessly encroaching on the life-world of family, friends and community. The invisible hand is clutching at the invisible heart and slowly choking it.

Thus the story of New Capitalism's effect on the family is just part of a wider story of what is happening to all non-market relations between people. Bonds of respect, civility and trust between people are being weakened, and relations based on competition, self-interest and suspicion are growing. Social cohesion is strained. None of these processes appears in dramatic form, and the process is slow, but its direction is unmistakable and relentless.

The New Capitalism is ecologically unsustainable

The New Capitalism is a high-energy and high-growth economy which is unsustainable. This model of economic development, pursued by the advanced industrial countries and by the new industrial economies such as China, is slowly destroying the biological and ecological bases on which human life depends. Capitalism has been enormously productive, and the New Capitalism even more so. The world economy quadrupled in the last half-century, and is set to do the same in the next. The global population expanded from 1.5 billion to 6 billion in the last 100 years. With this development has come extraordinary advances in the wellbeing of many people in the West whose lifestyle is the benchmark for billions of others. But the cost of this industrialisation has been, and will be, high.

Most alarming is climate change induced by fossil fuel use. This is inducing the shifting of climatic zones, global warming, loss of biodiversity, extreme weather events and impacts on human health.[5] From a third to half of the world's forests are estimated to have gone, together with about half the areas of mangroves and other wetlands. Chemical use is massively expanding, with 2–3 billion kilograms of pesticides released each year. One quarter of bird species have become extinct—a symbol of the extensive loss of biodiversity of other species too. Three-quarters of the world's fisheries are at capacity or over-fished.[6]

Global environmental problems have been hard to deal with for two interrelated reasons. First, they are unlike other problems with which traditional sets of political ideas are designed to grapple: they are both qualitatively different and simply too big and too complex. Democracy, neo-liberalism, socialism and other philosophies have neither the explanatory framework nor the terms to analyse what is going on. They are systems of ideas which deal with power and relations between humans. What is needed are new approaches that grapple with humanity's relations with nature: our need to live off nature's 'surplus' and not destroy its capital, to use the language of economists.

Second, while various elites control and benefit from the economy, their greed and power alone is not the main problem. Unsustainable growth is driven by the popular desire for a better material living standard. Moves towards a more sustainable economy will meet widespread resistance from many ordinary people, not just wealthy elites. For this reason, the battle to introduce sustainability will ultimately require persuasive efforts to change popular notions of progress and what constitutes the good life. This debate has already begun, with studies by Clive Hamilton and others which indicate that, in spite of the increase in material wealth in the advanced industrial world, people are no more happy and are sometimes less happy than their forebears.[7] Consumption no longer occurs in order to meet human needs; its purpose is to manufacture identity, Hamilton says. Because of this, 'there is an intimate relationship between the creation of self in consumer capitalism and the destruction of the natural world . . . Protecting the natural world requires not only far reaching changes in the way we use the natural environment: it calls for the radical transformation of ourselves'.[8]

Major environmental problems have made an impact only on the consciousness of a minority so far. But they will become better known to most people as the consequences begin to bite deeply. Well before we reach any apocalyptic period, a series of environmental crises seem likely to emerge which will exacerbate a series of familiar non-environmental problems. One is conflict between nations. Attempts to regulate over-fishing, for example, will sharply increase rivalries. Attempts to reduce fossil fuel consumption will be strongly resisted by many countries. Environmental refugees will grow. Another problem posed by environmental crises will be the exacerbation of social inequalities between people as they compete for scarce resources. The re-emergence of a politics of inequality shows the need for a new political vision to encompass 'old' issues along with the new.

New Capitalism and values

The New Capitalism develops the instrumental values of rationality and efficiency in the economy to their highest level. In the advanced industrial nations, this has delivered a society of material plenty unprecedented in history. Rationality, in the form of scientific knowledge, has brought extraordinary benefits in terms of health and wellbeing. But a society based largely on rationalism has its down-sides. It values economic growth for its own sake when indications are emerging that it damages wellbeing.[9] It promotes values associated with hyper-consumerism and the spread of the commercial values of instrumental rationality into parts of life once considered beyond the 'economy'.

In the world of New Capitalism, all human needs are slowly being commodified, including in those areas once thought to have a transcendent element: not just family life and personal relationships, but also our relationship with the natural world, aspects of education, physical and intellectual achievement, the arts, and so on. The values associated with these aspects of life—human values—are corroded at the same time that material affluence has reached its highest level.

A similar evolution was described by the German sociologist Max Weber as 'rationalisation'—a long-term process in which rational and scientific methods and values replace the non-rational side of life. Initially, he applied this to the early years of capitalism in which the centrality of religion and religious values were displaced and the society became devalued—or, to use his term, 'disenchanted'. The long-term significance of this is that religious ideas were, crucially, the source of ethics and values.

Thus the process of rationalisation and secularisation of society that accompanied the rise of the modern industrial economies involved the shrinking of that part of the world in which values, rather than rationality, ruled. Moreover, rationality itself became increasingly narrowed to a particular kind of instrumental, mean–ends rationality. This is the world of disloyal companies, thinning social relations, commodified care and public moral vacuity. At its deepest and least tangible level, this process of devaluation moves us closer to a condition of cultural meaninglessness in which the intrinsic value and meaning of values or actions are subordinated to a rational quest for efficiency and control.[10]

This process is fuelling a slow-burning moral crisis which is expressed in a variety of ways. At the political level, there is a new interest in ethics and values by the public. As well, there is a desire to revive notions of a culturally defined common good, and to value

246 Beyond Right and Left

social cohesion and national identity. On another level, there is a renewed search for spiritual meaning expressed in multiple ways from the growth of Buddhism and 'New Age' beliefs to the desire for spiritual certainty that comes from fundamentalist religion, whether Islamic or Christian. A desire for meaning and an assertion of intrinsic values also fuels the overtly secular movement to preserve the environment. Yet this is not a simply political movement; rather, it encompasses a transcendent element. The broad support which it has gathered all over the world draws on a non-rational, emotional desire to protect nature. More ominously, others who search for meaning in a commodified world support populist movements which look to the authenticity of their own culture and blame outsiders for their spiritual pain and unhappiness.

A new vision beyond Right and Left

So far the ideas in this book have traversed a wide variety of issues and areas, from current Australian politics to classical political philosophies, to major issues of our time such as the family and cultural identity. No doubt some will think I have touched on far too many issues and areas in far too little depth. But my purpose has been to broadly survey the fate of the central ideas of Right and Left, to describe the flaws and strengths on both sides, and to sketch a way forward for a new kind of progressive politics. As I have said, these are 'first words', not last words, and I hope this book will provoke a lively debate.

Throughout this book, I have advocated a series of apparently contradictory notions. The neo-liberals, whose economic ideas I have criticised, are philosophical universalists. They strive for a single global market with goods freely bought and sold by the universal global consumer. In this logic, local languages, customs and traditions will all eventually be supplanted by a single human identity. This is the 300-year trajectory of economic modernisation.

But, while decrying neo-liberal economic universalism, I favour another kind of universalism. At a global level, humanity faces a range of risks which arise from the atmosphere, oceans and lands on which we all depend. The case for seeing common human interests and developing shared values is strong. At the local level, in discussing ethnic identity and multiculturalism I argue that we are in danger of losing a sense of shared humanity and need to reconceptualise our goal as a synthesised national identity with agreed core values as well as a recognition of diversity.

My position on the politics of universalism and difference, then, differs from many progressive intellectuals who seem to assume that cultural difference and diversity are always good and that aspiring to universal values supports a stifling uniformity or worse. On the other hand, I insist on recognising difference when it comes to discussing men and women. It seems plain to me that essential differences exist between the male human and the female human, as well as a great deal of commonality. So I am critical of assumptions that equality must largely be defined as the sameness or uniformity of men and women because this ignores difference.

As a former Marxist, I recognise the utopian elements of its vision of a future society, while acknowledging that a number of socialist ideas have permeated mainstream Western thought, enriching its notions of equality, justice and civilised standards of life. To some on the Left, the most contradictory (and heretical) idea in this book is the reconsideration of certain aspects of conservative philosophy—in particular, that a 'green' outlook embodies several key conservative concepts such as heritage, stewardship and scepticism about grand experiments on nature.

But being a critic and commentator of the strengths and weaknesses of the ideas of Right and Left is not enough. I now want to move more directly to what I see as a positive way forward— that is, in the form of a political outlook which can inspire people to help make the world a better place. Before outlining this, there is a proviso. The purpose of sketching this political outlook is not

to recreate a new ideology in the sense of a new systematic architecture of ideas, an all-explanatory framework, a theory of history
and a political program. The old ideas, like liberalism and socialism,
were elaborate philosophies which offered a key to unlocking the
meaning of history and the future. They proposed solutions that
were relevant in all situations. In the light of current neo-liberalism,
as well as the historical experience of socialism, it would be foolish
to follow such an approach today. But the alternative to this kind
of total world view is not incoherence, nor is it a random collection
of ideas.

Somewhere between grand theory and incoherence, it is possible
to formulate a broad political outlook based on values. I prefer to
call such an outlook a 'vision'. The kind of vision which comes out
of the ideas I have developed in this book is based on human values,
and I prefer to call this vision a 'new humanism'.

A hybrid vision of humanism

Why humanism? The case for traditional humanism is strong but
open to criticism. Traditional humanism emphasises a commitment
to the interests and needs of human beings. Placing human needs
at the centre of this world view means establishing a concrete
reference point for measuring wellbeing, rather than an abstract
principle—whether it is liberty or equality. It also means acknowledging an inevitable complexity. The good society must satisfy needs
which pull in opposite directions—for diversity and autonomy as
well as for solidarity and community. The good society is thus a
balance between state, markets and civil society. Human needs are
both physical and psychological, and arise from our status as
evolved creatures. Making our needs foundational not only means
aspiring to fulfil them at the personal and social level. It also means
rejecting the social theories that suggest human beings are completely
malleable and therefore perfectible. This is because our needs are

an expression of our evolved nature, which has limits and is not completely plastic.

Traditional humanism expresses a moral idea of the preciousness of all humans. It is a statement that the value of humans derives from worldly circumstances and not from divine origin or the possession of a soul. Traditional humanism asserts the equal worth of all humans. It expresses a belief that human reasoning is a better guide to knowledge than relying on custom or religious belief. It is a claim that, in determining the truth, no one has a special claim by virtue of their authority. It favours equality of people and autonomy of individuals.

Traditional humanism emphasises the fundamental similarities between people; whatever the nationality or culture in which we grow up, we are members of a common humanity. It is a planetary vision. It favours tolerance because it recognises diversity and difference without ignoring commonalities. As a set of ideas, humanism is the possession of neither the Right nor the Left.

But why *new* humanism? Traditional humanism of the Enlightenment is not enough, and certain interpretations of humanism can be wrongheaded or even dangerous. There are at least four ways in which this has occurred. First, focusing on human needs exclusively can reinforce the attitude that humans should and can conquer the natural world with impunity. A narrow, short-term human-centred world view can lead to the disregard of the ecological interdependence of all life forms. This approach to humanism has little to say on cruelty to animals, for example. We need a planet fit for humans, and this means that human needs must be moderated to fit in with the requirements of the planet. Among other things, creating a sustainable society based on human values will necessitate stopping the growth of human population and accepting limits on human material desires.

Second, like many other sets of ideas, humanism can be ethnocentric—expressing a view, for example, in which 'humans' are defined as living in European and Christian societies and others are less than fully human. The ideal of a common humanity which is the common ground of the planet's people, regardless of the enormously diverse cultures in which they live, is vital here.

Similarly, a pseudo-humanism has existed for a long time which assumes humans are males. Masculine qualities and tendencies are accepted as the norm against which women are judged as different and inferior. The autonomous individual with calculating self-interest tends to conform to a masculine model, whereas the person enmeshed in webs of relationships who feels obligations of care conforms to a feminine model. These opposite tendencies need to be rebalanced in favour of the feminine so that we can reach a humanist world view which is a hybrid of both. Reason and rationality are not enough to explain the world or to give humans a moral sense. Emotions and instincts are real and central to the human experience.

Fourth, by damning religious belief, humanism also tends to reject any spiritual dimension to human life, although this is a core characteristic of humans and their societies. This spiritual dimension is most obviously expressed in religion, but it also appears elsewhere. Creativity and an aesthetic sense are often expressions of this. So too is a sense of transcendence and interdependence with the natural world. The belief in a higher ethical good is often tied to the various senses of a spiritual dimension to life. Atheism is not an essential part of a new humanism.

In proposing the ideas of new humanism, I have identified valuable aspects of liberalism, socialism and conservatism. These are important in fleshing out new humanist values. I now want to signal two new sources of ideas from which a new humanism can be enriched. These are, first, caring values—sometimes expressed as an 'ethic of care'; and second, conservation values associated with ecological sustainability and humans' interdependence with other living things on the planet.

Caring values

I touched on the idea of an ethic of care and caring values in Chapter 7. The idea developed out of a particular strand of feminism which supports a wider, public role for women, but also sees great value in the caring and nurturing traditionally performed by women. Such feminists argue that a central problem of patriarchal societies is that this caring activity is under-valued and denigrated, both at the level of the family and that of the society.

Caring is important because it names a human activity with a deep moral dimension which is often invisible in daily life, and which is ignored in most political and social theory. A focus on caring values is vital in any new philosophy beyond Right and Left. It enriches the more traditional notions of equality and justice, as well as adding a new concept to the idea of a good society involving emotion as well as reason. Some have argued that it provides a new dimension to social and political theory, and to philosophy in general. Caring is a deeply human practice—more basic than production, exchange or contracting—and such a recognition can be 'a painful, worrying and ultimately humbling fact'.[11]

While caring values have not yet been integrated into a political philosophy, some forms of social caring have been with us for a while. I would argue that caring values are at the heart of a variety of social reforms around the welfare state, for which both the traditional left and the social liberals have fought.[12] Some early founders of the welfare state consciously argued that the 'maternal' values of care and compassion from the family should be extended to the state, and the 'masculine' values of autonomy and equality extended into the family.[13] The idea of caring values has a wider applicability than the family, the caring professions and the welfare state. The ethos of caring can be applied to the relationship between humans and nature, embracing the need to care for the complex biological systems which sustain life on the planet. These kinds of caring values offer an important new element in an outlook such as new humanism. They involve a far broader concept than existing notions of caring, which often insist that women must always prefer to perform caring labour before considering their own individual needs.

In an outlook like new humanism, the philosophic ideal of caring would become as frequent and as important as the philosophic ideal of equality. And, like the vexed notion of equality, there will always be a continual debate about what it means in given circumstances.

Conservation values

Conserving the biological bases of life is not a problem that any traditional political philosophy has ever had to deal with until recently. For a series of obvious reasons, any new philosophy beyond Right and Left must deal with this difficult problem. At its most profound level, this involves thinking about humans' relationship to nature. Or rather, it means being aware of humans' position as *part* of nature, since the ecological crises reminds us that we are a species of animals, and as inescapably dependent on clean air, habitat, drinkable water and productive soil as all other animals. We live on the skin of a planet within a biosphere consisting of the lands, seas, atmosphere, rivers, forests and all the living organisms they support and within which we survive. All of these interact to produce oxygen, to nurture life and recycle wastes (such as carbon dioxide). In both an evolutionary sense and a practical sense, they are central to defining who we are as a species. They are a heritage *par excellence*.

Conservation values emphasise that the current human inhabitants of the planet are stewards of the biosphere, which is part of a heritage for succeeding generations of humans. This is actually a very old idea, expressed in conservative philosophy most famously by Edmund

Burke's view that society was a contract 'not only between those who are living but between those who are living, those who are dead and those to be born'. This is the opposite to the short-term view of neo-liberalism, which discards traditions of all kinds, including that of our environmental heritage.[14]

Conservation values are those which deem as right actions which tend to protect and sustain the biosphere. They deem as wrong those actions which permanently damage the biosphere. They emphasise the holistic and interconnected nature of the biological heritage of which we are part. Conservation values entail being guided by the intrinsic logic of these natural processes—for instance, in designing an economy, rather than solely relying on imposed rationalistic measures. They promote empathy with the natural world and see it as having intrinsic value. Conservation values may actually have some basis in the human psyche. Some speculate that humans need to relate to nature for reasons other than physical sustenance, and that this innate need encompasses 'the human craving for aesthetic, intellectual, cognitive and even spiritual meaning and satisfaction'.[15]

The conservation, or 'green', values which will enrich a new humanist approach are found in neither liberalism nor socialism—which have a shared view of endless progress and which assume no limits need be placed on the economy or on humans' needs. By contrast, conservation values involve a recognition of limits and the concept of 'enough'. Conservatives prefer the 'sufficient to the superabundant', as Oakeshott says. The concept of 'enough' is an important assertion in the face of the radicalism of neo-liberal economics and its growth imperative. The intersection of conservation and 'green' values with aspects of conservative philosophy is paradoxical, yet it is a sign of the new times we live in.[16] Conservatism of a 'green' kind and conservation values are opposed to 'the ever more invasive intrusions of a world system that can afford to leave nothing alone, but that must open new pathways to profit deep in the still unexploited fastnesses of the heart, the secret depths of the psyche . . . to be radical now is to say that we have had enough of the industrialisation of humanity'.[17] To be radical now is to be conservative, in a new sense.

The new humanism is a broad philosophical view of the world. For it to be relevant to politics and contemporary society, it needs to be expressed in a more concrete, less abstract form which has an application to politics. In my view, this is best described in terms of a new moral framework as a basis for political action.

A new moral framework

A new moral framework means putting human values at the centre of a political vision rather than theories of rights or class or of cultural or gender identity. It means developing a language of right and wrong which both connects with the lived experience of many people and is tied to social reform. It is the main way that the values of new humanism can be popularised, and the main way that the culture wars can be fought.

Such a framework is necessary because the intellectual frameworks and cultural and class identities which used to underpin bodies like the Labor Party and the Left have eroded, and nothing has replaced them, as I outlined in Chapter 5. The Greens, of course, have a moral vision of sorts, but it lacks coherence between its constituent parts— in other words, it tends to be a grab-bag of nice ideas. As well, it is in constant danger of marginalisation, reflecting the Greens' activist origins. The social liberals of the Right also have a moral vision, though it has been debilitated by its reliance on state-centred solutions to social problems and by the rise of the neo-liberal Right.

The territory of moral values is one on which some people— particularly intellectuals—feel uncomfortable. 'Morality' has so often been used as a club to enforce narrow sexual standards. In popular discourse, the territory of morality has almost totally been colonised by the moral conservatives. None of this should dissuade us, however. A moral outlook simply entails that ultimately judgments are made in terms of right and wrong, and at bottom most political philosophies are built on moral assumptions.[18] Avoiding the territory of moral values simply allows the Right to continue to stake it out as their own, and thereby maintain its broader political ascendancy.

The language of morality is not entirely absent from progressive politics. Shame is a universal and ancient feeling, and people on the Left sometimes say they feel ashamed of what is done in their name or the name of Australia. When they do articulate their beliefs in moral terms, progressives are often shrill and unconvincing to all but the converted. At other times, some on the cultural Left seem morally relativistic. My purpose is not to moralise or be moralistic in a 'holier than thou' way, but to set out a broad framework of values as a basis for political action.

The outlining of this moral framework for politics will be a natural development in some ways because it picks up on some issues which progressives have always fought for, and which many still do. But it will also be difficult for some because it means abandoning old ways of thinking (such as those based on class, or on material deprivation).

Adopting this approach means accepting that many of the social and political issues in Australia are actually moral questions, and can be defined in ways that highlight progressive values. This approach means finding a moral vocabulary and language to address these issues. Concepts such as responsibility, fairness and respect are important in defining responses to major social and political issues, and even traditional moral terms such as honour, loyalty, duty and service can express progressive ideals—depending on how they are defined.

Adopting such an approach will result in the articulation of a new popular common sense which will help progressives win back ground from the Right.

The new moral framework which I advocate has four different dimensions. First, it means *connecting a moral stance—which begins at a personal level—to social goals.* The Right defines morality as limited to individual behaviour, to virtuous conduct and to personal character. It then tries to make private behaviour and decisions (over abortion, homosexuality, etc.) into public matters that deserve moral condemnation. In this, the Right is utterly wrong. But it is right about one thing: public morality is important. Those who define public morality, its content and its extent are those who help set the political agenda.[19] The flip side of the Right's moral war is that it seeks to make public matters into private matters. Social problems like poverty or unemployment are blamed on personal failures or lack of discipline. It tends to favour private provision rather than public provision for education, health, and similar things. Similarly, the Right downplays the important public consequences of corporate behaviour (towards employees and the environment) and regards corporate morality as a private matter—for shareholders and CEOs or for private negotiation with employees.

The challenge is to *define public morality* and to set a moral agenda—and so far the Right is winning this battle. This is not surprising, since progressive thought does not systematically engage on this ground. It should, though. Matters of social justice are moral issues and are part of a moral framework of caring and of providing security. Too often, the language of policy technicalities and abstract notions like equality are employed in the public debate rather than the language of right and wrong. For example, strong feelings rightly exist over exorbitant salaries for top executives. Wealth inequalities should be made matters of public morality in the interests of the poor and lower paid. Implementing tax cuts for the rich and the comfortable should be seen as a moral wrong. Paying your fair share of tax should be (and is, by many people today) seen as support for the common good, and tax avoiders should be damned as selfish and greedy.

Winning the popular debate over public morality means pointing out deeper consequences. It means highlighting the moral consequences of unrestrained markets and competition for society.[20] For example, analyst David Callahan, from the public policy group

Demos, argues that a 'culture of cheating' has arisen in countries where free-market policy has triumphed. Plagiarism by students, tax evasion, workplace theft, music piracy, drug-enhanced sport, fraud by doctors, lawyers and by journalists, and, most of all, corporate scandals and cheating—these symptoms are well known and can be woven into a powerful narrative defining a new kind of public morality. Winning the debate on public morality means damning the further commercialisation of sports, the arts, universities and the growth of 'industries' like advertising and gambling. Unless a new and positive moral agenda is proposed, the Right will continue to win.

The second dimension is about *projecting a moral vision of the nation built around core values.* The political Right has done much to define who is Australian and what are Australian values. Patriotism has been traditionally mobilised by the Right to the extent that the word itself is almost synonymous with a boastful pride and hostility to other nations. Today, the love affair with unrestrained globalisation has meant that the neo-liberal Right has abandoned its role as guardian of the nation. To 'compensate', it has revived backward cultural definitions of Australia, and promoted fear of refugees and a superficial patriotism.

To combat this, a politically progressive force which seeks mass support needs to project a different idea of 'Australianness'. We need to strongly define the Australian way as one of equality, fairness and tolerance. But, more than that, we need to identify positive ideals and national values of which we can all be proud, and to which we can legitimately expect all Australians (local and overseas born) to be loyal. This already happens to some extent, but still the main definers of loyalty to Australia have the loudest voices and the narrowest ideas of 'Australian values'. In turn, this encourages progressives to adopt a cosmopolitanism, which is fine as a personal attitude, but is articulated in high-minded and abstract notions that often fail to connect with many people. When articulated in a culture war, this cosmopolitanism fails to translate adequately, and appears remote and elitist to many Australians who take pride in their country. Its values need to be articulated in a national framework. It is no longer sensible to celebrate cultural diversity without also asserting the need for core values common to all members of the nation. Projecting a national pride and identity does not automatically mean promoting Anglo-Celtic values or denying Australia's Indigenous heritage. It means drawing a distinction between an assimilation which discards the cultures of the Indigenous and non-English-speaking, and an evolving hybrid national identity which values the cultural mix, but also projects agreed common values.

A sense of national identity encourages social cohesion, which is a necessary condition for the continued operation of a welfare state based on the redistribution of wealth. That is, if the middle class and the rich feel no sense that 'us' includes the poor, they will become very hostile to paying taxes to support 'them'. This has occurred to some degree already, but in countries where the poor are not from the same ethnicity as the middle and rich, it has proceeded much further—with disastrous consequences. For such reasons, it is vital to build bonds of commonality in a synthetic common culture. In a similar way, in spite of globalisation, the nation remains vital as the forum for the exercise of democracy, the administration of justice and the law and a range of other institutional practices. Given this, what other political vocabulary do we have to talk in popular terms about the common good and the public interest?

What would a progressive ideal of national identity mean in practice? One sample concerns the popularity of environmental issues. Put simply, such concerns have appealed to many peoples' love of and pride in Australia. In the popular mind, campaigns on environmental issues mean protecting the country they love from the ravages of those who narrowly value only commercial self-interest. Preserving rivers, mountains, rainforests and desert landscapes appeals to a legitimate national pride in a wild and beautiful land.

The third dimension of this moral framework concerns the *centrality of caring and caring values.* Dependence is part of the human condition—as children, as aged adults, in illness or in disability. So is caring for others. But caring is devalued and largely invisible in our society. When it is recognised in a private context, it is seen as the natural role of women, not men. When it is recognised in the economy, it is commodified and carers are paid poorly for their work.

While neo-liberals see the economy as an entirely separate realm from that of moral obligations, a new moral framework would see strong connections between them. The radicalism of neo-liberal economics, which refashions society along free-market lines, does not 'conserve', but forces change. The Right thus has a major vulnerability because it also claims to stand for family values which support secure and stable family lives. Because most people associate caring values with their families, a new moral framework would assert that family values of caring and the needs of children need to be injected into economic policies. One part of this means that it should not be necessary for both parents to work fulltime while children are young. Another part means raising the social expectation that fathers will be full-time caregivers for a significant period in their children's early years. Both government and society should make a bigger commitment to the years of early childhood.

But to achieve such changes requires a new kind of social movement, and the reframing of a popular debate. What we need is a 'right to care' movement around three issues.[21] The first is that families be permitted and helped to care for their members. This involves a workplace challenge to rigid schedules, long hours, mandatory overtime and career expectations that make no allowance for those with family responsibilities; it also means changes to tax and welfare policies to support families when one parent chooses to care for children at home. Second, recognising the social value of care means raising wages and strengthening the career paths of care workers (incidentally benefiting the cared-for). Third, the right to care means delivering care to those who need it. That means recognising that good standards of health-care must be available for all, regardless of income, and that high-quality child care and home care are vital social needs.

A movement on this basis could be very powerful because it would unite unusual bedfellows—not just welfare and women's groups and trade unions, but religious and pro-family groups. For some feminists, support for care at home may be a sticking point. For some pro-family groups, opposition to further deregulation of the 'labour market' may be a sticking point. But the value of a new kind of united movement should overcome such doctrinaire approaches.

The fourth dimension of the new moral framework incorporates *conservation values*. These values, which I mentioned earlier, aim to emphasise the notion that we are part of nature, that we must act as stewards of a biological heritage. Indeed, Australians are the one people in the world with stewardship of an entire continent. Conservation values also emphasise what we share as humans, both in nature and in communities, rather than simply what we may gain through self-interest. Conservation values also favour prudence and careful scrutiny of proposals that we should gamble our future on such risky things as unlimited economic growth and genetic manipulation.[22]

I call these values conservation values rather than environmental values for quite deliberate reasons. I believe 'conservation' better expresses the philosophical attitude we need to address the natural world and its problems. This is more in tune with the popular beliefs of most ordinary people than the beliefs of either radical neo-liberalism or radical environmentalism. Conservation values share similar attitudes to a certain kind of old-fashioned conservatism now cast adrift by the Right. One of the negatives of the emergent green politics is that a significant minority of its supporters often articulate policies which sound like old Left ideas merely under a new flag, rather than something much more innovative and challenging. A new moral framework therefore emphasises conservation as a way of highlighting the genuinely new qualities of green politics.

This approach is vital, since mobilising vast public support for changes in economic and social policy will ultimately determine who wins this modern conflict over values.

For this reason, the conservation dimension of a new moral framework will allow a more effective intervention in the challenging process of creating a sustainable economy, which is likely to become a major issue in coming decades as climate change and a host of other issues begin to bite more deeply. One of the questions here involves how to reduce the use of non-renewable resources, how to make recycling work on a grand scale and how to move towards using renewable energy.

Governments will have a vital role to play, but one of the issues which we must face is the need to put a high 'market value' on resources. Their wasteful use and poor levels of recycling depend on there being a fresh supply of cheap resources on tap. When natural resources are more expensive, individual behaviour and corporate practices change. It becomes sensible and profitable to carefully reuse and recycle resources. Renewable sources of energy become more 'economic'. All of this entails the emergence of problems about equality, since high-priced resources will exacerbate differences in wealth and income. While a higher market price is needed, so too are laws and policies designed to minimise inequalities or to provide minimum citizens' entitlements. All of this will be part of an important battle to urge business and industry, as well as consumers, to adopt sustainable practices. This will require not only a popular movement, but also committed governments and allies within the business community, including far-sighted business leaders and shareholder activists.

A new moral framework and the future

The new moral framework is a challenge to the Right on its own grounds of conservatism. It is a challenge to the Left to fundamentally rethink its values and reconfigure them as a defence of social solidarity, the environment, and regulated civil society which is antithetical to market-based commercial values. Such a framework is broad and open, not tightly prescriptive. Within such a framework, there is plenty of room for negotiation and compromise.

The articulation of this framework should be outspoken and populist. It is not a prescription for a meek and mild middle way, or for a 'third way'. Social evils should be named and shamed. It should be a muscular moral framework which aims to shape and create a new political agenda. The nature of the emerging issues requires this. Resolving the tension between work and family life, for example, will involve major conflicts because these changes will be vigorously opposed by most employers and entrenched interests. Similarly, the promotion of a genuinely sustainable economy will involve conflict over established methods within industry, and over the attitudes and the lifestyles of most people. These will be all the more intense as climate change becomes more palpable.

As I've said before, this new moral framework is very much 'first words', not the last word on sketching a new politics beyond Right and Left. It attempts to incorporate some of the values and insights of Right and Left into a synthesis, while adding new elements. My sketch of such a framework may not be right in every aspect, but I am convinced its broad parameters are the best response to the ascendancy of neo-liberal politics, the death of socialism and of social liberalism, and to the new, emerging challenges in the real world. The moral framework which I propose is a political framework, in the sense that it is about persuasion and political action as well as the integrity of ideas for their own sake. It is designed to be useful to grassroots individuals and organisations, and to local political activity, as well as being articulated in broad public debate by parties with parliamentary representation. At both the grassroots level and on the national stage, this kind of values-based politics is the way forward beyond Right and Left.

Notes

1 Beyond Right and Left

1 Mark Latham, *From the Suburbs: Building a Nation from our Neighborhoods*, Pluto Press, Sydney, 2003, p. 19.
2 Michael Pusey, *The Experience of Middle Australia: The Dark Side of Economic Reform*, Cambridge University Press, Cambridge, 2003. See esp. pp. 114–17 and 176–78.
3 Geoffrey Barker, 'The elites strike back: Dissecting Howard's neo-Liberal triumph', *Australian Financial Review*, 13 March 2004.
4 Clive Hamilton, *Growth Fetish*, Allen & Unwin, Sydney, 2003, pp. x–xiii.
5 Julia Gillard, 'Winning the culture war', *The Sydney Papers*, Summer, 2003.

2 A world made by markets

1 Richard Neville, *Amerika Psycho*, Ocean Press, Melbourne, 2003, p. 6.
2 Thomas Frank, *One Market Under God: Extreme Capitalism, Market Populism and the End of Economic Democracy*, Vintage, London, 2002, p. xvi.
3 Karl Polyani, *The Great Transformation*, Beacon Press, Boston, 1957.
4 Polyani, *The Great Transformation*, p. 57.
5 Polyani, *The Great Transformation*, p. 55.
6 Polyani, *The Great Transformation*, p. 73.
7 John Gray, *False Dawn: The Delusions of Global Capitalism*, Granta Books, London, 1998, pp. 70, 72.
8 Lester Thurow, *The Future of Capitalism: How Today's Economic Forces Shape Tomorrow's World*, Allen & Unwin, Sydney, 1996, p. 313.
9 Naomi Klein, *No Logo*, Flamingo, London, 2001, p. 21.

10   Much of this section comes from Ian Watson, John Buchanan, Iain Campbell and Chris Briggs, *Fragmented Futures: New Challenges in Working Life*, The Federation Press, Sydney, 2003.

11   The material on hours and stress is from Watson et al., pp. 84–104.

12   Watson et al., *Fragmented Futures*, pp. 32–46.

13   Cited in Klein, *No Logo*, p. 9.

14   Klein, *No Logo*, p. 37.

15   Simon Canning, 'Kids Grow fat on junk food ads', *Australian*, 4 March 2004.

16   Stephen Kline, *Out of the Garden: Toys, TV and Children's Culture in the Age of Marketing*, Verso, London, 1995, p. 19.

17   Kline, *Out of the Garden*, p. 13.

18   Tracy Newlands and Stephen Frith, *Innocent Advertising? Corporate Sponsorship in Australian Schools*, New College Institute for Values Research, University of New South Wales, Sydney, 1996.

19   Newlands and Frith, *Innocent Advertising?*, p. 62.

20   Peter Gotting, 'Ploys give advertisers a different bang for their buck', *Sydney Morning Herald*, 14 January 2003.

21   Garry Maddox, 'Movies that try to make you buy are stealing the show', *Sydney Morning Herald*, 14 January 2003.

22   *Daily Telegraph* (London), 4 September 2001.

23   David Leser, 'Skinned!', *Good Weekend* (*Sydney Morning Herald*), 13 November 1999.

24   David Leser, 'Skinned!'

25   Larry Writer, *Never Before, Never Again*, Macmillan, Sydney, 1995, Preface.

26   John Goldlust, *Playing for Keeps: Sport, the Media and Society*, Longman Cheshire, Melbourne, 1987, p. 145.

27   Graeme Samuel, 'Footy wouldn't be fun without a level playing field', *Australian*, 26 August 2002.

28   John Daly, 'A sporting life', in *Year Book Australia, 2002*, Australian Bureau of Statistics, Canberra, 2002.

29   Cited in Chin-Tao Wu, *Privatising Culture: Corporate Art Intervention since the 1980s*, Verso, London, p. 269.

30   Cited in Wu, *Privatising Culture*, p. 270.

31   Wu, *Privatising Culture*, p. 270.

32   Carole Kayrooz, Pamela Kinnear and Paul Preston, *Academic Freedom and Commercialisation of Australian Universities*, Discussion Paper No. 37, The Australia Institute, Canberra, 2001.

33   Judith Brett, 'Competition and collegiality' *Australian Universities' Review*, vol. 40, no. 2, 1997.

34 The Hilmer statement was reported in the *Australian*, 7 November 2002. The other newspaper executive is the chairman of West Australian Newspapers, Trevor Eastwood, reported in the *Australian*, 25 November 1999.

35 Nancy Folbre, *The Invisible Heart: Economics and Family Values*, The New Press, New York, 2001.

36 Folbre, *The Invisible Heart*, p. 1.

37 'Overall women's share of aggregate hours has risen from 30 per cent in 1982 to 36 per cent in 2002. The largest growth has occurred among married (including de facto) women, whose aggregate hours have grown by 76 per cent, while men's have increased by only 26 per cent.' Barbara Pocock, *The Work/Life Collision*, The Federation Press, Sydney, 2003, p. 21.

38 Pocock, *The Work/Life Collision*, pp. 22–23.

39 Arlie Russell Hochschild, *The Time Bind: When Work Becomes Home and Home Becomes Work*, Metropolitan Books, New York, 1997, p. 221.

40 Hochschild, *The Time Bind*, pp. 10–11.

41 Adele Horin, 'When making money is child's play', *Sydney Morning Herald*, 4–5 October 2003.

42 Andrew Norton, 'Liberalism and the Liberal Party of Australia', in Paul Boreham et al., *The Politics of Australian Society: Political Issues for the New Century*, Pearson Education, Sydney, 2000, p. 30.

43 Marian Sawer, 'Populism and public choice in Australia and Canada: Converting equality seekers into "special interests"', Paper at Us and Them: Anti-Elitism in Australia, Workshop Sponsored by The Academy of Social Sciences, July 2003, Australian National University, Canberra.

44 This section is drawn largely from James Gustave Speth, *Red Sky at Morning: America and the Crisis of the Global Environment*, Yale University Press, New Haven, 2004, pp. 13ff.

45 David Korten, *When Corporations Rule the World*, Kumarian Press, West Hartford, 1995, p. 76.

46 Elizabeth Becker, 'WTO move puts cloud over farm subsidies', *New York Times*, 28 April 2004.

47 Joseph E. Stiglitz, *Globalization and its Discontents*, Allen Lane/The Penguin Press, Melbourne, 2002, p. ix.

48 Stiglitz, *Globalization*, p. 4.

49 Stiglitz, *Globalization*, p. 47.

50 Stiglitz, *Globalization*, pp. 54–58.

51 Stiglitz, *Globalization*, pp. 85–86.

52 Stiglitiz, *Globalization*, p. 216.

3   The triumph of an idea

1   Daniel Yergin and Joseph Stanislaw, *The Commanding Heights: The Battle for the World Economy*, Simon and Schuster, New York, 2002.

2   Richard Cockett, 'The New Right and the 1960s: The dialectics of liberation', in Geoff Andrews, Richard Cockett, Alan Hooper, Michael Williams (eds), *New Left, New Right and Beyond: Taking the Sixties Seriously*, Macmillan, London, 1999, p. 94.

3   Cited in Jim Tomlinson, *Hayek and the Market*, Pluto Press, London, 1990, pp. x–xi,

4   For an account of social liberalism and its effect on Australian politics, see Marian Sawer, *The Ethical State? Social Liberalism in Australia*, Melbourne University Press, Melbourne, 2003.

5   The best account of the overturning of traditional conservative politics is Judith Brett, *Australian Liberals and the Moral Middle Class*, Cambridge University Press, Cambridge, 2003.

6   Gregory Melleuish, *A Short History of Australian Liberalism*, CIS Occasional Paper No. 74, Sydney, 2001, pp. vii–viii.

7   *Australian*, 13 July 1978. For a detailed explanation of how Murdoch used the *Australian* to help set a political agenda, see my article, 'Rupert Murdoch and the culture war', *Australian Book Review*, February 2004.

8   Peregrine Worsthorne, *Australian*, 17 May 1979.

9   Max Harris, *Australian*, 3–4 November 1979.

10   John Hyde, *Dry. In Defence of Economic Freedom*, Institute of Public Affairs, 2002.

11   Paul Kelly, *The End of Certainty*, Allen & Unwin, Sydney, 1992, p. 36.

12   Wolfgang Kasper et al., *Australia at the Crossroads*, Harcourt Brace Jovanovich, Sydney, 1980, pp. 345–46.

13   F.A. Hayek, *Social Justice, Socialism and Democracy*, CIS Occasional Paper No. 2, Sydney, 1979, pp. 5–6.

14   F.A. Hayek, *Social Justice*, pp. 39, 32.

15   Charles Kemp, like many of the old Right, was wary of the New Right. See Chapter 4.

16   It's something that the Left of politics could well emulate, rather than 'exposing' the backers of the think-tanks as if this was a knockout argument.

17   David Kemp, 'Liberalism and Conservatism in Australia since 1944', in Brian Head and James Walter (eds), *Intellectual Movements and Australian Society*, Oxford University Press, Melbourne, 1988, p. 340.

18   Paul Sheehan, 'The Right Strikes Back', *Sydney Morning Herald*, 2 March 1985.

19   *Australian*, 15 March 1983; 19–20 March 1983.

20   Kelly, *The End of Certainty*, p. 243.

21   Cited in Kelly, *The End of Certainty*, p. 267.

22   Kelly, *The End of Certainty*, p. 239.

23   Cited in Kelly, *The End of Certainty*, p. 391.

24   *Sydney Morning Herald*, 29 August 1987.

25   Barry Jones, 'The Hawke government: An assessment from the inside', in Susan Ryan and Troy Bramston, *The Hawke Government: A Critical Retrospective*, Pluto Press, Melbourne, 2003, p. 425.

26   *Australian*, 4 March 2003.

27   Michael Costa and Mark Duffy, 'Labor and economic rationalism', in Chris James, Chris Jones and Andrew Norton (eds), *A Defence of Economic Rationalism*, Allen & Unwin, Sydney, 1993, p. 130.

28   F.A. Hayek, *The Road to Serfdom*, Routledge and Kegan Paul, London, 1962, p. 79.

29   See F.A. Hayek, *The Constitution of Liberty*, Routledge & Kegan Paul, London, 1960 (1976), Ch. 4.

30   Tomlinson, *Hayek and the Market*, p. 13. Hayek shared the prize with social-democratic economist Gunnar Myrdal.

31   Hayek, *The Constitution of Liberty*, p. 128.

32   Hayek, *The Constitution of Liberty*, p. 16.

33   Hayek, *The Constitution of Liberty*, p. 85.

34   Thomas Sowell, *A Conflict of Visions*, Basic Books, New York, 2002, Ch. 8.

35   Hayek's theories of natural and of cultural evolution are not sharply separated—the evolution of intelligence is the basis of individual creativity, and so of the evolution of the market. Moreover, as his views developed, he ceased to distinguish between the natural and social sciences, instead drawing the line between sciences that study relatively simple things and those that study complex phenomena. (Bruce Caldwell, *Hayek's Challenge*, University of Chicago Press, Chicago, 2004, pp. 301–06)

36   Hayek, *The Constitution of Liberty*, p. 79.

37   F.A. Hayek, *The Fatal Conceit: The Errors of Socialism*, Volume One of *Collected Works of FA Hayek*, W. Bartley (ed.), University of Chicago Press, Chicago, 1998, p. 12.

38   Hayek, *The Fatal Conceit*, p. 13.

39   Hayek, *The Fatal Conceit*, p. 18.

40   Also included are 'social contract' theorists who see the state as founded upon a rational agreement of citizens, but Hayek overlooks the fact that, among social contract theorists, there are some important 'pure' liberals—most notably John Locke—whose ideas he claims to be 'rescuing'.

41   Presumably, this kind of reforming rationalism, in liberal guise, undermined the natural need for workers to work 70-hour weeks and for children to

work in coal mines as occurred in nineteenth-century England. Hayek rarely addressed such issues, but his praise for the lost world of nineteenth-century liberalism was constant.

42 See Tomlinson, *Hayek and the Market*, pp. 64–65 and chs 3 and 6; also Chandran Kukathas, *Hayek and Modern Liberalism*, Clarendon Press, Oxford, 1989.

43 Kukathas, *Hayek and Modern Liberalism*, pp. 206–15.

44 Simon Marginson, *The Free Market: A Study of Hayek, Friedman and Buchanan and their Effects on the Public Good*, Public Sector Research Centre Monograph No. 1, University of New South Wales, Sydney, 1992, p. 95.

4   Neo-cons, ex-cons and the death of the old Right

1 Anthony Giddens, *Beyond Left and Right: The Future of Radical Politics*, Polity Press, Cambridge, 1994.

2 Trevor Blackwell and Jeremy Seabrook, *The Revolt Against Change: Towards a Conserving Radicalism*, Vintage, London, 1993, pp. 3–4.

3 *Sydney Morning Herald*, 22 July 2002.

4 Patrick Weller, *Malcolm Fraser PM: A Study in Prime Ministerial Power in Australia*, Penguin, Melbourne, 1989, p. 397; Graham Little, 'Malcolm Fraser: A strong leader revisited', in Judith Brett (ed.), *Political Lives*, Allen & Unwin, Sydney 1997, p. 61.

5 Malcolm Fraser, *Common Ground: Issues that Should Bind and Not Divide Us*, Viking, Melbourne, 2002, pp. 54–55.

6 Robert Manne, 'The End of the Cold War and Us', *Quadrant*, vol. 34, no. 3, March 1990.

7 Manne's description of these events in *Sydney Morning Herald*, 17 November 1997.

8 Robert Manne, 'In Denial: The Stolen Generations and the Right', *Australian Quarterly Essay*, vol. 1, no. 1, Black Inc., Melbourne, 2000.

9 Corey Robin, 'The ex-cons: Right wing thinkers go Left', *Lingua Franca*, vol. 11, no. 1, February 2001.

10 I use the terms liberalism and conservatism in quite specific ways. Both ideas are dogged by a classificatory tangle. In Australia, liberalism has meant both 'left-wing liberalism' and 'social liberalism' of the Right, today echoed in the name 'Liberal Party'. Historically, conservatism is a catch-all term for the Right, but actual conservatism has been a weak political tradition in Australia. This is confused by the fact that early free-traders were sometimes described as 'conservatives' in contrast to social liberals like Alfred Deakin. In the United States, the term 'liberalism' is used almost exclusively to mean 'left-liberalism' to describe those who support government guarantees

of civil rights and the welfare state. As in Australia, 'conservative' tends to be a catch-all term for the Right, which actually includes many conflicting strands. In Britain, what liberalism tends to be associated with is now called 'social liberalism', and in the 1980s 'conservatism' changed its meaning from 'One Nation' Tory beliefs towards neo-liberal Thatcherism. This book prefers to use these terms defined by their meaning in political philosophy rather than common usage. In the sense used in this book, liberalism is a philosophy arising from opposition to the absolutist state, which emphasised the liberty of the individual. Modern liberalism, however, has many meanings and a battle for the true heirs of liberalism is proceeding. By conservatism I tend to mean the ideas developed by thinkers such as Edmund Burke, and carried on by Michael Oakeshott and Roger Scruton. Conservatism tends to be associated with ethnicity, nationalism and religion in ways that often distinguish it from liberalism. Two excellent books on liberalism and conservatism in Australia are Judith Brett, *Australian Liberals and the Moral Middle Class from Alfred Deakin to John Howard* (Cambridge University Press, Melbourne, 2003) and Marian Sawer, *The Ethical State? Social Liberalism in Australia* (Melbourne University Press, Melbourne, 2003).

11   See his columns in the *Australian* of 2 June 1987, 9 June 1987 and 14 February 1989.

12   C.D. Kemp, 'Those Terrible 80 Years?', *Quadrant*, November 1991.

13   One Nation Party, National Rural and Regional Policy, 29 September 1998, <www.gwb.com.au/onenation>.

14   See note 10.

15   Petro Georgiou, 'Menzies, liberalism and social justice', The 1999 Menzies Lecture, Monash University, <home.vicnet.net.au/~victorp/liberals/victoria/georgioumenzieslecture.htm>.

16   Professor Peter Baume AO, 'Philosophical Liberalism', The Robert Nestdale Memorial Lecture, 1994.

17   Marian Wilkinson and David Marr, 'Howard, Beazley, Lashed Over Race', *Sydney Morning Herald*, 8 November 2001.

18   Marian Sawer, *The Ethical State? Social Liberalism in Australia*, Melbourne University Press, Melbourne, 2003.

19   Sawer, *The Ethical State*, p. 4.

20   Sawer, *The Ethical State*, p. 4.

21   Sawer, *The Ethical State*, pp. 35–36.

22   Sawer, *The Ethical State*, pp. 58–59.

23   Paul Kelly, *The End of Certainty*, Allen & Unwin, Sydney, 1992, 1994, p. 111.

24   Sawer, *The Ethical State*, p. 74 on old-age pensions and pp. 19–21 on general support for the welfare state.

25   Sawer, *The Ethical State*, esp. chs 5 and 6.

26   Elizabeth Drew, 'The Neocons in Power', *The New York Review of Books*, 12 June 2003.

27   Scott McConnell, 'Betrayal of the Right', from *The American Conservative*, reprinted in the *Australian*, 26 October 2004.

28   *New York Times*, 8 September 2002, cited in *The American Conservative*, 5 June 2003, online edition, <www.amconmag.com>.

29   Michael Lind, *Up From Conservatism: Why the Right is Wrong for America*, The Free Press, New York, 1996, p. 3.

30   Owen Harries, 'What Conservatism Means', *The American Conservative*, 17 November 2003.

31   Robert Manne, 'The Rift in Conservative Politics', in Robert Manne and John Carroll, *Shutdown: The Failure of Economic Rationalism and How to Rescue Australia*, Text Publishing, Melbourne, 1992, pp. 57–58.

32   Roger Scruton, *The Meaning of Conservatism*, Palgrave, 2001, p. 1.

33   There is disagreement on whether Burke was a conservative. Hayek, who also rejects the notion of abstract rights, claims Burke as part of the British liberal tradition, as do others including Lord Acton. Hayek's justification is, first, that Burke remained a Whig and, second, that the very fact of having a rational account of conservatism meant he departed from that tradition itself, which Hayek sees as consisting only in a set of dispositions. See F.A. Hayek, *The Constitution of Liberty*, Routledge and Kegan Paul, London, 1960 (1976), p. 407 and its Appendix 'Why I am not a Conservative'. I shall remain with the more conventional classification of Burke as a conservative. However, it is useful to keep in mind that the term 'liberalism' was not widely used until the early nineteenth century.

34   Edmund Burke, *Reflections on the Revolution in France*, Penguin, Harmondsworth, 1969.

35   Burke, *Reflections*.

36   'But I cannot stand forward and give praise or blame to anything which relates to human actions, and human concerns, on a simple view of the object, as it stands stripped of every relation, in all the nakedness and solitude of metaphysical abstraction. Circumstances (which with some gentlemen pass for nothing) give in reality to every political principle its distinguishing color and discriminating effect.' (Burke, *Reflections*)

37   To a common heritage we owe, in the words of Roger Scruton, 'a humble recognition that we are not the producers but the products of our world. We must strive to be worthy of an inheritance we did not create and to amend it only when we have first understood it'. Roger Scruton, 'Rousseau

and the origins of liberalism', in Hilton Kramer (ed.), *The Betrayal of Liberalism*, Ivan R. Dee, Chicago, 1999.

38 Thomas Sowell, *A Conflict of Visions*, Basic Books, New York, 2002, Ch. 2.

39 Sowell, *A Conflict of Visions*, pp. 31–32.

40 John Gray, *Heresies*, Granta Books, London, 2004, p. 123.

41 One exception is the pre-Enlightenment liberalism of British philosopher John Locke, which grounded equality and liberty in a conception of human nature. This in turn gave rise to the tradition of 'natural law'. This is now being revived, for instance, by lawyer Geoffrey Robertson as a conceptual basis for international human rights law.

42 One left-wing thinker who also advances this view is Peter Singer, *A Darwinian Left: Politics, Evolution and Cooperation*, Weidenfeld & Nicolson, London, 1999.

43 Anthony Giddens, *Beyond Left and Right: The Future of Radical Politics*, Polity Press, Cambridge, 1998.

44 Torbjorn Tannsjo, *Conservatism for Our Time*, Routledge, London, 1990, p. ix.

45 See, for example, Francis Fukuyama, *The Great Disruption*, Profile Books, London, 1999; and Eva Cox and Peter Caldwell (among other contributors), in Ian Winter (ed.), *Social Capital and Public Policy in Australia*, Australian Institute of Family Studies, Melbourne, 2000.

46 Pierre Bourdieu, 'The Essence of Neoliberalism', in *Le Monde Diplomatique*, December 1998.

47 John Gray, *False Dawn: The Delusions of Global Capitalism*, Granta Books, London, p. 3.

48 Gray, *False Dawn*, p. 17.

49 Gray, *False Dawn*, p. 38.

50 Gray, *False Dawn*, pp. 70–72.

51 Gray, *False Dawn*, p. 199.

52 *The American Conservative*, 21 June 2004.

53 Francis Fukuyama, *Our Posthuman Future: Consequences of the Biotechnology Revolution*, Profile Books, London, 2003.

54 Fukuyama, *Our Posthuman Future*, p. 9.

55 Fukuyama, *Our Posthuman Future*, p. 101.

56 Michael Oakeshott, *Rationalism in Politics and Other Essays*, Methuen, London, 1962, pp. 168–69.

57 Blackwell and Seabrook, *The Revolt Against Change*, p. 77.

58 Obviously combined with measures of equality, ensuring that those on lower incomes do not bear a disproportionate cost.

5   What was socialism?

1   Russell Jacoby, *The End of Utopia: Politics and Culture in an Age of Apathy*, Basic Books, New York, 1999, p. 10.

2   The article was published as 'Tradition of miners a casualty in a class war', *Sydney Morning Herald*, 15 January 1986.

3   Russel Ward, *The Australian Legend*, Oxford University Press, Melbourne, 1978, pp. 16–17.

4   Judith Brett, *Australian Liberals and the Moral Middle Class*, Cambridge University Press, Cambridge, 2003, pp. 203–04.

5   Cited in Brett, *Australian Liberals*, p. 204.

6   Though just what constitutes a 'socially conservative' view is a matter of definition. Too often, liberals and leftists sweepingly condemn those with different views on race and nation, as we will see in Chapter 8.

7   Clive Bean and Ian McAllister, 'Voting behaviour', in Marian Simms and John Warhust (eds), *Howard's Agenda: The 1998 Australian Election*, University of Queensland Press, Brisbane, 2000, p. 181.

8   See, for example, Michael Thompson, *Labor Without Class: The Gentrification of the ALP*, Pluto Press, Melbourne, 1999.

9   ABS Press Release, 31 March 2003 '6310.0 Employee Earnings, benefits and trade union membership'; ABS Press Release '6325.0 Union membership down', 3 February 1997.

10   Jorge Castaneda, *Utopia Unarmed: The Latin American Left After the Cold War*, Vintage Books, New York, 1994.

11   M. Hardt and A. Negri, *Empire*, Harvard University Press, Cambridge, MA, 2000.

12   I am not referring here to the far more successful components of the New Left, such as the women's movement and other non-class based social movements.

13   A major report commissioned by the Soviet Politburo, was reproduced under the title 'The Novosibirsk Report' in *Survey*, vol. 28, no. 1, 1984.)

14   Mikhail Gorbachev, *Memoirs*, Transworld Publishers, London, 1996, pp. 217, 277.

15   Does China demonstrate that extensive state-owned industries can be combined with a market? At first glance it does, and hence may be thought to negate the lesson of the collapse of the Soviet Union, but the guarantor of this situation is the complete absence of political democracy and individual freedoms.

16   Alec Nove, *The Economics of Feasible Socialism Revisited*, HarperCollins, London, 1991, see Part I, 'The legacy of Marx', esp. p. 20.

17   Francis Fukuyama, *The End of History and the Last Man*, Free Press, New York, 1992.

18   Erik Olin Wright, 'Introduction', in Samuel Bowles and Herbert Gintis, *Recasting Egalitarianism: New Rules for Communities, States and Markets*, Verso, London, 1998, p. xi. He acknowledges that Right and Left remain divided on the mix of market and non-market forms. The Left, however, has a special problem: 'Many on the Left have significantly softened their traditional hostility to market institutions acknowledging that strong market mechanisms are important for certain kinds of efficiency considerations and that excessive restrictions on voluntary exchanges can produce all sorts of undesirable consequences. While many people may continue to worry about the consequences of unfettered markets, there is much less confidence on the Left today about how to properly design such fetters so as to reap the virtues of markets while avoiding the negative consequences.'

19   Eric Aarons, *What's Right?*, Rosenberg Publishing, Sydney, 2003, pp. 28–38.

20   Aarons, *What's Right?*, p. 37.

21   Jurgen Habermas, 'What does socialism mean today? The revolutions of recuperation and the need for new thinking', in Robin Blackburn (ed.), *After the Fall: The Failure of Communism and the Future of Socialism*, Verso, London, 1991, pp. 33–35.

22   Andrew Gamble, *An Introduction to Modern Social and Political Thought*, Macmillan, London, 1981, pp. 102–03.

23   Eugene Kamenka, 'Socialism and Utopia', in Eugene Kamenka (ed.), *Utopias: Papers from the Annual Symposium of the Australian Academy of the Humanities*, Oxford University Press, Melbourne, 1987.

24   Anne Whitehead, *Paradise Mislaid: In Search of the Australian Tribe in Paraguay*, University of Queensland Press, Brisbane, 1997.

25   With the benefits of hindsight and experience, we can now see that, though they patronisingly criticised 'utopian socialism', Marx and Engels themselves created a form of utopianism, combining high ideals with an unrealistic projection of how a just society could be constructed.

26   Donald Sassoon, *One Hundred Years of Socialism: The West European Left in the Twentieth Century*, Fontana, Melbourne, 1997. p. 9.

27   For example, Frederick Engels said: 'The emancipation of women becomes possible only when women are enabled to take part in production on a large social scale, and when domestic duties requires their attention only to a minor degree. And this has become possible only as a result of modern large-scale industry, which not only permits of the participation of women in production in large numbers, but actually calls for it, and, moreover, strives to convert domestic work also into a public industry.'

Frederick Engels, 'The Origin of the Family, Private Property and the State', in Karl Marx and Frederick Engels, *Selected Works*, Progress Publishers, Moscow, 1958, p. 311.

28   Karl Marx, 'Theses on Feuerbach', in Karl Marx and Frederick Engels, *Selected Works*, p. 404.

29   See, for example, Steven Pinker, *The Blank Slate: The Modern Denial of Human Nature*, Penguin Books, London, 2002; Robert Wright, *The Moral Animal: Why We Are the Way We Are*, Abacus, London, 1996.

30   Peter Singer, *A Darwinian Left: Politics, Evolution and Cooperation*, Weidenfeld & Nicolson, London, 1999, chapters 3 and 4.

31   Pinker, *The Blank Slate*, p. ix.

32   Peter Singer, *A Darwinian Left: Politics Evolution and Cooperation*, Weidenfeld & Nicolson, London, 1999.

33   Singer, *A Darwinian Left*, p. 37.

34   Clive Hamilton, *Growth Fetish*, Allen & Unwin, Sydney, 2003.

35   Hamilton, *Growth Fetish*, pp. x–xi.

6   The culture war and moral politics

1   Michael Costello, *Australian*, 30 January 2004.

2   *Age*, 22 January 2004.

3   *Australian*, 7 August 2002.

4   Tony Abbott, 'The moral case for the Howard government', Speech to the Young Liberals issued by the Minister for Health and Ageing, 23 January 2004. (Extract also published in *Sydney Morning Herald*, 23 January 2004.)

5   John Garnaut, 'Federalism isn't working: Abbott' *Sydney Morning Herald*, 24 January 2005.

6   In this sense, a culture war is very similar to the concept of a battle for 'hegemony', first articulated by the Italian Marxist Antonio Gramsci who argued that the working class needed to exercise intellectual and moral leadership.

7   Tim Dymond, 'A history of the "new class" concept', in Marian Sawer and Barry Hindess (eds), *Us and Them: Anti-Elitism in Australia*, API Network, Curtin University, Perth, 2004. See also David McKnight, 'Rupert Murdoch and the culture war', *Australian Book Review*, February 2004; 'A world hungry for a new philosophy', *Journalism Studies*, vol. 4. no. 3, 2003.

8   Jonathan Zimmerman, *Whose America? Culture Wars in Public Schools*, Harvard University Press, Cambridge, MA, 2002, p. 214.

9   See, for instance, Jean Kirkpatrick, 'Neoconservatism as a response to the counter-culture'; see also the influence of Leo Strauss in Kenneth Weinstein, 'Philosophic Roots: The role of Leo Strauss'. Both articles are in Irwin Stelzer (ed.), *Neoconservatism*, Atlantic Books, London, 2004.

10 David Brock, *Blinded by the Right: The Conscience of an Ex-Conservative*, Crown Publishers, New York, 2003, pp. 56–58.

11 *Washington Times*, 22 May 1989, cited in Richard Bolton (ed.), *Culture Wars: Documents from the Recent Controversies in the Arts*, The New Press, New York, 1992.

12 Richard Jensen, 'The culture wars, 1965–1995: A historian's map', *Journal of Social History*, vol. 29, mid-winter, 1995.

13 This account of the convention is from Brock, *Blinded by the Right*, pp. 121–23.

14 Jensen, 'The culture wars'.

15 Jensen, 'The culture wars'.

16 *Australian*, 22 January 2004.

17 See Marion Maddox, *God Under Howard*, Allen & Unwin, Sydney, 2004.

18 Don Watson, *Recollections of a Bleeding Heart: A Portrait of Paul Keating PM*, Random House, Sydney, 2002, pp. 91–93.

19 John Howard, 'The role of government: A Modern Liberal approach', Menzies Research Centre, 1995 National Lecture Series, <www.australianpolitics.com>.

20 David Barnett with Pru Goward, *John Howard: Prime Minister*, Viking, Ringwood, 1997, p. 697.

21 Barnett with Goward, *John Howard*, p. 704.

22 Jonathan King with David Iggulden, *The Battle for the Bicentenary*, Hutchison Australia, Sydney, 1989.

23 This is set out in remarkable detail in Robert Manne, *In Denial: The Stolen Generations and the Right*, Quarterly Essay Issue 1, Black Inc., Melbourne, 2001.

24 Robert Manne, *The Barren Years: John Howard and Australian Political Culture*, Text Publishing, Melbourne, 2001, pp. 134–35.

25 For several detailed accounts, see Marian Sawer and Barry Hindess (eds), *Us and Them: Anti-Elitism in Australia*, API Network, Perth, 2004.

26 Barnett with Goward, *John Howard*, p. 188.

27 Judith Brett, *Australian Liberals and the Moral Middle Class*, Cambridge University Press, Cambridge, 2003, p. 189.

28 Brett, *Australian Liberals*, pp. 189–90.

29 See for example, Keith Windschuttle, 'The cultural war on western civilisation', *New Criterion*, January 2002.

30 Jack Waterford, 'You Can't Say That', *The Independent Monthly*, May 1993.

31 Phillip Adams (ed.), *The Retreat from Tolerance: A Snapshot of Australian Society*, ABC Books, Sydney, 1997.

32   McKenzie Wark, 'Free speech, cheap talk and the virtual republic', in Adams (ed.), *The Retreat from Tolerance*, p. 176.

33   Adams (ed.), *The Retreat from Tolerance*, pp. 21–22.

34   The original phrase comes from the German student leader Rudi Dutschke, whose reference to the 'long march' comes from the tactical retreat in the 1930s made by the armed guerrillas of the Chinese Communist Party under Mao Tse-Tung.

35   Michael Walzer, 'What's going on?', *Dissent*, Winter, 1996.

36   Walzer, 'What's going on?', p. 7.

37   Cited by Carol Johnson, 'Anti-elitist discourse in Australia: International influences and comparisons', in Sawer and Hindess, *Us and Them*, pp. 126–27.

38   Lindsay Tanner, *Crowded Lives*, Pluto Press, Melbourne, 2003, p. 34.

39   Noel Pearson, 'On the human right to misery, mass incarceration and early death', Dr Charles Perkins Memorial Oration, 2001.

40   Pearson, 'On the Human Right'.

41   See his speech at the Annual Bob Hawke Lecture, published in *Campus Review*, December 2002, and at <www.hawkecentre.unisa.edu.au>.

42   Noel Pearson, 'The light on the hill', Ben Chifley Memorial Lecture, Bathurst, 12 August 2000.

43   Pearson, 'The light on the hill'.

44   Marcia Langton, 'A new deal? Indigenous development and the politics of recovery', Dr Charles Perkins Memorial Lecture, 4 October 2002.

45   Aden Ridgeway, 'Practical blueprint fails Blacks', *Australian*, 12 June 2001.

46   'Black leaders clash on dole "poison"', *Sydney Morning Herald*, 1 May 1999.

47   Warren Snowdon, 'Noel Pearson speaks for Cape York', *Age*, 6 June 2002.

48   A similar intervention and a demand for rethinking have been made in Rosemary Neill, *White Out: How Politics is Killing Black Australia*, Allen & Unwin, Sydney, 2002, and in Peter Sutton, 'The Politics of Suffering: Indigenous policy in Australia since the 1970s', *Anthropological Forum*, vol. 11, no. 2, 2001.

49   Eva Cox, *A Truly Civil Society*, 1995 Boyer Lectures, ABC Books, Sydney, 1995, pp. 15, 29.

50   See David McKnight, 'Stuck in Noam Man's Land', *Sydney Morning Herald*, 26–27 December 2001; David McKnight, 'Bali, the Left and anti-imperialism, *Arena*, February 2003.

51   The following is from George Lakoff, *Moral Politics: What Conservatives Know that Liberals Don't*, University of Chicago Press, Chicago, 1996, pp. 67–69.

52   Lakoff, *Moral Politics*, p. 155.

53   Lakoff, *Moral Politics*, p. 336.

Chapter 7   Rethinking family values

1   Ilse's mother preferred not to be named.
2   In the late 1960s, as a seventeen-year-old, I remember attending meetings of my bushwalking club in the wood-panelled rooms of a Feminist Society in King Street, Sydney . . .
3   Belinda Probert, 'Grateful slaves or self-made women? A matter of choice or policy?', Clare Burton Memorial Lecture, 2001.
4   Anne Summers, *The End of Equality: Work, Babies and Women's Choices in 21st Century Australia*, Random House, Sydney, 2003, p. 2.
5   Bob Gregory, 'Can this be the Promised Land?', *Dissent*, no. 9, Spring, 2002.
6   Barbara Pocock, *The Work/Life Collision*, The Federation Press, Sydney, 2003, p. 73.
7   Malcolm Turnbull, in Lucy Sullivan, *The Influence of Income Equity on the Total Fertility Rate*, Menzies Research Centre, Canberra, 2003, p. 3.
8   *Valuing Parenthood: Options for Paid Maternity Leave*, <www.hreoc.gov.au/sex_discrimination>.
9   The problem with the baby payment is that it does not necessarily give mothers a paid break, and there is no guarantee it will be used for that purpose.
10 Ann Crittenden, *The Price of Motherhood: Why the Most Important Job in the World is Still the Least Valued*, Henry Holt and Co., New York, 2001, p. 3.
11 Crittenden, *The Price of Motherhood*, p. 7.
12 Elizabeth Windschuttle, 'Wages for Mothers?' *Refractory Girl*, Summer, 1974, p. 46.
13 Pocock, *The Work/Life Collision*, p. 19.
14 'Overall women's share of aggregate hours has risen from 30 per cent in 1982 to 36 per cent in 2002. The largest growth has occurred among married (including de facto) women whose aggregate hours have grown by 76 per cent, while men's have increased by only 26 per cent.' Pocock, *The Work/Life Collision*, p. 21.
15 Pocock, *The Work/Life Collision*, pp. 22–23.
16 Pocock, *The Work/Life Collision*, p. 1.
17 Pocock, *The Work/Life Collision*, p. 55.
18 Pocock, *The Work/Life Collision*, p. 25.
19 Pocock, *The Work/Life Collision*, pp. 81, 90.
20 Pocock, *The Work/Life Collision*, pp. 78, 89.
21 Pocock, *The Work/Life Collision*, p. 66.
22 Pocock, *The Work/Life Collision*, pp. 66–67.
23 Summers, *The End of Equality*, pp. 7–8.
24 Summers, *The End of Equality*, p. 46.

25   Summers, *The End of Equality*, p. 48.
26   Tanya Plibersek, 'Child care is not the answer if we're working when we need family time', *Sydney Morning Herald*, 29 December 2003.
27   Katherine Wilson, 'Stepford Wives, Howard style', *Overland*, no. 174, 2004, pp. 30–31.
28   Summers, *Then End of Equality*, p. 161.
29   Summers, *Then End of Equality*, p. 161.
30   Crittenden, *The Price of Motherhood*, p. 7.
31   Peter McDonald, 'Gender equity, social institutions and the future of fertility', *Journal of Population Research*, vol. 17, no. 1, 2000.
32   McDonald, 'Gender equity', p. 12.
33   M.D.R. Evans and Jonathan Kelley, 'Employment for mothers of pre-school children: Evidence from Australia and 23 other nations', *People and Place*, vol. 9, no. 3, 2001.
34   Anne Manne, 'Women's preferences, fertility and family policy: The case for diversity', *People and Place*, vol. 9, no. 4, 2001, pp. 17–19.
35   Catherine Hakim, 'Five feminist myths about women's employment', *British Journal of Sociology*, vol. 46, no. 3, 1995.
36   The results are summarised in Catherine Hakim, 'Taking women seriously', *People and Place*, vol. 9, no. 4, 2001.
37   Hakim, 'Taking women seriously', p. 2.
38   Hakim, 'Taking women seriously', p. 5.
39   Pocock, *The Work/Life Collision*, p. 29.
40   G. Greer, *The Whole Woman*, Doubleday, Sydney, 1999, pp. 1–2.
41   Greer, *The Whole Woman*, p. 197.
42   Greer, *The Whole Woman*, p. 205.
43   Lauri Umansky, *Motherhood Reconceived: Feminism and the Legacy of the Sixties*, New York University Press, New York, 1996, p. 115.
44   It did, however, result in many other kinds of campaigns, often around women's bodies, health and violence against women.
45   Carol Gilligan, *In a Different Voice: Psychological Theory and Women's Development*, Harvard University Press, Cambridge, MA, 1993.
46   See, for instance, Mary Jeanne Larrabee (ed.), *An Ethic of Care*, Routledge, New York, 1993; Joan Tronto, *Moral Boundaries: A Political Argument for an Ethic of Care*, Routledge, New York, 1993.
47   Crittenden, *The Price of Motherhood*, p. 71ff.
48   Crittenden, *The Price of Motherhood*, p. 9.
49   Pocock, *The Work/Life Collision*, p. 16.
50   Nancy Folbre, *The Invisible Heart: Economics and Family Values*, The New Press, New York, 2001.

8   We're all in the same boat

1   Much of this section is taken from David Marr and Marian Wilkinson, *Dark Victory*, Allen & Unwin, Sydney, 2003, chs 14–16, and from *Report of the Senate Select Committee on a Certain Maritime Incident*, <www.aph.gov.au/Senate/committee/maritime_incident_cttee/report>.

2   *Report of the Senate Select Committee*, p. 33.

3   Marr and Wilkinson, *Dark Victory*, p. 192.

4   Marr and Wilkinson, *Dark Victory*, p. 187, 189.

5   Todd Gitlin, *The Twilight of Common Dreams*, Metropolitan Books, New York, 1995, p. 91.

6   Judith Brett has set this out in her discussion of John Howard in *Australian Liberals and the Moral Middle Class*, Cambridge University Press, Cambridge, 2003, pp. 203–06.

7   Christian Joppke and Steven Lukes, 'Introduction: Multicultural questions', in Joppke and Lukes (eds), *Multicultural Questions*, Oxford University Press, Oxford, 1999, pp. 8–11.

8   The official response to FGM was to 'uphold human rights but remain respectful of diverse cultures, neither condemning nor romanticising the particular culture involved'. Ian Patrick, 'Responding to female genital mutilation: The Australian experience in context', *Australian Journal of Social Issues*, February 2001.

9   Patricia Easteal, *Shattered Dreams: Marital Violence Against Overseas Born Women in Australia*, Australian Government Publishing Service, Canberra, 1996.

10 Laksiri Jayasuriya, 'Rethinking Australian multiculturalism: Towards a new paradigm', *The Australian Quarterly*, Autumn, 1990, p. 50.

11 Jayasuriya, 'Rethinking Australian multiculturalism', p. 57.

12 Sunder Katwala 'Why I'm proud to be a mongrel Brit', *The Observer*, 11 April 2004.

13 *Australian Multiculturalism for a New Century: Towards Inclusiveness*, Australian Government, Canberra, 1999, p. 35.

14 *National Agenda for a Multicultural Australia: Sharing Our Future*, Australian Government Publishing Service, Canberra, 1989.

15 *Australian Multiculturalism for a New Century*, p. 37.

16 Ghassan Hage, *White Nation: Fantasies of White Supremacy in a Multicultural Society*, Pluto Press, Sydney, 1998, pp. 37–47.

17 Hage, *White Nation*, p. 21.

18 Hage, *White Nation*, p. 22. Hage has an idiosyncratic use of the term 'White', which he prefers to 'Anglo' since it conveys 'a far more dominant

mode of self-perception, although a largely unconscious one' by those whom the rest of us probably call Anglos or Anglo-Celts.

19 Miriam Dixson, *The Imaginary Australian: Anglo-Celts and Identity, 1788 to the Present*, University of New South Wales Press, Sydney, 1999.
20 Dixson, *The Imaginary Australian*, pp. 42–43.
21 Dixson, *The Imaginary Australian*, p. 6.
22 Dixson, *The Imaginary Australian*, p. 14.
23 *The Guardian*, 24 April 2004.
24 Mark Lopez, *The Origins of Multiculturalism in Australian Politics, 1945–1975*, Melbourne University Press, Melbourne, 2000, p. 450.
25 John Frow, 'No room for difference', *Courier-Mail*, 2 October 1999.
26 Hage, *White Nation*, p. 205.
27 This argument is made in Nancy Fraser, *Justus Interruptus: Critical Reflections on the 'Postsocialist' Condition*, Routledge, New York, 1997, p. 5.
28 Kenan Malik, 'Against multiculturalism', *New Humanist*, Summer, 2002, and on <www.kenanmalik.com>.
29 Malik, 'Against multiculturalism'.
30 Robert Hughes, *The Culture of Complaint: The Fraying of America*, Harvill, London, 1994, p. 99.
31 Robert Wright, *The Moral Animal: Evolutionary Psychology and Everyday Life*, Abacus, London, 1996, p. 8.
32 The developments are reported in both popular accounts and in books written by research scientists. In the first group are: Steven Pinker, *The Blank Slate: The Modern Denial of Human Nature*, Penguin, London, 2002; Matt Ridley, *Nature via Nurture: Genes, Experience and What Makes Us Human*, HarperCollins, New York, 2003; Peter Singer, *A Darwinian Left: Politics Evolution and Co-operation*, Weidenfeld & Nicolson, London, 1999; Robert Wright, *The Moral Animal: Evolutionary Psychology and Everyday Life*, Abacus, London 1996; in the second category are books such as: John Tooby and Leda Cosmides, *The Adapted Mind: Evolutionary Psychology and the Generation of Culture*, Oxford University Press, New York, 1992; Frans De Waal, *The Ape and the Sushi Master: Cultural Reflections of a Primatologist*, Penguin, London, 2002; Christopher Boehm, *Hierarchy in the Forest: The Evolution of Egalitarian Behaviour*, Harvard University Press, Cambridge, MA, 1999.
33 Pinker, *The Blank Slate*, pp. 294, 323.
34 Stephen Castles, *Issues for a Community Relations Strategy: A Report to the Office of Multicultural Affairs*, University of Wollongong, 1990, pp. 31–32.
35 Ien Ang, 'From anti-racism to interracial trust', Speech at the Beyond Tolerance: National Conference on Racism, March 2002, in Justin Healey (ed.), *Racism in Australia*, The Spinney Press, Thirroul, NSW, 2003.

36 See Pinker, *The Blank Slate*, chs 14–16; Wright *The Moral Animal*, chs 7, 9, 13; De Waal, *The Ape and the Sushi Master*, Ch. 10; Singer, *A Darwinian Left*, chs 3, 4.

37 Martha Nussbaum, 'Cosmopolitan Emotions?' *New Humanist*, Winter, 2001.

9 A new humanism

1 Malcolm Fraser, *Common Ground: Issues That Should Bind and Not Divide Us*, Viking, Melbourne, 2002, pp. 54–55.

2 John Gray, *Enlightenment's Wake: Politics and Culture at the Close of the Modern Age*, Routledge, London, 1995, p. 105.

3 Martha Nussbaum, *Sex and Social Justice*, Oxford University Press, New York, 1999, pp. 6–14.

4 F.A. Hayek, *The Fatal Conceit: The Errors of Socialism*, Volume One of Collected Works of F.A. Hayek. W. Bartley (ed.), University of Chicago Press, Chicago, 1998, p. 18.

5 UN Environment Program, *Global Environment Outlook 2000*, Earthscan Publications, London, 1999.

6 James Gustave Speth, *Red Sky at Morning*, Yale University Press, New Haven, 2004, pp. 13–15.

7 Clive Hamilton, *Growth Fetish*, Allen & Unwin, Sydney, 2003; Richard Eckersley, *Well and Good: Morality, Meaning and Happiness*, Text Publishing, Melbourne, 2005.

8 Hamilton, *Growth Fetish*, p. 97.

9 Eckersley, *Well and Good*.

10 Nicholas Gane, *Max Weber and Postmodern Theory: Rationalization versus Re-enchantment*, Palgrave, Houndsmith, 2002, p. 15.

11 Diemut Elisabet Bubeck, *Care, Gender and Justice*, Clarendon Press, Oxford, 1995, p. 12.

12 Marian Sawer highlights some of these, particularly pensions which recognised the unpaid caring work of women as a service to the community. She argues that social liberalism operated to 'feminise thinking about the state'. She adds: 'The 'nightwatchman state of *laissez faire* liberalism underwent a sex change as it developed into the welfare state, before eventually being denounced as the "nanny state" by the neo-liberals of the late twentieth century.' Marian Sawer, *The Ethical State: Social Liberalism in Australia*, Melbourne University Press, Melbourne, 2003, p. 5.

13 Sawer, *The Ethical State*, Ch. 5.

14   The confluence of environmental thought and classical conservatism is noted by a number of commentators, including Peter Hay, *Main Currents in Western Environmental Thought*, University of New South Wales Press, Sydney, 2002, pp. 179–82.

15   Stephen Kellert categorises nine dimensions of the 'biophilia tendency' among human experience, such as: wonder and awe combined with curiosity; well-being that comes from physical activity with an "outdoor" dimension; the aesthetic appeal of nature; a deep emotional attachment to certain individual parts of nature, often animals but sometimes places; feelings of ethical responsibility and spiritual reverence for the natural world, sometimes expressed as feeling part of nature; the "dominionistic" dimension where satisfaction is achieved at overcoming a challenge from nature. See Stephen Kellert and Edward O. Wilson, (eds), *The Biophilia Hypothesis*, Island Press, Washington, 1993, Ch. 2.

16   As John Gray says: 'Many of the central conceptions of traditional conservatism have a natural congruence with Green concerns: the Burkean idea of the social contract, not as an agreement among anonymous ephemeral individuals, but as a compact between the generations of the living, the dead and those yet unborn; Tory scepticism about progress and awareness of its ironies and illusions; conservative resistance to untried novelty and large-scale social experiments; and perhaps most especially, the traditional conservative tenet that individual flourishing can only occur in the context of forms of common life.' John Gray, *Beyond the New Right: Markets, Government and the Common Environment*, Routledge, London, 1993, p. 124.

17   Blackwell and Seabrook, *Revolt Against Change*, Vintage Books, London, 1993, p. 95.

18   Some try to avoid using the term morality by substituting terms like 'ethics' and 'ethical', with 'morality' confined to personal behaviour and 'ethical' describing social attributes (e.g. an ethical policy). But this is not a distinction I support, and it runs the danger of strengthening a discourse which makes it hard to communicate in popular terms with most people.

19   Developing these ideas was assisted by reading Robert Reich, *Reason: Why Liberals Will Win the Battle for America*, Alfred A. Knopf, New York, 2004, esp. Ch. 2.

20   David Callahan, 'Take back values', *The Nation* (New York), 9 February 2004.

21   This is adapted from ideas in Deborah Stone, 'Why we need a care movement', *The Nation*, 13 March 2000, p. 13.

22   Several ideas are drawn from John Gray, *Enlightenment's Wake: Politics and Culture at the Close of the Modern Age*, Routledge, London, 1995, Ch. 10.

Acknowledgements

Good books mostly come from the heart. That is to say, a writer has to be driven by passion, or some similar motivation, to undertake the long and solitary task of researching and writing.

This book is part of a journey I began when I first discovered politics as a high school student. I was drawn to radical politics at the University of Sydney during the heady days of activism against the Vietnam War. Vietnam seemed to hold the key to unlocking the meaning of politics more generally and for me it led to a long commitment to the Left. Many years have passed since those early days. I have not lost the idealism with which I began but, like most people, experience has partly tempered and partly altered my views.

Writing a book is always difficult but perhaps doubly so when you are trying to unpack and re-think your own views, passion and intellectual framework. Along the way I was helped by many people and by significant institutional support. In 2002 the then editor of the Spectrum section of the *Sydney Morning Herald*, Michael Visontay, published an article by me which prefigured this book. After the article appeared, a number of encouraging responses came from readers including publishers, spurring me to proceed with a book. I later spent five months as a Visiting Fellow at the Department of Government and International Relations at the University of Sydney. I thank Rod Tiffen for help with this. The most valuable support came from my own institution, the University of Technology, Sydney, which awarded me a one-year Readership in 2003–04. For that I am indebted to the then Dean of the Humanities Faculty, Professor Joyce Kirk, and to the then Pro-Vice Chancellor (Research), Professor Lesley Johnson.

For generous, critical comment and wise advice at every point I am deeply indebted to my partner and fellow writer Jane Mills.

I owe a substantial debt to Jean Curthoys for editorial advice, comments and a very large amount of research. I am also grateful to Madelaine Healy, Molly Tregoning, John Fisher and David Smith for research assistance.

Elizabeth Weiss from Allen & Unwin gave constant support, perceptive advice and intellectual input from the beginning to the end of this project. Eric Aarons provided important advice and read drafts of chapters at various stages. Valuable ideas for this book flowed from two seminars under the title 'Rethinking Progress' organised by the Research Initiative on International Activism at UTS and the Australia Institute in 2003.

I would also like to thank Richard Archer, Judith Brett, David Burchell, Rowan Cahill, Paul Gillen, Greg Giles, Nicky Hager, Rebecca Huntley, Andrew Jakubowicz, Jim Jose, Rebecca Kaiser, Peter Lewis, Anne Manne, Tony Moore, Margaret Mulvihill, Richard Neville, Penny O'Donnell, Barbara Pocock, Nick Rushworth, Graeme Smith, Lindsay Tanner and John Wishart. Some were supportive, others more critical, none bears responsibility for the content. For their kind words supporting this book I also wish to thank Robert Manne, Clive Hamilton and Margo Kingston.

Much of this book was researched and written in the Fisher Library at the University of Sydney and at the Blake Library at the University of Technology, Sydney. I thank the staff at both institutions. Thanks to Geoff and Carolyn Banbury of Bungendore for hospitality and to the friends who lent me houses at Coledale and Blackheath for writing.

Every long project I have worked on has been researched and written with the accompaniment of certain music and songs which have stuck in my head long after publication. In this case, they include: 'Desert Blues—Ambiances du Sahara', 'The Wassoulou Sound—Women of Mali', 'Die Dreigroschenoper, Berlin 1930', David Lumsdaine' s 'Cambewarra Mountain', Paul Simon's 'Rhythm of the Saints', as well as a great deal of well-known classical music.

David McKnight
July 2005

David McKnight can be contacted at www.beyondrightandleft.com.au

Index

democracy
  relativist approach 227
  rethought 120–21
deregulation 20, 53, 59, 60, 78, 96
difference
  principle of 227–8
  recognising 247
differentiation 125
Dixson, Miriam 223–6
Dole, Bob 83
'domestic labour'
  socialist solution 126
  see also housework
'dries' 56–7

Easteal, Patricia 216
ecology
  crisis 43–4
  interdependence 249, 252
  unsustainable 242–4
economic liberalism
  glory days 51
  impact of 7
  Right radicalism 9
economic planning, central see central
  planning
economic rationalism see neo-liberalism
economies
  market-driven 21–4
  relation to society 22–3
  see also free markets; markets
education
  history curriculum, (US) 145
  teaching values 135–6
egalitarianism
  Australian culture 107–9
  immorality of 57
  Liberal Party code 211
  radical 205
elites, suspicion of 11–12
'emotional asceticism' 40
emotions
  appeal of conservatism 88–92
  culture war 141–2
  multiculturalism 222
  social fabric 88
empathy 205, 227, 229–30
employment
  changing conditions 26–7, 97
  commodification 25

empowerment of people 79
End of History, The 118
Engels, Frederick 122
Englishness, celebration of 225
Enlightenment
  challenge to authority 87
  influence of ideas 92, 102, 229
  Left's rejection of 226–7
  rationalist ideals 96
  Scottish 73
environment
  global issues 6, 243–4
  heritage 252–53
  market values 43–5
  popularity of issues 258
environment movement and conservatism
  98–104
equal opportunity programs 173
equal rights 173
equality
  of cultures 228
  degrees of 131
  employment-focused 185–6
  'gender equity' model 187–8
  idea of 183–7
  within liberty 66–7
  rethinking 201
  see also inequality
'essentialism' 193–4
ethical issues 7
ethics, new interest in 245–6
ethnic communities 150–1
ethnic identification 202, 209–12,
  231–5
ethnocentrism 206, 209, 233, 249–50
Eurocentrism 226–27
European settlement 148
externalised costs 44–5

'fair go' 81–2
family
  changed expectations 139
  commodification 40–2
  crucial role 166
  cultural Left views 168
  dual-incomes 180, 191
  'gender equity' model 187–8
  Howard government policy 183
  impact of capitalism 38–40
  models of 167, 189–91